Insurgent Mexico

INSURGENT MEXICO

INSURGENT MEXICO

BY
JOHN REED

NEW YORK AND LONDON
D. APPLETON AND COMPANY
1914

To

PROFESSOR CHARLES TOWNSEND COPELAND

of

HARVARD UNIVERSITY

Dear Copey:

I remember you thought it strange that my first trip abroad didn't make me want to write about what I saw there. But since then I have visited a country which stimulated me to express it in words. And as I wrote these impressions of Mexico I couldn't help but think that I never would have seen what I did see had it not been for your teaching me.

I can only add my word to what so many who are writing already have told you: That to listen to you is to learn how to see the hidden beauty of the visible world; that to be your friend is to try to be intellectually honest.

So I dedicate this book to you with the understanding that you shall take as your own the parts that please you, and forgive me the rest.

As ever,
Jack.

New York,
July 3, 1914.

CONTENTS

PART IV. A PEOPLE IN ARMS

PART V. CARRANZA—AN IMPRESSION

PART VI. MEXICAN NIGHTS

INSURGENT MEXICO

ON THE BORDER

MERCADO'S Federal army, after its dramatic and terrible retreat four hundred miles across the desert when Chihuahua was abandoned, lay three months at Ojinaga on the Rio Grande.

At Presidio, on the American side of the river, one could climb to the flat mud roof of the Post Office and look across the mile or so of low scrub growing in the sand to the shallow, yellow stream; and beyond to the low *mesa*, where the town was, sticking sharply up out of a scorched desert, ringed round with bare, savage mountains.

One could see the square, gray adobe houses of Ojinaga, with here and there the Oriental cupola of an old Spanish church. It was a desolate land, without trees. You expected minarets. By day, Federal soldiers in shabby white uniforms swarmed about the place desultorily digging trenches, for Villa and his victorious Constitutionalists were rumored to be on the way. You got sudden glints, where the sun flashed on field guns; strange, thick clouds of smoke rose straight in the still air.

Toward evening, when the sun went down with the flare of a blast furnace, patrols of cavalry rode sharply

1

across the skyline to the night outposts. And after dark, mysterious fires burned in the town.

There were thirty-five hundred men in Ojinaga. This was all that remained of Mercado's army of ten thousand and the five thousand which Pascual Orozco had marched north from Mexico City to reinforce him. Of this thirty-five hundred, forty-five were majors, twenty-one colonels, and eleven generals.

I wanted to interview General Mercado; but one of the newspapers had printed something displeasing to General Salazar, and he had forbidden the reporters the town. I sent a polite request to General Mercado. The note was intercepted by General Orozco, who sent back the following reply:

ESTEEMED AND HONORED SIR: If you set foot inside of Ojinaga, I will stand you sideways against a wall, and with my own hand take great pleasure in shooting furrows in your back.

But after all I waded the river one day and went up into the town. Luckily, I did not meet General Orozco. No one seemed to object to my entrance. All the sentries I saw were taking a siesta on the shady side of adobe walls. But almost immediately I encountered a courteous officer named Hernandez, to whom I explained that I wished to see General Mercado.

Without inquiring as to my identity, he scowled, folded his arms, and burst out:

"I am General Orozco's chief of staff, and I will not take you to see General Mercado!"

ON THE BORDER

I said nothing. In a few minutes he explained:

"General Orozco hates General Mercado! He does not deign to go to General Mercado's cuartel, and General Mercado does not *dare* to come to General Orozco's cuartel! He is a coward. He ran away from Tierra Blanca, and then he ran away from Chihuahua!"

"What other Generals don't you like?" I asked.

He caught himself and slanted an angry look at me, and then grinned:

"*Quien sabe. . . . ?*"

I saw General Mercado, a fat, pathetic, worried, undecided little man, who blubbered and blustered a long tale about how the United States army had come across the river and helped Villa to win the battle of Tierra Blanca.

The white, dusty streets of the town, piled high with filth and fodder, the ancient windowless church with its three enormous Spanish bells hanging on a rack outside and a cloud of blue incense crawling out of the black doorway, where the women camp followers of the army prayed for victory day and night, lay in hot, breathless sun. Five times had Ojinaga been lost and taken. Hardly a house that had a roof, and all the walls gaped with cannon-shot. In these bare, gutted rooms lived the soldiers, their women, their horses, their chickens and pigs, raided from the surrounding country. Guns were stacked in the corners, saddles piled in the dust. The soldiers were in rags; scarcely one possessed a complete uniform. They squatted around little fires in their doorways, boiling corn-husks and dried meat. They were almost starving.

Along the main street passed an unbroken procession of sick, exhausted, starving people, driven from the interior by fear of the approaching rebels, a journey of eight days over the most terrible desert in the world. They were stopped by a hundred soldiers along the street, and robbed of every possession that took the Federals' fancy. Then they passed on to the river, and on the American side they had to run the gantlet of the United States customs and immigration officials and the Army Border Patrol, who searched them for arms.

Hundreds of refugees poured across the river, some on horseback driving cattle before them, some in wagons, and others on foot. The inspectors were not very gentle.

"Come down off that wagon!" one would shout to a Mexican woman with a bundle in her arm.

"But, señor, for what reason? . . ." she would begin.

"Come down there or I'll pull you down!" he would yell.

They made an unnecessarily careful and brutal search of the men and of the women, too.

As I stood there, a woman waded across the ford, her skirts lifted unconcernedly to her thighs. She wore a voluminous shawl, which was humped up in front as if she were carrying something in it.

"Hi, there!" shouted a customs man. "What have you got under your shawl?"

4

ON THE BORDER

She slowly opened the front of her dress, and answered placidly:

"I don't know, señor. It may be a girl, or it may be a boy."

These were metropolitan days for Presidio, a straggling and indescribably desolate village of about fifteen adobe houses, scattered without much plan in the deep sand and cotton-wood scrub along the river bottom. Old Kleinmann, the German store-keeper, made a fortune a day outfitting refugees and supplying the Federal army across the river with provisions. He had three beautiful adolescent daughters whom he kept locked up in the attic of the store, because a flock of amorous Mexicans and ardent cow-punchers prowled around like dogs, drawn from many miles away by the fame of these damsels. Half the time he spent working furiously in the store, stripped to the waist; and the remainder, rushing around with a large gun strapped to his waist, warning off the suitors.

At all times of the day and night, throngs of unarmed Federal soldiers from across the river swarmed in the store and the pool hall. Among them circulated dark, ominous persons with an important air, secret agents of the Rebels and the Federals. Around in the brush camped hundreds of destitute refugees, and you could not walk around a corner at night without stumbling over a plot or a counterplot. There were Texas rangers, and United States troopers, and agents of American corporations trying to get secret instructions to their employees in the interior.

INSURGENT MEXICO

One MacKenzie stamped about the Post Office in a high dudgeon. It appeared that he had important letters for the American Smelting and Refining Company mines in Santa Eulalia.

"Old Mercado insists on opening and reading all letters that pass through his lines," he shouted indignantly.

"But," I said, "he will let them pass, won't he?"

"Certainly," he answered. "But do you think the American Smelting and Refining Company will submit to having its letters opened and read by a damned greaser? It's an outrage when an American corporation can't send a private letter to its employees! If this don't bring Intervention," he finished, darkly, "I don't know what will!"

There were all sorts of drummers for arms and ammunition companies, smugglers and *contrabandistas*; also a small, bantam man, the salesman for a portrait company, which made crayon enlargements from photographs at $5 apiece. He was scurrying around among the Mexicans, getting thousands of orders for pictures which were to be paid for upon delivery, and which, of course, could never be delivered. It was his first experience among Mexicans, and he was highly gratified by the hundreds of orders he had received. You see, a Mexican would just as soon order a portrait, or a piano, or an automobile as not, so long as he does not have to pay for it. It gives him a sense of wealth.

The little agent for crayon enlargements made one comment on the Mexican revolution. He said that General Huerta must be a fine man, because he understood he was distantly connected, on his mother's side, with the distinguished Carey family of Virginia!

The American bank of the river was patroled twice a day by details of cavalry, conscientiously paralleled on the Mexican side by companies of horsemen. Both parties watched each other narrowly across the Border. Every once in a while a Mexican, unable to restrain his nervousness, took a pot-shot at the Americans, and a small battle ensued as both parties scattered into the brush. A little way above Presidio were stationed two troops of the Negro Ninth Cavalry. One colored trooper, watering his horse on the bank of the river, was accosted by an English-speaking Mexican squatting on the opposite shore:

"Hey, coon!" he shouted, derisively, "when are you damned Gringos going to cross that line?"

"Chile!" responded the Negro. "We ain't agoin' to cross that line at all. We're just goin' to pick up that line an' carry it right down to the Big Ditch!"

Sometimes a rich refugee, with a good deal of gold sewed in his saddle-blankets, would get across the river without the Federals discovering it. There were six big, high-power automobiles in Presidio waiting for just such a victim. They would soak him one hundred dollars gold to make a trip to the railroad; and on the way, somewhere in the desolate wastes south of Marfa, he was almost sure to be held up by masked men and everything taken away from him. Upon these occasions the High Sheriff of Presidio County would bluster into town on a small pinto horse,—a figure true to the best tradition of "The Girl of the Golden West."

7

He had read all Owen Wister's novels, and knew what a Western sheriff ought to look like: two revolvers on the hip, one slung under his arm, a large knife in his left boot, and an enormous shotgun over his saddle. His conversation was larded with the most fearful oaths, and he never caught any criminal. He spent all of his time enforcing the Presidio County law against carrying firearms and playing poker; and at night, after the day's work was done, you could always find him sitting in at a quiet game in the back of Kleinmann's store.

War and rumors of war kept Presidio at a fever heat. We all knew that sooner or later the Constitutionalist army would come overland from Chihuahua and attack Ojinaga. In fact, the major in command of the Border Patrol had already been approached by the Federal generals in a body to make arrangements for the retreat of the Federal army from Ojinaga under such circumstances. They said that when the rebels attacked they would want to resist for a respectable length of time,—say two hours,—and that then they would like permission to come across the river.

We knew that some twenty-five miles southward, at La Mula Pass, five hundred rebel volunteers guarded the only road from Ojinaga through the mountains. One day a courier sneaked through the Federal lines and across the river with important news. He said that the military band of the Federal army had been marching around the country practicing their music, and had been captured by the Constitutionalists, who stood them up in the market-place with rifles pointed

8

at their heads, and made them play twelve hours at a stretch. "Thus," continued the message, "the hardships of life in the desert have been somewhat alleviated." We could never discover just how it was that the band happened to be practicing all alone twenty-two miles from Ojinaga in the desert.

For a month longer the Federals remained at Ojinaga, and Presidio throve. Then Villa, at the head of his army, appeared over a rise of the desert. The Federals resisted a respectable length of time—just two hours, or, to be exact, until Villa himself at the head of a battery galloped right up to the muzzles of the guns,—and then poured across the river in wild rout, were herded in a vast corral by the American soldiers, and afterward imprisoned in a barbed-wire stockade at Fort Bliss, Texas.

But by that time I was already far down in Mexico, riding across the desert with a hundred ragged Constitutionalist troopers on my way to the front.

PART ONE

DESERT WAR

CHAPTER I

URBINA'S COUNTRY

A PEDDLER from Parral came into town with a mule-load of *macuche*,—you smoke *macuche* when you can't get tobacco,—and we strolled down with the rest of the population to get the news. This was in Magistral, a Durango mountain village three days' ride from the railroad. Somebody bought a little *macuche*, the rest of us borrowed from him, and we sent a boy for some corn-shucks. Everybody lit up, squatting around the peddler three deep; for it was weeks since the town had heard of the Revolution. He was full of the most alarming rumors: that the Federals had broken out of Torreon and were headed this way, burning ranches and murdering *pacificos;* that the United States troops had crossed the Rio Grande; that Huerta had resigned; that Huerta was coming north to take charge of the Federal troops in person; that Pascual Orozco had been shot at Ojinaga; that Pascual Orozco was coming south with ten thousand *colorados.* He retailed these reports with a wealth of dramatic gesture, stamping around until his heavy brown-and-gold sombrero wabbled on his head, tossing his faded blue blanket over his shoulder, firing imaginary rifles and drawing imaginary swords,

13

while his audience murmured: *"Ma!"* and *"Adio!"* But the most interesting rumor was that General Urbina would leave for the front in two days.

A hostile Arab named Antonio Swayfeta happened to be driving to Parral in a two-wheeled gig the next morning, and allowed me to go with him as far as Las Nieves, where the General lives. By afternoon we had climbed out of the mountains to the great upland plain of Northern Durango, and were jogging down the mile-long waves of yellow prairie, stretching away so far that the grazing cattle dwindled into dots and finally disappeared at the base of the wrinkled purple mountains that seemed close enough to hit with a thrown stone. The Arab's hostility had thawed, and he poured out his life's story, not one word of which I could understand. But the drift of it, I gathered, was largely commercial. He had once been to El Paso and regarded it as the world's most beautiful city. But business was better in Mexico. They say that there are few Jews in Mexico because they cannot stand the competition of the Arabs.

We passed only one human being all that day—a ragged old man astride a burro, wrapped in a red-and-black checked serape, though without trousers, and hugging the broken stock of a rifle. Spitting, he volunteered that he was a soldier; that after three years of deliberation he had finally decided to join the Revolution and fight for Libertad. But at his first battle a cannon had been fired, the first he had ever heard; he had immediately started for his home in El Oro, where

14

he intended to descend into a gold-mine and stay there
until the war was over. . . .

We fell silent, Antonio and I. Occasionally he addressed the mule in faultless Castilian. Once he informed me that that mule was "all heart" (*pura cora-
zon*). The sun hung for a moment on the crest of the
red porphyry mountains, and dropped behind them;
the turquoise cup of sky held an orange powder of
clouds. Then all the rolling leagues of desert glowed
and came near in the soft light. Ahead suddenly
reared the solid fortress of a big rancho, such as one
comes on once a day in that vast land,—a mighty
square of blank walls, with loop-holed towers at the
corners, and an iron-studded gate. It stood grim and
forbidding upon a little bare hill, like any castle, its
adobe corrals around it; and below, in what had been
a dry arroyo all day, the sunken river came to the surface in a pool, and disappeared again in the sand. Thin
lines of smoke from within rose straight into the high
last sunshine. From the river to the gate moved the
tiny black figures of women with water-jars on their
heads: and two wild horsemen galloped some cattle
toward the corrals. Now the western mountains were
blue velvet, and the pale sky a blood-stained canopy of
watered silk. But by the time we reached the great
gate of the rancho, above was only a shower of stars.

Antonio called for Don Jesus. It is always safe
to call for Don Jesus at a rancho, for that is invaria-
bly the *administrador's* name. He finally appeared, a
magnificently tall man in tight trousers, purple silk
undershirt, and a gray sombrero heavily loaded with

15

silver braid; and invited us in. The inside of the wall consisted of houses, running all the way around. Along the walls and over the doors hung festoons of jerked meat, and strings of peppers, and drying clothes. Three young girls crossed the square in single file, balancing *ollas* of water on their heads, shouting to each other in the raucous voices of Mexican women. At one house a woman crouched, nursing her baby; next door another kneeled to the interminable labor of) grinding corn-meal in a stone trough. The men-folk squatted before little corn-husk fires, bundled in their faded serapes, smoking their *hojas* as they watched the women work. As we unharnessed they rose and gathered around, with soft-voiced "*Bueno noches*," curious and friendly. Where did we come from? Where going? What did we have of news? Had the Maderistas taken Ojinaga yet? Was it true that Orozco was coming to kill the *pacificos?* Did we know Panfilo Silveyra? He was a *sergento*, one of Urbina's men. He came from that house, was the cousin of this man. Ah, there was too much war!

Antonio departed to bargain for corn for the mule. "A *tanito*—just a little corn," he whined. "Surely Don Jesus wouldn't charge him anything. . . . Just so much corn as a mule could eat . . . !" At one of the houses I negotiated for dinner. The woman spread out both her hands. "We are all so poor now," she said. "A little water, some beans—*tortillas*. . . . It is all we eat in this house. . . ." Milk? No. Eggs? No. Meat? No. Coffee? *Valgame Dios*, no! I ventured that with this money they might be purchased at one of the other houses. *"Quien sabe?"* replied she dreamily. At this moment arrived the husband and upbraided her for her lack of hospitality. "My house is at your orders," he said magnificently, and begged a cigarette. Then he squatted down while she brought forward the two family chairs and bade us seat ourselves. The room was of good proportions, with a dirt floor and a ceiling of heavy beams, the adobe showing through. Walls and ceiling were whitewashed, and, to the naked eye, spotlessly clean. In one corner was a big iron bed, and in the other a Singer sewing machine, as in every other house I saw in Mexico. There was also a spindle-legged table, upon which stood a picture-postcard of Our Lady of Guadelupe, with a candle burning before it. Above this, on the wall, hung an indecent illustration clipped from the pages of *Le Rire*, in a silver-gilt frame—evidently an object of the highest veneration.

Arrived now various uncles, cousins, and *compadres*, wondering casually if we dragged any cigarros. At her husband's command, the woman brought a live coal in her fingers. We smoked. It grew late. There developed a lively argument as to who would go and buy provisions for our dinner. Finally they compromised on the woman; and soon Antonio and I sat in the kitchen, while she crouched upon the altar-like adobe platform in the corner, cooking over the open fire. The smoke enveloped up, pouring out the door. Occasionally a pig or a few hens would wander in from the outside, or a sheep would make a dash for the *tortilla* meal, until the angry voice of the master of the house reminded the woman that she was not doing five or six things at once. And she would rise wearily and belabor the animal with a flaming brand.

All through our supper—jerked meat fiery with *chile*, fried eggs, *tortillas*, *frijoles*, and bitter black coffee, —the entire male population of the rancho bore us company, in the room and out. It seemed that some were especially prejudiced against the Church. "Priests without shame," cried one, "who come when we are so poor and take away a tenth of what we have!"

"And us paying a quarter to the Government for this cursed war!" . . .

"Shut your mouth!" shrilled the woman. "It is for God! God must eat, the same as we. . . ."

Her husband smiled a superior smile. He had once been to Jimenez and was considered a man of the world.

"God does not eat," he remarked with finality. "The *curas* grow fat on us."

"Why do you give it?" I asked.

"It is the law," said several at once.

And not one would believe that that law was repealed in Mexico in the year 1857!

I asked them about General Urbina. "A good man, all heart." And another: "He is very brave. The bullets bound off him like rain from a sombrero. . . ." "He is the cousin of my woman's first husband's sister." "He is *bueno para los negocios del campo*" (that is to say, he is a highly successful bandit and highwayman). And finally one said proudly: "A few years

18

ago he was just a peon like us; and now he is a General and a rich man."

But I shall not soon forget the hunger-pinched body and bare feet of an old man with the face of a saint, who said slowly: "The Revolucion is good. When it is done we shall starve never, never, never, if God is served. But it is long, and we have no food to eat, or clothes to wear. For the master has gone away from the hacienda, and we have no tools or animals to do our work with, and the soldiers take all our corn and drive away the cattle. . . ."

"Why don't the *pacificos* fight?"

He shrugged his shoulders. "Now they do not need us. They have no rifles for us, or horses. They are winning. And who shall feed them if we do not plant corn? No, señor. But if the Revolucion loses, then there will be no more *pacificos*. Then we will rise, with our knives and our horsewhips. . . . The Revolucion will not lose. . . ."

As Antonio and I rolled up in our blankets on the floor of the granary, they were singing. One of the young bucks had procured a guitar somewhere, and two voices, clinging to each other in that peculiar strident Mexican "barber-shop" harmony, were whining loudly something about a *"trista historia d'amor."* . . .

The rancho was one of many belonging to the Hacienda of El Canotillo, and all next day we drove through its wide lands, which covered more than two million

19

acres, I was told. The *hacendado*, a wealthy Spaniard, had fled the country two years before.

"Who is owner now?"

"General Urbina," said Antonio. And it was so, as I soon saw. The great haciendas of Northern Durango, an area greater than the State of New Jersey, had been confiscated for the Constitutionalist government by the General, who ruled them with his own agents, and, it was said, divided fifty-fifty with the Revolution.

We drove steadily all day, only stopping long enough to eat a few *tortillas*. And along about sundown we saw the brown mud wall that hemmed El Canotillo round, with its city of little houses, and the ancient pink tower of its church among the alamo trees,— miles away at the foot of the mountains. The village of Las Nieves, a straggling collection of adobes the exact color of the earth of which they are built, lay before us, like some strange growth of the desert. A flashing river, without a trace of green along its banks to contrast it with the scorched plain, made a semicircle around the town. And as we splashed across the ford, between the women kneeling there at their washing, the sun suddenly went behind the western mountains. Immediately a deluge of yellow light, thick as water, drowned the earth, and a golden mist rose from the ground, in which the cattle floated legless.

I knew that the price for such a journey as Antonio had carried me was at least ten pesos, and he was an Arab to boot. But when I offered him money, he threw his arms around me and burst into tears. . . . God bless you, excellent Arab! You are right; business is better in Mexico.

CHAPTER II

THE LION OF DURANGO AT HOME

A T General Urbina's door sat an old peon with four cartridge-belts around him, engaged in the genial occupation of filling corrugated iron bombs with gunpowder. He jerked his thumb toward the patio. The General's house, corrals and store-rooms ran around all four sides of a space as big as a city block, swarming with pigs, chickens and half-naked children. Two goats and three magnificent pea-cocks gazed pensively down from the roof. In and out of the sitting-room, whence came the phonographic strains of the "Dollar Princess," stalked a train of hens. An old woman came from the kitchen and dumped a bucket of garbage on the ground; all the pigs made a squealing rush for it. In a corner of the house-wall sat the General's baby daughter, chewing on a cartridge. A group of men stood or sprawled on the ground around a well in the center of the patio. The General himself sat in their midst, in a broken wicker arm-chair, feeding *tortillas* to a tame deer and a lame black sheep. Before him knelt a peon, pouring from a canvas sack some hundreds of Mauser cartridges.

To my explanations the General returned no answer. He gave me a limp hand, immediately withdrawing it, but did not rise. A broad, medium-sized man of dark mahogany complexion, with a sparse black beard up to his cheek-bones, that didn't hide the wide, thin, expressionless mouth, the gaping nostrils, the shiny, small, humorous, animal eyes. For a good five minutes he never took them from mine. I produced my papers.

"I don't know how to read," said the General suddenly, motioning to his secretary. "So you want to go with me to battle?" he shot at me in the coarsest Spanish. "Many bullets!" I said nothing. "*Muy bien!* But I don't know when I shall go. Maybe in five days. Now eat!"

"Thanks, my general, I've already eaten."

"Go and eat," he repeated calmly. "*Andale!*"

A dirty little man they all called Doctor escorted me to the dining-room. He had once been an apothecary in Parral, but was now a Major. We were to sleep together that night, he said. But before we reached the dining-room there was a shout of "Doctor!" A wounded man had arrived, a peasant with his sombrero in his hand, and a blood-clotted handkerchief around his head. The little doctor became all efficiency. He dispatched a boy for the family scissors, another for a bucket of water from the well. He sharpened with his knife a stick he picked up from the ground. Seating the man on a box, he took off the bandage, revealing a cut about two inches long, caked with dirt and dried blood. First he cut off the hair around the wound, jabbing the points of the scissors carelessly into it. The man drew in his breath sharply, but did

22

not move. Then the doctor slowly *cut the clotted blood away from the top*, whistling cheerfully to himself. "Yes," he remarked, "it is an interesting life, the doctor's." He peered closely at the vomiting blood; the peasant sat like a sick stone. "And it is a life full of nobility," continued the doctor. "Alleviating the sufferings of others." Here he picked up the sharpened stick, thrust it deep in, *and slowly worked it the entire length of the cut!*

"Pah! The animal has fainted!" said the doctor. "Here, hold him up while I wash it!" With that he lifted the bucket and poured its contents over the head of the patient, the water and blood dribbling down over his clothes. "These ignorant peons," said the doctor, binding up the wound in its original bandage, "have no courage. It´is the intelligence that makes the soul, eh?" . . .

When the peasant came to, I asked: "Are you a soldier?" The man smiled a sweet, deprecating smile.

"No, señor, I am only a *pacífico*," he said. "I live in the Canotillo, where my house is at your orders. . . ."

Some time later—a good deal—we all sat down to supper. There was Lieutenant-Colonel Pablo Seañes, a frank, engaging youth of twenty-six, with five bullets in him to pay for the three years' fighting. His conversation was sprinkled with soldierly curses, and his pronunciation was a little indistinct, the result of a bullet on the jaw-bone and a tongue almost cut in two by a sword. He was a demon in the field, they said, and a killer (*muy matador*) after it. At the first taking of Torreon, Pablo and two other officers, Major

Fierro and Captain Borunda, had executed alone eighty unarmed prisoners, each man shooting them down with his revolver until his hand got tired pulling the trigger.

"*Oiga!*" Pablo said. "Where is the best institute for the study of hypnotism in the United States? . . . As soon as this cursed war is over I am going to study to become a hypnotist. . . ." With that he turned and began to make passes at Lieutenant Borrega, who was called derisively "The Lion of the Sierras," because of his prodigious boasting. The latter jerked out his revolver: "I want no business with the devil!" he screamed, amid the uproarious laughter of the others.

Then there was Captain Fernando, a grizzled giant of a man in tight trousers, who had fought twenty-one battles. He took the keenest delight in my fragmentary Spanish, and every word I spoke sent him into bellows of laughter that shook down the adobe from the ceiling. He had never been out of Durango, and declared that there was a great sea between the United States and Mexico, and that he believed all the rest of the earth to be water. Next to him sat Longinos Güereca, with a row of decayed teeth across his round, gentle face every time he smiled, and a record for simple bravery that was famous throughout the army. He was twenty-one, and already First Captain. He told me that last night his own men had tried to kill him. . . . Then came Patricio, the best rider of wild horses in the State, and Fidencio next to him, a pure-blooded Indian seven feet tall, who always fought standing up. And last Raphael Zalarzo, a tiny hunchback that Urbina carried in his train to amuse him, like any medieval Italian duke.

When we had burned our throats with the last *enchilada*, and scooped up our last *frijole* with a *tortilla*,—forks and spoons being unknown,—the gentlemen each took a mouthful of water, gargled it, and spat it on the floor. As I came out into the patio, I saw the figure of the General emerge from his bedroom door, staggering slightly. In his hand he carried a revolver. He stood for a moment in the light of another door, then suddenly went in, banging it behind him.

I was already in bed when the doctor came into the room. In the other bed reposed the Lion of the Sierras and his momentary mistress, now loudly snoring.

"Yes," said the Doctor, "there has been some little trouble. The General has not been able to walk for two months from rheumatism. . . . And sometimes he is in great pain, and comforts himself with *aguardiente*. . . . To-night he tried to shoot his mother. He always tries to shoot his mother . . . . because he loves her very much." The Doctor peeped at himself in the mirror, and twisted his mustache. "This Revolucion. Do not mistake. It is a fight of the poor against the rich. I was very poor before the Revolucion and now I am very rich." He pondered a moment, and then began removing his clothes. Through his filthy undershirt the Doctor honored me with his one English sentence: "I have mooch lices," he said, with a proud smile. . . .

I went out at dawn and walked around Las Nieves. The town belongs to General Urbina, people, houses, animals and immortal souls. At Las Nieves he and he alone wields the high justice and the low. The town's only store is in his house, and I bought some cigarettes from the Lion of the Sierras, who was detailed store-clerk for the day. In the patio the General was talking with his mistress, a beautiful, aristocratic-looking woman, with a voice like a hand-saw. When he noticed me he came up and shook hands, saying that he'd like to have me take some pictures of him. I said that that was my purpose in life, and asked him if he thought he would leave soon for the front. "In about ten days, I think," he answered. I began to get uncomfortable.

"I appreciate your hospitality, my General," I told him, "but my work demands that I be where I can see the actual advance upon Torreon. If it is convenient, I should like to go back to Chihuahua and join General Villa, who will soon go south." Urbina's expression didn't change, but he shot at me: "What is it that you don't like here? You are in your own house! Do you want cigarettes? Do you want *aguardiente*, or *sotol*, or cognac? Do you want a woman to warm your bed at night? Everything you want I can give you! Do you want a pistol? A horse? Do you want money?" He jerked a handful of silver dollars from his pocket and threw them jingling on the ground at my feet.

I said: "Nowhere in Mexico am I so happy and contented as in this house." And I was prepared to go further.

For the next hour I took photographs of General Urbina: General Urbina on foot, with and without sword; General Urbina on three different horses; General Urbina with and without his family; General Urbina's three children, on horseback and off; General Urbina's mother, and his mistress; the entire family, armed with swords and revolvers, including the phonograph, produced for the purpose, one of the children holding a placard upon which was inked: "General Tomas Urbina R."

CHAPTER III

THE GENERAL GOES TO WAR

WE had finished breakfast and I was resigning myself to the ten days in Las Nieves, when the General suddenly changed his mind. He came out of his room, roaring orders. In five minutes the house was all bustle and confusion,—officers rushing to pack their serapes, *mozos* and troopers saddling horses, peons with armfuls of rifles rushing to and fro. Patricio harnessed five mules to the great coach,—an exact copy of the Deadwood Stage. A courier rode out on the run to summon the Tropa, which was quartered at the Canotillo. Rafaelito loaded the General's baggage into the coach; it consisted of a typewriter, four swords, one of them bearing the emblem of the Knights of Pythias, three uniforms, the General's branding-iron, and a twelve-gallon demijohn of *sotol*.

And there came the Tropa, a ragged smoke of brown dust miles along the road. Ahead flew a little, squat, black figure, with the Mexican flag streaming over him; he wore a floppy sombrero loaded with five pounds of tarnished gold braid,—once probably the pride of some imperial *hacendado*. Following him closely were Manuel Paredes, with riding boots up to his hips, fastened with silver buckles the size of dollars, beating his mount with the flat of a saber; Isidro Amayo, making his horse buck by flapping a hat in his eyes; José Valiente, ringing his immense silver spurs inlaid with turquoises; Jesus Mancilla, his flashing brass chain around his neck; Julian Reyes, with colored pictures of Christ and the Virgin fastened to the front of his sombrero; a struggling tangle of six behind, with Antonio Guzman trying to lasso them, the coils of his horsehair rope soaring out of the dust. They came on the dead run, all Indian shouts and cracking revolvers, until they were only a hundred feet away, then jerked their little cow-ponies cruelly to a staggering halt with bleeding mouths, a whirling confusion of men, horses and dust.

This was the Tropa when I first saw them. About a hundred, they were, in all stages of picturesque raggedness; some wore overalls, others the *charro* jackets of peons, while one or two sported tight *vaquero* trousers. A few had shoes, most of them only cowhide sandals, and the rest were barefooted. Sabas Gutierrez was garbed in an ancient frockcoat, split up the back for riding. Rifles slung at their saddles, four or five cartridge-belts crossed over their chests, high, flapping sombreros, immense spurs chiming as they rode, bright-colored serapes strapped on behind—this was their uniform.

The General was with his mother. Outside the door crouched his mistress, weeping, her three children around her. For almost an hour we waited, then Urbina suddenly burst out of the door. With scarcely a look at his family, he leaped on his great, gray charger, and spurred furiously into the street. Juan Sanchez blew a blast on his cracked bugle, and the Tropa, with the General at its head, took the Canotillo road.

In the meanwhile Patricio and I loaded three cases of dynamite and a case of bombs into the boot of the coach. I got up beside Patricio, the peons let go of the mules' heads, and the long whip curled around their bellies. Galloping, we whirled out of the village, and took the steep bank of the river at twenty miles an hour. Away on the other side, the Tropa trotted along a more direct road. The Canotillo we passed without stopping.

"*Arré mulas! Putas! Hijas de la Ho——!*" yelled Patricio, the whip hissing. The *Camino Real* was a mere track on uneven ground; every time we took a little arroyo the dynamite came down with a sickening crash. Suddenly a rope broke, and one case bounced off the coach and fell upon rocks. It was a cool morning, however, and we strapped it on again safely. . . .

Almost every hundred yards along the road were little heaps of stones, surmounted by wooden crosses,— each one the memorial of a murder. And occasionally a tall, whitewashed cross uprose in the middle of a side-road, to protect some little desert rancho from the visits of the devil. Black shiny chaparral, the height of a mule's back, scraped the side of the coach; Spanish bayonet and the great barrel-cactus watched us like sentinels from the skyline of the desert. And always the mighty Mexican vultures circled over us, as if they knew we were going to war.

Late in the afternoon the stone wall which bounds the million acres of the Hacienda of Torreon de Cañas swung into sight on our left, marching across deserts and mountains like the Great Wall of China, for more than thirty miles; and, soon afterward, the hacienda itself. The Tropa had dismounted around the Big House. They said that General Urbina had suddenly been taken violently sick, and would probably be unable to leave his bed for a week.

The Casa Grande, a magnificent porticoed palace but one story high, covered the entire top of a desert rise. From its doorway one could see fifteen miles of yellow, rolling plain, and, beyond, the interminable ranges of bare mountains piled upon each other. Back of it lay the great corrals and stables, where the Tropa's evening fires already sent up myriad columns of yellow smoke. Below, in the hollow, more than a hundred peons' houses made a vast open square, where children and animals romped together, and the women kneeled at their eternal grinding of corn. Out on the desert a troop of *vaqueros* rode slowly home; and from the river, a mile away, the endless chain of black-shawled women carried water on their heads. . . . It is impossible to imagine how close to nature the peons live on these great haciendas. Their very houses are built of the earth upon which they stand, baked by the sun. Their food is the corn they grow; their drink the water from the dwindled river, carried painfully upon their heads; the clothes they wear are spun from the wool, and their sandals cut from the hide of a newly slaughtered steer. The animals are their constant companions, familiars of their houses. Light and darkness are their day and night. When a man and a woman fall in love they fly to each other without the formalities of a courtship,—and when they are tired of each other they simply part. Marriage is very costly (six pesos to the priest), and is considered a very swagger extra; but it is no more binding than the most casual attachment. And of course jealousy is a stabbing matter.

We dined in one of the lofty, barren *salas* of the Casa Grande; a room with a ceiling eighteen feet high, and walls of noble proportions, covered with cheap American wallpaper. A gigantic mahogany sideboard occupied one side of the place, but we had no knives and forks. There was a tiny fireplace, in which a fire was never lighted, yet the chill of death abode there day and night. The room next door was hung with heavy, spotted brocade, though there was no rug on the concrete floor. No pipes and no plumbing in all the house,—you went to the well or the river for water. And candles the only light! Of course the *dueño* had long fled the country; but the hacienda in its prime must have been as splendid and as uncomfortable as a medieval castle.

The *cura* or priest of the hacienda church presided at dinner. To him were brought the choicest viands, which he sometimes passed to his favorites after helping himself. We drank *sotol* and *aguamiel*, while the *cura* made away with a whole bottle of looted anisette. Exhilarated by this, His Reverence descanted upon the virtues of the confessional, especially where young girls were concerned. He also made us understand that he possessed certain feudal rights over new brides. "The girls, here," he said, "are very passionate. . . ."

I noticed that the rest didn't laugh much at this, though they were outwardly respectful. After we were out of the room, José Valiente hissed, shaking so that he could hardly speak: "I know the dirty——! And my sister . . . ! The Revolucion will have something to say about these *curas!*" Two high Constitutionalist officers afterward hinted at a little-known program to drive the priests out of Mexico; and Villa's hostility to the *curas* is well known.

Patricio was harnessing the coach when I came out in the morning, and the Tropa were saddling up. The doctor, who was remaining with the General, strolled up to my friend, Trooper Juan Vallejo.

"That's a pretty horse you've got there," he said, "and a nice rifle. Lend them to me."

"But I haven't any other——" began Juan.

"I am your superior officer," returned the doctor. And that was the last we ever saw of doctor, horse and rifle.

I said farewell to the General, who was lying in torture in bed, sending bulletins to his mother by telephone every fifteen minutes. "May you journey happily," he said. "Write the truth. I commend you to Pablito."

CHAPTER IV

LA TROPA ON THE MARCH

AND so I got inside the coach, with Rafaelito, Pablo Seañes, and his mistress. She was a strange creature. Young, slender, and beautiful, she was poison and a stone to everybody but Pablo. I never saw her smile and never heard her say a gentle word. Sometimes she treated us with dull ferocity; sometimes with bestial indifference. But Pablo she cradled like a baby. When he lay across the seat with his head in her lap, she would hug it fiercely to her breast, making noises like a tigress with her young.

Patricio handed down his guitar from the box, where he kept it, and to Rafael's accompaniment the Lieutenant-Colonel sang love-ballads in a cracked voice. Every Mexican knows hundreds of these. They are not written down, but often composed extemporaneously, and handed along by word of mouth. Some of them are

33

very beautiful, some grotesque, and others as satirical as any French popular song. He sang:

> "*Exiled I wandered through the world—*
> *Exiled by the government.*
> *I came back at the end of the year,*
> *Drawn by the fondness of love.*
> *I went away with the purpose*
> *Of staying away forever.*
> *And the love of a woman was the only thing*
> *That made me come back.*"

And then "*Los Hijos de la Noche*":

> "*I am of the children of the night*
> *Who wander aimlessly in the darkness.*
> *The beautiful moon with its golden rays*
> *Is the companion of my sorrows.*

> "*I am going to lose myself from thee,*
> *Exhausted with weeping;*
> *I am going sailing, sailing,*
> *By the shores of the sea.*

> "*You will see at the time of our parting*
> *I will not allow you to love another.*
> *For if so it should be, I would ruin your face,*
> *And many blows we would give one another.*

> "*So I am going to become an American.*
> *Go with God, Antonia.*

LA TROPA ON THE MARCH

Say farewell to my friends.
O may the Americans allow me to pass
And open a saloon
On the other side of the River!"

The Hacienda of El Centro turned out to give us lunch. And there Fidencio offered me his horse to ride for the afternoon.

The Tropa had already ridden on ahead, and I could see them, strung out for half a mile in the black mesquite brush, the tiny red-white-and-green flag bobbing at their head. The mountains had withdrawn somewhere beyond the horizon, and we rode in the midst of a great bowl of desert, rolling up at the edges to meet the furnace-blue of the Mexican sky. Now that I was out of the coach, a great silence, and a peace beyond anything I ever felt, wrapped me around. It is almost impossible to get objective about the desert; you sink into it,—become a part of it. Galloping along, I soon caught up with the Tropa.

"Aye, meester!" they shouted. "Here comes meester on a horse! *Que tal*, meester? How goes it? Are you going to fight with us?"

But Captain Fernando at the head of the column turned and roared: "Come here, meester!" The big man was grinning with delight. "You shall ride with me," he shouted, clapping me on the back. "Drink, now," and he produced a bottle of *sotol* about half full. "Drink it all. Show you're a man." "It's too much," I laughed. "Drink it," yelled the chorus as the Tropa crowded up to see. I drank it. A howl of

laughter and applause went up. Fernando leaned
over and gripped my hand. "Good for you, *compañero!*" he bellowed, rolling with mirth. The men
crowded around, amused and interested. Was I going
to fight with them? Where did I come from? What
was I doing? Most of them had never heard of reporters, and one hazarded the opinion darkly that I
was a Gringo and a Porfirista, and ought to be shot.

The rest, however, were entirely opposed to this view.
No Porfirista would possibly drink that much *sotol* at
a gulp. Isidro Amayo declared that he had been in
a brigade in the first Revolution which was accompanied by a reporter, and that he was called *Corre-
sponsal de Guerra*. Did I like Mexico? I said: "I
am very fond of Mexico. I like Mexicans too. And I
like *sotol, aguardiente, mescal, tequila, pulque*, and
other Mexican customs!" They shouted with laughter.

Captain Fernando leaned over and patted my arm.
"Now you are with the men (*los hombres*.) When we
win the Revolucion it will be a government by the men,
—not by the rich. We are riding over the lands of
the men. They used to belong to the rich, but now
they belong to me and to the *compañeros*."

"And you will be the army?" I asked.

"When the Revolucion is won," was the astonishing
reply, "there will be no more army. The men are sick
of armies. It is by armies that Don Porfirio robbed
us."

"But if the United States should invade Mexico?"

A perfect storm broke everywhere. "We are more
valiente than the Americanos—The cursed Gringos

36

would get no further south than Juarez—Let's see them try it—We'd drive them back over the Border on the run, and burn their capital the next day . . .!"

"No," said Fernando, "you have more money and more soldiers. But the men would protect us. We need no army. The men would be fighting for their houses and their women."

"What are you fighting for?" I asked. Juan Sanchez, the color-bearer, looked at me curiously. "Why, it is good, fighting. You don't have to work in the mines . . . !"

Manuel Paredes said: "We are fighting to restore Francisco I. Madero to the Presidency." This extraordinary statement is printed in the program of the Revolution. And everywhere the Constitutionalist soldiers are known as "Maderistas." "I knew him," continued Manuel, slowly. "He was always laughing, always."

"Yes," said another, "whenever there was any trouble with a man, and all the rest wanted to fight him or put him in prison, Pancho Madero said: 'Just let me talk to him a few minutes. I can bring him around.' "

"He loved *bailes*," an Indian said. "Many a time I've seen him dance all night, and all the next day, and the next night. He used to come to the great Haciendas and make speeches. When he began the peons hated him; when he ended they were crying. . . ."

Here a man broke out into a droning, irregular tune, such as always accompanies the popular ballads that spring up in thousands on every occasion:

INSURGENT MEXICO

"In Nineteen hundred and ten
Madero was imprisoned
In the National Palace
The eighteenth of February

"Four days he was imprisoned
In the Hall of the Intendancy
Because he did not wish
To renounce the Presidency

"Then Blanquet and Felix Diaz
Martyred him there
They were the hangmen
Feeding on his hate.

"They crushed. . . .
Until he fainted
With play of cruelty
To make him resign.

"Then with hot irons
They burned him without mercy
And only unconsciousness
Calmed the awful flames.

"But it was all in vain
Because his mighty courage
Preferred rather to die
His was a great heart!

LA TROPA ON THE MARCH

"This was the end of the life
Of him who was the redeemer
Of the Indian Republic
And of all the poor.

"They took him out of the Palace
And tell us he was killed in an assault
What a cynicism!
What a shameless lie!

"O Street of Lecumberri
Your cheerfulness has ended forever
For through you passed Madero
To the Penitentiary.

"That twenty-second of February
Will always be remembered in the Indian Republic.
God has pardoned him
And the Virgin of Guadelupe.

"Good-bye Beautiful Mexico
Where our leader died
Good-bye to the palace
Whence he issued a living corpse

"Señores, there is nothing eternal
Nor anything sincere in life
See what happened to Don Francisco I. Madero!"

39

By the time he was half-way through, the entire Tropa was humming the tune, and when he finished there was a moment of jingling silence.

"We are fighting," said Isidro Amayo, "for Libertad."

"What do you mean by Libertad?"

"Libertad is when I can *do what I want!*"

"But suppose it hurts somebody else?"

He shot back at me Benito Juarez' great sentence: "Peace is the respect for the rights of others!"

I wasn't prepared for that. It startled me, this barefooted *mestizo's* conception of Liberty. I submit that it is the only correct definition of Liberty—*to do what I want to!* Americans quote it to me triumphantly as an instance of Mexican irresponsibility. But I think it is a better definition than ours—Liberty is the right to do what the Courts want. Every Mexican schoolboy knows the definition of peace and seems to understand pretty well what it means, too. But, they say, Mexicans don't want peace. That is a lie, and a foolish one. Let Americans take the trouble to go through the Maderista army, asking whether they want peace or not! The people are sick of war.

But, just to be square, I'll have to report Juan Sanchez' remark:

"Is there war in the United States now?" he asked.

"No," I said untruthfully.

"No war at all?" He meditated for a moment. "How do you pass the time, then . . . ?"

Just about then somebody saw a coyote sneaking through the brush, and the entire Tropa gave chase with a whoop. They scattered rollicking over the desert, the late sun flashing from cartridge-belts and spurs, the ends of their bright serapes flying out behind. Beyond them, the scorched world sloped gently up, and a range of far lilac mountains jumped in the heat waves like a bucking horse. By here, if tradition is right, passed the steel-armored Spaniards in their search for gold, a blaze of crimson and silver that has left the desert cold and dull ever since. And, topping a rise, we came upon the first sight of the Hacienda of La Mimbrera, a walled enclosure of houses strong enough to stand a siege, stretching steeply down a hill, with the magnificent Casa Grande at the top.

In front of this house, which had been sacked and burned by Orozco's General, Che Che Campa, two years before, the coach was drawn up. A huge fire had been kindled, and ten *compañeros* were slaughtering sheep. Into the red glare of the firelight they staggered, with the struggling, squealing sheep in their arms, its blood fountaining upon the ground, shining in the fierce light like something phosphorescent.

The officers and I dined in the house of the *administrador* Don Jesus, the most beautiful specimen of manhood I have ever seen. He was much over six feet tall, slender, white-skinned—a pure Spanish type of the highest breed. At one end of his dining-room, I remember, hung a placard embroidered in red, white and green: "Viva Mexico!" and at the other, a second, which read: "Viva Jesus!"

It was after dinner, as I stood at the fire, wondering where I was to sleep, that Captain Fernando touched me on the arm.

"Will you sleep with the *compañeros?*"

We walked across the great open square, in the furious light of the desert stars, to a stone store-house set apart. Inside, a few candles stuck against the wall illumined the rifles stacked in the corners, the saddles on the floor, and the blanket-rolled *compañeros* with their heads on them. One or two were awake, talking and smoking. In a corner, three sat muffled in their serapes, playing cards. Five or six had voices and a guitar. They were singing "Pascual Orozco," beginning:

"They say that Pascual Orozco has turned his coat
Because Don Terrazzas seduced him;
They gave him many millions and they bought him
And sent him to overthrow the government.

"Orozco believed it
And to the war he went;
But the Maderista cannon
Was his calamity.

"If to thy window shall come Porfirio Diaz,
Give him for charity some cold tortillas;
If to thy window shall come General Huerta,
Spit in his face and slam the door.

"If to thy window shall come Inez Salazar,
Lock your trunk so that he can't steal;
If to thy window shall come Maclovio Herrera,
Give him dinner and put the cloth on the table."

LA TROPA ON THE MARCH

They didn't distinguish me at first, but soon one of the card-players said: "Here comes Meester!" At that the others roused, and woke the rest. "That's right—it's good to sleep with the *hombres*—take this place, *amigo*—here's my saddle—here there is no crookedness —here a man goes straight. . . ."

"May you pass a happy night, *compañero*," they said. "Till morning, then."

Pretty soon somebody shut the door. The room became full of smoke and fetid with human breath. What little silence was left from the chorus of snoring was entirely obliterated by the singing, which kept up, I guess, until dawn. The *compañeros* had fleas. . . .

But I rolled up in my blankets and lay down upon the concrete floor very happily. And I slept better than I had before in Mexico.

At dawn we were in the saddle, larking up a steep roll of barren desert to get warm. It was bitter cold. The Tropa were wrapped in serapes up to their eyes, so that they looked like colored toadstools under their great sombreros. The level rays of the sun, burning as they fell upon my face, caught them unaware, glorifying the serapes to more brilliant colors than they possessed. Isidro Amayo's was of deep blue and yellow spirals; Juan Sanchez had one brick red, Captain Fernando's was green and cerise; against them flashed a purple and black zigzag pattern. . . .

We looked back to see the coach pulled to a stop, and Patricio waving to us. Two of the mules had given out, raw from the traces, and tottering with the

43

fatigue of the last two days. The Tropa scattered to look for mules. Soon they came back, driving two great beautiful animals that had never seen harness. No sooner had they smelled the coach than they made a desperate break for freedom. And now the Tropa instantly went back to their native profession—they became *vaqueros*. It was a pretty sight, the rope-coils swinging in the air, the sudden snake-like shoot of the loops, the little horses bracing themselves against the shock of the running mule. Those mules were demons. Time after time they broke the *riatas;* twice they overturned horse and rider. Pablo came to the rescue. He got on Sabas's horse, drove in the spurs, and went after one mule. In three minutes he had roped him by the leg, thrown him, and tied him. Then he took the second with equal dispatch. It was not for nothing that Pablo was Lieutenant-Colonel at twenty-six. Not only could he fight better than his men, but he could ride better, rope better, shoot better, chop wood better, and dance better.

The mules' legs were tied, and they were dragged with ropes to the coach, where the harness was slipped on them in spite of their frantic struggles. When all was ready, Patricio got on the box, seized the whip, and told us to cut away. The wild animals scrambled to their feet, bucking and squealing. Above the uproar came the crack of the heavy whip, and Patricio's bellow: *"Andale! hijos de la Gran' Ch——!"* and they jerked forward, running, the big coach taking the arroyos like an express train. Soon it vanished behind its own pall of dust, and appeared hours afterward, crawling up the side of a great hill, miles away. . . .

Panchito was eleven years old, already a trooper with a rifle too heavy for him, and a horse that they had to lift him on. His *compadre* was Victoriano, a veteran of fourteen. Seven others of the Tropa were under seventeen. And there was a sullen, Indian-faced woman, riding side-saddle, who wore two cartridge-belts. She rode with the *hombres*—slept with them in the cuartels.

"Why are you fighting?" I asked her.

She jerked her head toward the fierce figure of Julian Reyes.

"Because he is," she answered. "He who stands under a good tree is sheltered by a good shade."

"A good rooster will crow in any chicken-coop," capped Isidro.

"A parrot is green all over," chimed in someone else.

"Faces we see, but hearts we do not comprehend," said José, sentimentally.

At noon we roped a steer, and cut his throat. And because there was no time to build a fire, we ripped the meat from the carcase and ate it raw.

"*Oiga*, meester," shouted José. "Do the United States soldiers eat raw meat?"

I said I didn't think they did.

"It is good for the *hombres*. In the campaign we have no time for anything but *carne crudo*. It makes us brave."

By late afternoon we had caught up with the coach, and galloped with it down through the dry arroyo and up through the other side, past the great *ribota* court that flanks the Hacienda of La Zarca. Unlike La Mimbrera, the Casa Grande here stands on a level place, with the peons' houses in long rows at its flanks, and a flat desert barren of chaparral for twenty miles in front. Che Che Campa also paid a visit to La Zarca. The big house is a black and gaping ruin.

CHAPTER V

WHITE NIGHTS AT ZARCA

OF course, I took up quarters at the cuartel. And right here I want to mention one fact. Americans had insisted that the Mexican was fundamentally dishonest—that I might expect to have my outfit stolen the first day out. Now for two weeks I lived with as rough a band of ex-outlaws as there was in the army. They were without discipline and without education. They were, many of them, Gringo-haters. They had not been paid a cent for six weeks, and some were so desperately poor that they couldn't boast sandals or serapes. I was a stranger with a good outfit, unarmed. I had a hundred and fifty pesos, which I put conspicuously at the head of my bed when I slept. And I never lost a thing. But more than that, I was not permitted to pay for my food; and in a company where money was scarce and tobacco al-

46

most unknown, I was kept supplied with all I could smoke by the *compañeros*. Every suggestion from me that I should pay for it was an insult.

The only thing possible was to hire music for a *baile*. Long after Juan Sanchez and I rolled up in our blankets that night, we could hear the rhythm of the music, and the shouts of the dancers. It must have been midnight when somebody threw open the door and yelled: "Meester! *Oiga*, meester! Are you asleep? Come to the *baile! Arriba! Andale!*"

"Too sleepy!" I said. After some further argument the messenger departed, but in ten minutes back he came. "El Capitan Fernando orders you to come at once! *Vamonos!*" Now the others woke up. "Come to the *baile*, meester!" they shouted. Juan Sanchez sat up and began pulling on his shoes. "Now we're off!" said he. "The meester is going to dance! Captain's orders! Come on, meester!"

"I'll go if all the Tropa does," I said. They raised a yell at that, and the night was full of chuckling men pulling on their clothes.

Twenty of us reached the house in a body. The mob of peons blocking door and window opened to let us pass. "The meester!" they cried. "The meester's going to dance!"

Capitan Fernando threw his arms about me, roaring: "Here he comes, the *compañero!* Dance now! Go to it! They're going to dance the *jota!*"

"But I don't know how to dance the *jota!*"

Patricio, flushed and panting, seized me by the arm.

47

"Come on, it's easy! I'll introduce you to the best girl in the Zarca!"

There was nothing to do. The window was jammed with faces, and a hundred tried to crowd in at the door. It was an ordinary room in a peon's house, whitewashed, with a humpy dirt floor. In the light of two candles sat the musicians. The music struck up *"Puentes á Chihuahua."* A grinning silence fell. I gathered the young lady under my arm, and started the preliminary march around the room customary before the dance begins. We waltzed painfully for a moment or two, and suddenly they all began to yell: *"Ora! Ora!* Now!"

"What do you do now?"

"Vuelta! Vuelta! Loose her!" a perfect yell.

"But I don't know how!"

"The fool doesn't know how to dance," cried one. Another began the mocking song:

> *"The Gringos all are fools,*
> *They've never been in Sonora,*
> *And when they want to say: 'Diez Reales,'*
> *They call it 'Dollar an' a quarta' . . . ."*

But Patricio bounded into the middle of the floor, and Sabas after him; each seized a *muchacha* from the line of women sitting along one end of the room. And as I led my partner back to her seat, they *"vuelta'd."* First a few waltz steps,—then the man whirled away from the girl, snapping his fingers, throwing one arm up to cover his face, while the girl

48

put one hand on her hip and danced after him. They approached each other, receded, danced around each other. The girls were dumpy and dull, Indian-faced and awkward, bowed at the shoulder from much grinding of corn and washing of clothes. Some of the men had on heavy boots, some none; many wore pistols and cartridge-belts, and a few carried rifles slung from their shoulders.

The dance was always preceded by a grand march-around; then, after the couple had danced twice the circuit of the room, they walked again. There were two-steps, waltz and mazurka beside the *jota*. Each girl kept her eyes on the ground, never spoke, and stumbled heavily after you. Add to this a dirt floor full of arroyos, and you have a form of torture unequaled anywhere in the world. It seemed to me I danced for hours, spurred on by the chorus: "Dance, meester! *No floje!* Keep it up! Don't quit!"

Later there was another *jota*, and here's where I almost got into trouble. I danced this one successfully —with another girl. And afterward, when I asked my original partner to two-step, she was furiously angry.

"You shamed me before them all," said she. "*You* —you said you didn't know how to dance the *jota!*" As we marched around the room, she appealed to her friends: "Domingo! Juan! Come out and take me away from this Gringo! He won't dare to do anything!"

Half a dozen of them started onto the floor, and the rest looked on. It was a ticklish moment. But all

at once the good Fernando glided in front, a revolver
in his hand.

"The Americano is my friend!" said he. "Get back
there and mind your business! . . ."

The horses were tired, so we rested a day in La
Zarca. Behind the Casa Grande lay a ruined garden,
full of gray alamo trees, figs, vines, and great barrel-
cactuses. It was walled around by high adobe walls on
three sides, over one of which the ancient white tower
of the church floated in the blue sky. The fourth
side opened upon a reservoir of yellow water, and beyond it stretched the western desert, miles upon miles
of tawny desolation. Trooper Marin and I lay under
a fig tree, watching the vultures sail over us on quiet
wing. Suddenly the silence was broken by loud, swift
music.

Pablo had found a pianola in the church, where it
had escaped Che Che Campa's notice the previous year;
with it was one roll, the "Merry Widow Waltz." Nothing would do but that we carry the instrument out into
the ruined patio. We took turns playing the thing
all day long; Rafaelito volunteering the information
that the "Merry Widow" was Mexico's most popular
piece. A Mexican, he said, had composed it.

The finding of the pianola suggested that we give
another baile that night, in the portico of the Casa
Grande itself. Candles were stuck upon the pillars, the
faint light flickering upon broken walls, burned and
blackened doorways, the riot of wild vines that had
twisted unchecked around the roof-beams. The en-

tire patio was crowded with blanketed men, making holiday, even yet a little uncomfortable in the great house which they had never been allowed to enter. As soon as the orchestra had finished a dance, the pianola immediately took up the task. Dance followed dance, without any rest. A barrel of *sotol* further complicated things. As the evening wore on the assembly got more and more exhilarated. Sabas, who was Pablo's orderly, led off with Pablo's mistress. I followed. Immediately afterward Pablo hit her on the head with the butt end of his revolver, and said he'd shoot her if she danced with anyone else, and her partner too. After sitting some moments meditating, Sabas rose, pulled his revolver, and informed the harpist that he had played a wrong note. Then he shot at him. Other *compañeros* disarmed Sabas, who immediately went to sleep in the middle of the dance-floor.

The interest in Meester's dancing soon shifted to other phenomena. I sat down beside Julian Reyes, he with the Christ and Virgin on the front of his sombrero. He was far gone in *sotol*—his eyes burned like a fanatic's.

He turned on me suddenly:

"Are you going to fight with us?"

"No," I said. "I am a correspondent. I am forbidden to fight."

"It is a lie," he cried. "You don't fight because you are afraid to fight. In the face of God, our Cause is Just."

"Yes, I know that. But my orders are not to fight."

"What do I care for orders?" he shrieked. "We

want no correspondents. We want no words printed in
a book. We want rifles and killing, and if we die we
shall be caught up among the saints! Coward! Huertista! . . ."

"That's enough!" cried someone, and I looked up to
see Longinos Güereca standing over me. "Julian
Reyes, you know nothing. This *compañero* comes thousands of miles by the sea and the land to tell his countrymen the truth of the fight for Liberty. He goes
into battle without arms, he's braver than you are, because you have a rifle. Get out now, and don't bother
him any more!"

He sat down where Julian had been, smiled his home-
ly, gentle smile, and took both my hands in his.

"We shall be *compadres*, eh?" said Longinos Güereca. "We shall sleep in the same blankets, and always
be together. And when we get to the Cadena I shall
take you to my home, and my father shall make you
my brother. . . . I will show you the lost gold-mines
of the Spaniards, the richest mines in the world. . . .
We'll work them together, eh? . . . We'll be rich,
eh? . . ."

And from that time on until the end, Longinos
Güereca and I were always together.

But the *baile* grew wilder and wilder. Orchestra
and pianola alternated without a break. Everybody
was drunk now. Pablo was boasting horribly of killing
defenseless prisoners. Occasionally, some insult would
be passed, and there would be a snapping of rifle levers
all over the place. Then perhaps the poor exhausted

women would begin to go home; and what an ominous
shout would go up: *"No vaya!* Don't go! Stop!
Come back here and dance! Come back here!" And
the dejected procession would halt and straggle back.
At four o'clock, when somebody started the report that
a Gringo Huertista spy was among us, I decided to
go to bed. But the *baile* kept up until seven. . . .

CHAPTER VI

"QUIEN VIVE?"

AT dawn I woke to the sound of shooting, and a
cracked bugle blowing wildly. Juan Sanchez
stood in front of the cuartel, sounding Reveille;
he didn't know which call Reveille was, so he played
them all.

Patricio had roped a steer for breakfast. The animal started on a plunging, bellowing run for the desert,
Patricio's horse galloping alongside. The rest of the
Tropa, only their eyes showing over their serapes,
kneeled with their rifles to their shoulders. Crash!
In that still air, the enormous sound of guns labored
heavily up. The running steer jerked sideways,—his
screaming reached us faintly. Crash! He fell head-
long. His feet kicked in the air. Patricio's pony
jerked roughly up, and his serape flapped like a ban-
ner. Just then the enormous sun rose bodily out of
the east, pouring clear light over the barren plain like
a sea. . . .

Pablo emerged from the Casa Grande, leaning on his wife's shoulder.

"I am going to be very ill," he groaned, suiting the action to the word. "Juan Reed will ride my horse."

He got into the coach, weakly took the guitar, and sang:

"I remained at the foot of a green maguey
My ungrateful love went away with another.
I awoke to the song of the lark:
Oh, what a hangover I have, and the barkeeps won't
*   trust me!*

"O God, take away this sickness,
I feel as if I were surely going to die—
The Virgin of pulque and whisky must save me:
O what a hangover, and nothing to drink! . . ."

It is some sixty-five miles from La Zarca to the Hacienda of La Cadena, where the Tropa was to be stationed. We rode it in one day, without water and without food. The coach soon left us far behind. Pretty soon, the barrenness of the land gave way to spiny, hostile vegetation,—the cactus and the mesquite. We strung out along a deep rut between the gigantic chaparral, choked with the mighty cloud of alkali dust, scratched and torn by the thorny brush. Sometimes emerging in an open space, we could see the straight road climbing the summits of the rolling desert, until the eye couldn't follow it; but we knew it must be there, still farther and farther again. Not a breath of wind stirred. The vertical sun beat down with a fury that made one reel. And most of the troop, who had been drunk the night before, began to suffer terribly. Their lips glazed, cracked, turned dark blue. I didn't hear a single word of complaint; but there was nothing of the lighthearted joking and rollicking of other days. José Valiente taught me how to chew mesquite twigs, but that didn't help much.

When we had been riding for hours, Fidencio pointed ahead, saying huskily: "Here comes a *christiano!*" When you realize that word *christiano*, which now means simply Man, is descended among the Indians from immeasurable antiquity,—and when the man that says it looks exactly as Guatemozin might have looked, it gives you curious sensations. The *christiano* in question was a very aged Indian driving a burro. No, he said, he didn't carry any water. But Sabas leaped from his horse and tumbled the old man's pack on the ground.

"Ah!" he cried; "fine! *Tres piedras!*" and held up a root of the *sotol* plant, which looks like a varnished century-plant, and oozes with intoxicating juices. We divided it as you divide an artichoke. Pretty soon everybody felt better. . . .

It was at the end of the afternoon that we rounded a shoulder of the desert and saw ahead the gigantic ashen alamo trees that surrounded the spring of the Hacienda of Santo Domingo. A pillar of brown dust, like the smoke of a burning city, rose from the corral, where *vaqueros* were roping horses. Desolate and alone stood the Casa Grande, burned by Che Che Campa a year ago. And by the spring, at the foot of the alamo trees, a dozen wandering peddlers squatted around their fire, their burros munching corn. From the fountain to the adobe houses and back moved an endless chain of women water-carriers,—the symbol of northern Mexico.

"Water!" we shouted, joyously, galloping down the hill. The coach-horses were already at the spring with Patricio. Leaping from their saddles, the Tropa threw themselves on their bellies. Men and horses indiscriminately thrust in their heads, and drank and drank. . . . It was the most glorious sensation I have ever felt.

"Who has a cigarro?" cried somebody. For a few blessed minutes we lay on our backs smoking. The sound of music—gay music—made me sit up. And there, across my vision, moved the strangest procession in the world. First came a ragged peon carrying the flowering branch of some tree. Behind him, another bore upon his head a little box that looked like a coffin, painted in broad strips of blue, pink and silver. There followed four men, carrying a sort of canopy made of gay-colored bunting. A woman walked beneath it, though the canopy hid her down to the waist; but on top lay the body of a little girl, with bare feet and little brown hands crossed on her breast. There was a wreath of paper flowers in her hair, and her whole body was heaped with them. A harpist brought up the rear, playing a popular waltz called "*Recuerdos de Durango.*" The funeral procession moved slowly and gaily along, passing the *ribota* court, where the players never ceased their handball game,

"QUIEN VIVE?"

to the little Campo Santo. "Bah!" spat Julian Reyes
furiously. "That is a blasphemy to the dead!"

In the late sunshine the desert was a glowing thing.
We rode in a silent, enchanted land, that seemed some
kingdom under the sea. All around were great cactuses
colored red, blue, purple, yellow, as coral is on the
ocean bed. Behind us, to the west, the coach rolled
along in a glory of dust like Elijah's chariot. . . .
Eastward, under a sky already darkening to stars,
were the rumpled mountains behind which lay La Cadena, the advance post of the Maderista army. It
was a land to love—this Mexico—a land to fight for.
The ballad-singers suddenly began the interminable
song of "The Bull-Fight," in which the Federal chiefs
are the bulls, and the Maderista generals the *torreros;*
and as I looked at the gay, lovable, humble *hombres*
who had given so much of their lives and of their comfort to the brave fight, I couldn't help but think of the
little speech Villa made to the foreigners who left Chihuahua in the first refugee train:

"This is the latest news for you to take to your people. There shall be no more palaces in Mexico. The
tortillas of the poor are better than the bread of the
rich. Come! . . ."

It was late night—past eleven—when the coach broke
down on a stretch of rocky road between high mountains. I stopped to get my blankets; and when I
started on again, the *compañeros* had long vanished
down the winding road. Somewhere near, I knew, was
La Cadena. At any minute now a sentinel might start

up out of the chaparral. For about a mile I descended a steep road that was often the dried bed of a river, winding down between high mountains. It was a black night, without stars, and bitter cold. Finally, the mountains opened into a vast plain, and across that I could faintly see the tremendous range of the Cadena, and the pass that the Tropa was to guard. Barely three leagues beyond that pass lay Mapimi, held by twelve hundred Federals. But the hacienda was still hidden by a roll of the desert.

I was quite upon it, without being challenged, before I saw it, an indistinct white square of buildings on the other side of a deep arroyo. And still no sentinel. "That's funny," I said to myself. "They don't keep very good watch here." I plunged down into the arroyo, and climbed up the other side. In one of the great rooms of the Casa Grande were lights and music. Peering through, I saw the indefatigable Sabas whirling in the mazes of the *jota*, and Isidro Amayo, and José Valiente. A *baile!* Just then a man with a gun lounged out of the lighted doorway.

"Quien vive?" he shouted, lazily.

"Madero!" I shouted.

"May he live!" returned the sentinel, and went back to the *baile.* . . .

AN OUTPOST OF THE REVOLUTION

CHAPTER VII

AN OUTPOST OF THE REVOLUTION

THERE were a hundred and fifty of us stationed at La Cadena, the advance guard of all the Maderista army to the West. Our business was to guard a pass, the Puerta de la Cadena; but the troops were quartered at the hacienda, ten miles away. It stood upon a little plateau, a deep arroyo on one side, at the bottom of which a sunken river came to the surface for perhaps a hundred yards, and vanished again. As far as the eye could reach up and down the broad valley was the fiercest kind of desert, —dried creek-beds, and a thicket of chaparral, cactus and sword plant.

Directly east lay the Puerta, breaking the tremendous mountain range that blotted out half the sky and extended north and south beyond vision, wrinkled like a giant's bed-clothes. The desert tilted up to meet the gap, and beyond was nothing but the fierce blue of stainless Mexican sky. From the Puerta you could see fifty miles across the vast arid plain that the Spaniards named *Llano de los Gigantes*, where the little mountains lie tumbled about; and four leagues away the low gray houses of Mapimi. There lay the enemy; twelve hundred *colorados*, or Federal irregulars, under the infamous Colonel Argumendo. The *colorados* are the bandits that made Orozco's revolution. They were so called because their flag was red, and because their hands were red with slaughter, too. They swept through Northern Mexico, burning, pillaging and robbing the poor. In Chihuahua, they cut the soles from the feet of one poor devil, and drove him a mile across the desert before he died. And I have seen a city of four thousand souls reduced to *five* after a visit by the *colorados*. When Villa took Torreon, there was no mercy for the *colorados;* they are always shot.

The first day we reached La Cadena, twelve of them rode up to reconnoiter. Twenty-five of the Tropa were on guard at the Puerta. They captured one *colorado*. They made him get off his horse, and took away his rifle, clothes and shoes. Then they made him run naked through a hundred yards of chaparral and cactus, shooting at him. Juan Sanchez finally dropped him, screaming, and thereby won the rifle, which he brought back as a present to me. The *colorado* they left to the great Mexican buzzards, which flap lazily above the desert all day long.

When all this happened, my *compadre*, Captain Longinos Güereca, and Trooper Juan Vallejo, and I, had borrowed the Colonel's coach for a trip to the dusty little rancho of Bruquilla,—Longinos' home. It lay four desert leagues to the north, where a spring burst miraculously out of a little white hill. Old Güereca was a white-haired peon in sandals. He had been born a slave on one of the great haciendas; but years of toil, too appalling to realize, had made him that rare being in Mexico, the independent owner of a small property. He had ten children,—soft, dark-skinned girls, and sons that looked like New England farmhands,—and a daughter in the grave.

The Güerecas were proud, ambitious, warm-hearted folk. Longinos said: "This is my dearly loved friend, Juan Reed, and my brother." And the old man and his wife put both their arms around me and patted me on the back, in the affectionate way Mexicans embrace.

"My family owes nothing to the Revolucion," said 'Gino, proudly. "Others have taken money and horses and wagons. The *jefes* of the army have become rich from the property of the great haciendas. The Güerecas have given all to the Maderistas, and have taken nothing but my rank. . . ."

The old man, however, was a little bitter. Holding up a horsehair rope, he said: "Three years ago I had four *riatas* like this. Now I have only one. One the *colorados* took, and the other Urbina's people took, and the last one José Bravo. . . . What difference does it make which side robs you?" But he didn't mean it all. He was immensely proud of his youngest son, the bravest officer in all the army.

We sat in the long adobe room, eating the most exquisite cheese, and *tortillas* with fresh goat-butter, —the deaf old mother apologizing in a loud voice for the poverty of the food, and her warlike son reciting his personal Iliad of the nine-days' fight around Torreon.

"We got so close," he was saying, "that the hot air and burning powder stung us in the face. We got too close to shoot, so we clubbed our rifles——"

Just then all the dogs began to bark at once. We leaped from our seats. One didn't know what to expect in the Cadena those days. It was a small boy on horseback, shouting that the *colorados* were entering the Puerta—and off he galloped.

Longinos roared to put the mules in the coach. The entire family fell to work with a fury, and in five minutes Longinos dropped on one knee and kissed his father's hand, and we were tearing down the road. "Don't be killed! Don't be killed! Don't be killed!" we could hear the Señora wailing.

We passed a wagon loaded with corn-stalks, with a whole family of women and children, two tin trunks, and an iron bed, perched on top. The man of the family rode a burro. Yes, the *colorados* were coming —thousands of them pouring through the Puerta. The last time the *colorados* had come they had killed his daughter. For three years there had been war in this valley, and he had not complained. Because it was for the Patria. Now they would go to the United States where—— But Juan lashed the mules cruelly, and we heard no more. Farther along was an old man without shoes, placidly driving some goats. Had he heard about the *colorados?* Well, there *had* been some gossip about *colorados*. Were they coming through the Puerta, and how many?

"*Pues, quien sabe, señor!*"

At last, yelling at the staggering mules, we came into camp just in time to see the victorious Tropa straggle in across the desert, firing off many more rounds of ammunition than they had used in the fight.

62

AN OUTPOST OF THE REVOLUTION

They moved low along the ground, scarcely higher on their broncos than the drab mesquite through which they flashed, all big sombreros and flapping gay serapes, the last sunshine on their lifted rifles.

That very night came a courier from General Urbina, saying that he was ill and wanted Pablo Seañes to come back. So off went the great coach, and Pablo's mistress, and Raphaelito, the hunchback, and Fidencio, and Patricio. Pablo said to me: "Juanito, if you want to come back with us, you shall sit beside me in the coach." Patricio and Raphaelito begged me to come. But I had got so far to the front now that I didn't want to turn back. Then the next day my friends and *compañeros* of the Tropa, whom I had learned to know so well in our march across the desert, received orders to move to Jarralitos. Only Juan Vallejo and Longinos Güereca stayed behind.

The Cadena's new garrison were a different kind of men. God knows where they came from, but it was a place where the troopers had literally starved. They were the most wretchedly poor peons that I have ever seen—about half of them didn't have serapes. Some fifty were known to be *nuevos* who had never smelt powder, about the same number were under a dreadfully incompetent old party named Major Salazar, and the remaining fifty were equipped with old carbines and ten rounds of ammunition apiece. Our commanding officer was Lieutenant-Colonel Petronilo Hernandez, who had been six years a Major in the Federal army until the murder of Madero drove him to the other side. He was a brave, good-hearted little man, with twisted

63

shoulders, but years of official army red tape had un-
fitted him to handle troops like these. Every morning
he issued an Order of the Day, distributing guards,
posting sentinels, and naming the officer on duty. Nobody ever read it. Officers in that army have nothing
to do with the disciplining or ordering of soldiers.
They are officers because they have been brave, and
their job is to fight at the head of their troop—that's
all. The soldiers all look up to some one General, under whom they are recruited, as to their feudal lord.
They call themselves his *gente*—his people; and an
officer of anybody else's *gente* hasn't much authority
over them. Petronilo was of Urbina's *gente;* but two-
thirds of the Cadena garrison belonged to Arrieta's
division. That's why there were no sentinels to the
west and north. Lieutenant-Colonel Alberto Redondo
guarded another pass four leagues to the south, so we
thought we were safe in that direction. True, twenty-
five men did outpost duty at the Puerta, and the
Puerta was strong. . . .

CHAPTER VIII

THE FIVE MUSKETEERS

THE Casa Grande of La Cadena had been sacked,
of course, by Che Che Campa the year before. In the patio were corraled the officers'
horses. We slept on the tiled floors of the rooms surrounding it. In the *sala* of the owner, once barbari-

cally decorated, pegs were driven into the walls to hang saddles and bridles on, rifles and sabers were stacked against the wall, and dirty blanket-rolls lay flung into the corner. At night a fire of corn-cobs was built in the middle of the floor, and we squatted around it, while Apolinario and fourteen-year-old Gil Tomas, who was once a *colorado*, told stories of the Bloody Three Years.

"At the taking of Durango," said Apolinario, "I was of the *gente* of Captain Borunda; he that they call the *Matador*, because he always shoots his prisoners. But when Urbina took Durango there weren't many prisoners. So Borunda, thirsty for blood, made the rounds of all the saloons. And in every one he would pick out some unarmed man and ask him if he were a Federal. 'No, señor,' the man would say. 'You deserve death because you have not told the truth!' yelled Borunda, pulling his gun. Bang!"

We all laughed heartily at this.

"That reminds me," broke in Gil, "of the time I fought with Rojas in Orozco's—(cursed be his mother!)—Revolucion. An old Porfirista officer deserted to our side, and Orozco sent him out to teach the *colorados* (animals!) how to drill. There was one droll fellow in our company. Oh! he had a fine sense of humor. He pretended he was too stupid to learn the manual of arms. So this cursed old Huertista—(may he fry in hell!)—made him drill alone.

" 'Shoulder arms!' The *compañero* did it all right.

" 'Present arms!' Perfectly.

" 'Port arms!' He acted like he didn't know how, so the old fool went around and took hold of the rifle.

" '*This* way!' says he, pulling on it.

" 'Oh!' says the fellow, '*that* way!' And he let him have the bayonet right in the chest. . . ."

After that Fernando Silveyra, the paymaster, recounted a few anecdotes of the *curas*, or priests, that sounded exactly like Touraine in the thirteenth century, or the feudal rights of landlords over their women tenants before the French Revolution. Fernando ought to have known, too, for he was brought up for the Church. There must have been about twenty of us sitting around that fire, all the way from the most miserably poor peon in the Tropa up to First Captain Longinos Güereca. There wasn't one of these men who had any religion at all, although once they had all been strict Catholics. But three years of war have taught the Mexican people many things. There will never be another Porfirio Diaz; there will never be another Orozco Revolution; and the Catholic Church in Mexico will never again be the voice of God.

Then Juan Santillanes, a twenty-two-year-old *subteniente*, who seriously informed me that he was descended from the great Spanish hero, Gil Blas, piped up the ancient disreputable ditty, which begins:

> "*I am Count Oliveros*
> *Of the Spanish artillery. . . .*"

Juan proudly displayed four bullet wounds. He had killed a few defenseless prisoners with his own gun,

66

he said; giving promise of growing up to be *muy mata-dor* (a great killer) some day. He boasted of being the strongest and bravest man in the army. His idea of humor seemed to be breaking eggs into the pocket of my coat. Juan was very young for his years, but very likable.

But the best friend I had beside 'Gino Güereca was Subteniente Luis Martinez. They called him "*Gachu-pine*"—the contemptuous name for Spaniards—because he might have stepped out of a portrait of some noble Spanish youth by Greco. Luis was pure race—sensitive, gay and high-spirited. He was only twenty, and had never been in battle. Around the contour of his face was a faint black beard.

He fingered it, grinning. "Nicanor and I made a bet that we wouldn't shave until we took Torreon. . . ."

Luis and I slept in different rooms. But at night, when the fire had gone out and the rest of the fellows were snoring, we sat at each other's blankets—one night in his cuartel, the one next to mine—talking about the world, our girls, and what we were going to be and to do when we really got at it. When the war was over, Luis was coming to the United States to visit me; and then we were both coming back to Durango City to visit the Martinez family. He showed me the photograph of a little baby, proudly boasting that he was an uncle already. "What will you do when the bullets begin to fly?" I asked him.

"*Quien sabe?*" he laughed. "I guess I'll run!"

It was late. The sentinel at the door had long since

gone to sleep. "Don't go," said Luis, grabbing my coat. "Let's gossip a little longer. . . ."

'Gino, Juan Santillanes, Silveyra, Luis, Juan Vallejo and I rode up the arroyo to bathe in a pool that was rumored to be there. It was a scorched river bed filled with white-hot sand, rimmed with dense mesquite and cactus. Every kilometer the hidden river showed itself for a little space, only to disappear at a crackling white rim of alkali. First came the horse pool, the troopers and their wretched ponies gathered around it; one or two squatting on the rim, scooping water up against the animals' sides with calabashes. . . . Above them kneeled the women at their eternal laundry on the stones. Beyond that the ancient path from the hacienda cut across, where the never-ending line of black-shawled women moved with water-jars on their heads. Still farther up were women bathers, wrapped round and round with yards of pale blue or white cotton, and naked brown babies splashing in the shallows. And, last of all, naked brown men, with sombreros on and bright-colored serapes draped over their shoulders, smoked their *hojas*, squatting on the rocks. We flushed a coyote up there, and scrambled steeply up to the desert, pulling at our revolvers. There he went! We spurred into the chaparral on the dead run, shooting and yelling. But of course he got away. And later, much later, we found the mythical pool—a cool, deep basin worn in the solid rock, with green weeds growing on the bottom.

When we got back, 'Gino Güereca became greatly excited, because his new *tordillo* horse had come from Bruquilla—a four-year-old stallion that his father had raised for him to ride at the head of his company.

"If he is dangerous," announced Juan Santillanes, as we hurried out, "I want to ride him first. I *love* to subdue dangerous horses!"

A mighty cloud of yellow dust filled all the corral, rising high into the still air. Through it appeared the dim chaotic shapes of many running horses. Their hoofs made dull thunder. Men were vaguely visible, all braced legs and swinging arms, handkerchiefs bound over their faces; wide-spreading rope coils lifted, circling. The big gray felt the loop tighten on his neck. He trumpeted and plunged; the *vaquero* twisted the rope around his hip, lying back almost to the ground, feet plowing the dirt. Another noose gripped the horse's hind legs—and he was down. They put a saddle on him and a rope halter.

"Want to ride him, Juanito?" grinned 'Gino.

"After you," answered Juan with dignity. "He's your horse. . . ."

But Juan Vallejo already was astride, shouting to them to loose the ropes. With a sort of squealing roar, the *tordillo* struggled up, and the earth trembled to his furious fight.

We dined in the ancient kitchen of the hacienda, sitting on stools around a packing box. The ceiling was a rich, greasy brown, from the smoke of generations of meals. One entire end of the room was taken up by immense adobe stoves, ovens, and fireplaces, with four or five ancient crones bending over them, stirring pots and turning *tortillas*. The fire was our only light, flickering strangely over the old women; lighting up the black wall, up which the smoke fled, to wreathe around the ceiling and finally pour from the window. There were Colonel Petronilo, his mistress, a strangely beautiful peasant woman with a pock-marked face, who always seemed to be laughing to herself about something; Don Tomas, Luis Martinez, Colonel Redondo, Major Salazar, Nicanor, and I. The Colonel's mistress seemed uncomfortable at the table; for a Mexican peasant woman is a servant in her house. But Don Petronilo always treated her as if she were a great lady.

Redondo had just been telling me about the girl he was going to marry. He showed me her picture. She was even then on her way to Chihuahua to get her wedding dress. "As soon as we take Torreon," he said.

"Oiga, señor!" Salazar touched me on the arm. "I have found out who you are. You are an agent of American business men who have vast interests in Mexico. I know *all* about American business. You are an agent of the trusts. You come down here to spy upon the movement of our troops, and then you will secretly send them word. Is it not true?"

"How could I secretly send anybody any word from here?" I asked. "We're four days' hard ride from a telegraph line."

"Ah, *I* know," he grinned cunningly, wabbling a finger at me. "I know many things; I have much in the head." He was standing up now. The Major suffered badly from gout; his legs were wrapped in yards and yards of woolen bandages, which made them look like *tamales*. "I know *all* about business. I have studied much in my youth. These American trusts are invading Mexico to rob the Mexican people——"

"You're mistaken, Major," interrupted Don Petronilo sharply. "This señor is my friend and my guest."

"Listen, *mi Coronel*," Salazar burst out with unexpected violence. "This señor is a spy. All Americans are Porfiristas and Huertistas. Take this warning before it is too late. I have much in the head. I am a very smart man. Take this Gringo out and shoot him —at once. Or you will regret it."

A clamor of voices burst out all together from the others, but it was interrupted by another sound—a shot, and then another, and men shouting.

Came a trooper running. "Mutiny in the ranks!" he cried. "They won't obey orders!"

"Who won't?" snapped Don Petronilo.

"The *gente* of Salazar!"

"Bad people!" exclaimed Nicanor as we ran. "They were *colorados* captured when we took Torreon. Joined us so we wouldn't kill 'em. Ordered out to-night to guard the Puerta!"

"Till to-morrow," said Salazar at this point, "I'm going to bed!"

The peons' houses at La Cadena, where the troops were quartered, enclosed a great square, like a walled town. There were two gates. At one we forced our way through a mob of women and peons fighting to get out. Inside, there were dim lights from doorways, and three or four little fires in the open air. A bunch of frightened horses crowded one another in a corner. Men ran wildly in and out of their cuartels, with rifles in their hands. In the center of the open space stood a group of about fifty men, mostly armed, as if to repel an attack.

"Guard those gates!" cried the Colonel. "Don't let anybody out without an order from me!" The running troops began to mass at the gates. Don Petronilo walked out alone into the middle of the square.

"What's the trouble, *compañeros?*" he asked quietly.

"They were going to kill us all!" yelled somebody from the darkness. "They wanted to escape! They were going to betray us to the *colorados!*"

"It's a lie!" cried those in the center. "We are not Don Petronilo's *gente!* Our *jefe* is Manuel Arrieta!"

Suddenly Longinos Güereca, unarmed, flashed by us and fell upon them furiously, wrenching away their rifles and throwing them far behind. For a moment it looked as if the rebels would turn on him, but they did not resist.

"Disarm them!" ordered Don Petronilo. "And lock them up!"

They herded the prisoners into one large room, with an armed guard at the door. And long after midnight I could hear them hilariously singing.

That left Don Petronilo with a hundred effectives, some extra horses with running sores on their backs, and two thousand rounds of ammunition, more or less. Salazar took himself off in the morning, after recommending that all his *gente* be shot; he was evidently greatly relieved to be rid of them. Juan Santillanes was in favor of execution, too. But Don Petronilo decided to send them to General Urbina for trial.

CHAPTER IX

THE LAST NIGHT

THE days at La Cadena were full of color. In the cold dawn, when the river pools were filmed with ice, a trooper would gallop into the great square with a plunging steer at the end of his rope. Fifty or sixty ragged soldiers, only their eyes showing between serapes and big sombreros, would begin an amateur bull-fight, to the roaring delight of the rest of the *compañeros*. They waved their blankets, shouting the correct bull-fight cries. One would twist the infuriated animal's tail. Another, more impatient, beat him with the flat of a sword. Instead of banderillas, they stuck daggers into his shoulder—his hot blood spattering them as he charged. And when at last he was down and the merciful knife in his brain, a mob fell upon the carcase, cutting and ripping, and bearing off chunks of raw meat to their cuartels. Then the white, burning sun would rise suddenly behind the Puerta, stinging your hands and face. And the pools of blood, the faded patterns of the serapes, the far reaches of umber desert glowed and became vivid. . . .

Don Petronilo had confiscated several coaches in the campaign. We borrowed them for many an excursion —the five of us. Once it was a trip to San Pedro del

Gallo to see a cock-fight, appropriately enough. Another time 'Gino Güereca and I went to see the fabulously rich lost mines of the Spaniards, which he knew. But we never got past Bruquilla—just lounged in the shade of the trees and ate cheese all day.

Late in the afternoon the Puerta guard trotted out to their post, the late sun soft on their rifles and cartridge-belts; and long after dark the detachment relieved came jingling in out of the mysterious dark.

The four peddlers whom I had seen in Santo Domingo arrived that night. They had four burro loads of *macuche* to sell the soldiers.

"It's meester!" they cried, when I came down to their little fire. "*Que tal*, meester? How goes it? Aren't you afraid of the *colorados?*"

"How is business?" I asked, accepting the heaped-up handful of *macuche* they gave me.

They laughed uproariously at this.

"Business! Far better for us if we had stayed in Santo Domingo! *This* Tropa couldn't buy one cigarro if they clubbed their money! . . ."

One of them began to sing that extraordinary ballad, "The Morning Song to Francisco Villa." He sang one verse, and then the next man sang a verse, and so on around, each man composing a dramatic account of the deeds of the Great Captain. For half an hour I lay there, watching them, as they squatted between their knees, serapes draped loosely from their shoulders, the firelight red on their simple, dark faces.

THE LAST NIGHT

While one man sang the others stared upon the ground,
wrapt in composition.

"*Here is Francisco Villa*
  With his chiefs and his officers,
  Who come to saddle the short-horns
  Of the Federal Army.

"*Get ready now, colorados,*
  Who have been talking so loud,
  For Villa and his soldiers
  Will soon take off your hides!

"*To-day has come your tamer,*
  The Father of Rooster Tamers,
  To run you out of Torreon—
  To the devil with your skins!

"*The rich with all their money*
  Have already got their lashing,
  As the soldiers of Urbina
  Can tell, and those of Maclovio Herrera.

"*Fly, fly away, little dove,*
  Fly over all the prairies,
  And say that Villa has come
  To drive them all out forever.

"*Ambition will ruin itself,*
  And justice will be the winner,
  For Villa has reached Torreon
  To punish the avaricious."

75

"Fly away, Royal Eagle,
These laurels carry to Villa,
For he has come to conquer
Bravo and all his colonels.

"Now you sons of the Mosquito,
Your pride will come to an end,
If Villa has come to Torreon,
It is because he could do it!

"Viva Villa and his soldiers!
Viva Herrera and his gente!
You have seen, wicked people,
What a brave man can do.

"With this now I say good-bye;
By the Rose of Castile,
Here is the end of my rhyme
To the great General Villa!"

After a while I slipped away, and I doubt if they even saw me go. They sang around their fire for more than three hours.

But in our cuartel there was other entertainment. The room was full of smoke from the fire on the floor. Through it I dimly made out some thirty or forty troopers squatting or sprawled at full length—perfectly silent as Silveyra read aloud a proclamation from the Governor of Durango forever condemning the lands of the great haciendas to be divided among the poor.

THE LAST NIGHT

He read:

"Considering: that the principal cause of discontent among the people in our State, which forced them to spring to arms in the year 1910, was the absolute lack of individual property; and that the rural classes have no means of subsistence in the present, nor any hope for the future, except to serve as peons on the haciendas of the great land owners, who have monopolized the soil of the State;

"Considering: that the principal branch of our national riches is agriculture, and that there can be no true progress in agriculture without that the majority of farmers have a personal interest in making the earth produce. . . .

"Considering, finally: that the rural towns have been reduced to the deepest misery, because the common lands which they once owned have gone to augment the property of the nearest hacienda, especially under the Dictatorship of Diaz; with which the inhabitants of the State lost their economic, political, and social independence, then passed from the rank of citizens to that of slaves, without the Government being able to lift the moral level through education, because the hacienda where they lived is private property. . . .

"Therefore, the Government of the State of Durango declares it a public necessity that the inhabitants of the towns and villages be the owners of agricultural lands. . . ."

When the paymaster had painfully waded through all the provisions that followed, telling how the land was to be applied for, etc., there was a silence.

"That," said Martinez, "is the Mexican Revolucion."

"It's just what Villa's doing in Chihuahua," I said. "It's great. All you fellows can have a farm now."

An amused chuckle ran around the circle. Then a little, bald-headed man, with yellow, stained whiskers, sat up and spoke.

"Not us," he said, "not the soldiers. After a Revolucion is done it wants no more soldiers. It is the *pacificos* who will get the land—those who did not fight. And the next generation. . . ." He paused and spread his torn sleeves to the fire. "I was a school teacher," he explained, "so I know that Revolucions, like Republics, are ungrateful. I have fought three years. At the end of the first Revolucion that great man, Father Madero, invited his soldiers to the Capital. He gave us clothes, and food, and bull-fights. We returned to our homes and found the greedy again in power."

"I ended the war with forty-five pesos," said a man.

"You were lucky," continued the schoolmaster. "No, it is not the troopers, the starved, unfed, common soldiers who profit by the Revolucion. Officers, yes—some—for they get fat on the blood of the Patria. But we—no."

"What on earth are you fighting for?" I cried.

"I have two little sons," he answered. "And *they* will get their land. And they will have other little sons. They, too, will never want for food. . . ." The little man grinned. "We have a proverb in Guadalajara: 'Do not wear a shirt of eleven yards, for he who wants to be a Redeemer will be crucified.'"

THE LAST NIGHT

"*I've* got no little son," said fourteen-year-old Gil Tomas, amid shouts of laughter. "I'm fighting so I can get a thirty-thirty rifle from some dead Federal, and a good horse that belonged to a millionaire."

Just for fun I asked a trooper with a photo button of Madero pinned to his coat who that was.

"*Pues, quien sabe, señor?*" he replied. "My captain told me he was a great saint. I fight because it is not so hard as to work."

"How often are you fellows paid?"

"We were paid three pesos just nine months ago to-night," said the schoolmaster, and they all nodded. "We are the real volunteers. The *gente* of Villa are professionals."

Then Luis Martinez got a guitar and sang a beautiful little love song, which he said a prostitute had made up one night in a *bordel*.

The last thing I remember of that memorable night was 'Gino Güereca lying near me in the dark, talking.

"To-morrow," he said, "I shall take you to the lost gold-mines of the Spaniards. They are hidden in a cañon in the Western mountains. Only the Indians know of them—and I. The Indians go there sometimes with knives and dig the raw gold out of the ground. We'll be rich. . . ."

CHAPTER X

THE COMING OF THE COLORADOS

BEFORE sunrise next morning, Fernando Silveyra, fully dressed, came into the room and said calmly to get up, that the *colorados* were coming. Juan Vallejo laughed: "How many, Fernando?"

"About a thousand," he answered in a quiet voice, rummaging for his bandolier.

The patio was unusually full of shouting men saddling horses. I saw Don Petronilo, half dressed, at his door, his mistress buckling on his sword. Juan Santillanes was pulling at his trousers with furious haste. There was a steady rattle of clicks as cartridges slipped into rifles. A score of soldiers ran to and fro aimlessly, asking everyone where something was.

I don't think we any of us really believed it. The little square of quiet sky over the patio gave promise of another hot day. Roosters crowed. A cow that was being milked bellowed. I felt hungry.

"How near are they?" I asked.

"Near."

"But the outpost—the guard at the Puerta?"

"Asleep," Fernando said, as he strapped on his cartridge-belt.

Pablo Arriola clanked in, crippled by his big spurs.

"A little bunch of twelve rode up. Our men thought it was only the daily reconnaissance. So after they

80

drove them back, the Puerta guard sat down to breakfast. Then Argumedo himself and hundreds—hundreds——"

"But twenty-five could hold that pass against an army until the rest got there. . . ."

"They're already past the Puerta," said Pablo, shouldering his saddle. He went out.

"The ——!" swore Juan Santillanes, spinning the chambers of his revolver. "Wait till I get at them!"

"Now meester's going to see some of those shots he wanted," cried Gil Tomas. "How about it, meester? Feel scared?"

Somehow the whole business didn't seem real. I said to myself, "You lucky devil, you're actually going to see a fight. That will round out the story." I loaded my camera and hurried out in front of the house.

There was nothing much to see there. A blinding sun rose right in the Puerta. Over the leagues and leagues of dark desert to the east nothing lived but the morning light. Not a movement. Not a sound. Yet somewhere out there a mere handful of men were desperately trying to hold off an army.

Thin smoke floated up in the breathless air from the houses of the peons. It was so still that the grinding of *tortilla* meal between two stones was distinctly audible—and the slow, minor song of some woman at her work way around the Casa Grande. Sheep were maaing to be let out of the corral. On the road to Santo Domingo, so far away that they were mere colored accents in the desert, the four peddlers sauntered behind their burros. Little knots of peons were

81

gathered in front of the hacienda, pointing and looking east. And around the gate of the big enclosure where the soldiers were quartered a few troopers held their horses by the bridle. That was all.

Occasionally the door of the Casa Grande vomited mounted men—two or three at a time—who galloped down the Puerta road with their rifles in their hands. I could follow them as they rose and fell over the waves of the desert, growing smaller all the time, until they mounted the last roll—where the white dust they kicked up caught the fierce light of the sun, and the eye couldn't stand it. They had taken my horse, and Juan Vallejo didn't have one. He stood beside me, cocking and firing his empty rifle.

"Look!" he shouted suddenly. The western face of the mountains that flanked the Puerta was in shadow still. Along their base, to the north and to the south, too, wriggled little thin lines of dust. They lengthened out—Oh so slowly. At first there was only one in each direction; then two others began, farther down, nearer, advancing relentlessly, like raveling in a stocking—like a crack in thin glass. The enemy, spreading wide around the battle, to take us in the flank!

Still the little knots of troopers poured from the Casa Grande, and spurred away. Pablo Arriola went, and Nicanor, waving to me brightly as they passed. Longinos Güereca rocketed out on his great *tordillo* horse, yet only half broken. The big gray put down his head and buck-jumped four times across the square.

"To-morrow for the mines," yelled 'Gino over his

shoulder. "I'm very busy to-day—very rich—the lost
mines of——" But he was too far away for me to
hear. Martinez followed him, shouting to me with a
grin that he felt scared to death. Then others. It
made about thirty so far. I remember that most of
them wore automobile goggles. Don Petronilo sat his
horse, with field-glasses to his eyes. I looked again
at the lines of dust—they were curving slowly down,
the sun glorifying them—like scimitars.

Don Tomas galloped past, Gil Tomas at his heels.
But someone was coming. A little running horse appeared on the rise, headed our way, the rider outlined
in a radiant dust. He was going at furious speed, dipping and rising over the rolling land. . . . And as he
spurred wildly up the little hill where we stood, we
saw a horror. A fan-shaped cascade of blood poured
from the front of him. The lower part of his mouth
was quite shot away by a soft-nosed bullet. He reined
up beside the colonel, and tried earnestly, terribly, to
tell him something; but nothing intelligible issued from
the ruin. Tears poured down the poor fellow's cheeks.
He gave a hoarse cry, and, driving his spurs deep in his
horse, fled up the Santo Domingo road. Others were
coming, too, on the dead run—those who had been the
Puerta guard. Two or three passed right through the
hacienda without stopping. The rest threw themselves
upon Don Petronilo, in a passion of rage. "More ammunition!" they cried. "More cartridges!"

Don Petronilo looked away. "There isn't any!"
The men went mad, cursing and hurling their guns on
the ground.

"Twenty-five more men at the Puerta," shouted the Colonel. In a few minutes half of the new men galloped out of their cuartel and took the eastern road. The near ends of the dust lines were now lost to view behind a swell of ground.

"Why don't you send them all, Don Petronilo?" I yelled.

"Because, my young friend, a whole company of *colorados* is riding down that arroyo. You can't see them from there, but I can."

He had no sooner spoken than a rider whirled around the corner of the house, pointing back over his shoulder to the south, whence he had come.

"They're coming that way, too," he cried. "Thousands! Through the other pass! Redondo had only five men on guard! They took them prisoner and got into the valley before he knew it!"

"*Valgame Dios!*" muttered Don Petronilo.

We turned south. Above the umber rise of desert loomed a mighty cloud of white dust, shining in the sun, like the biblical pillar of smoke.

"The rest of you fellows get out there and hold them off!" The last twenty-five leaped to their saddles and started southward.

Then suddenly the great gate of the walled square belched men and horses—men without rifles. The disarmed *gente* of Salazar! They milled around as if in a panic. "Give us our rifles!" they shouted. "Where's our ammunition?"

"Your rifles are in the cuartel," answered the Colonel, "but your cartridges are out there killing *colorados!*"

A great cry went up. "They've taken away our arms! They want to murder us!"

"How can we fight, man? What can we do without rifles?" screamed one man in Don Petronilo's face.

"Come on, *compañeros!* Let's go out and strangle 'em with our hands, the—*colorados!*" yelled one. Five struck spurs into their horses, and sped furiously toward the Puerta—without arms, without hope. It was magnificent!

"We'll all get killed!" said another. "Come on!" And the other forty-five swept wildly out on the road to Santo Domingo.

The twenty-five recruits that had been ordered to hold the southern side had ridden out about half a mile, and there stopped, seeming uncertain what to do. Now they caught sight of the disarmed fifty galloping for the mountains.

"The *compañeros* are fleeing! The *compañeros* are fleeing!"

For a moment there was a sharp exchange of cries. They looked at the dust cloud towering over them. They thought of the mighty army of merciless devils who made it. They hesitated, broke—and fled furiously through the chaparral toward the mountains.

I suddenly discovered that I had been hearing shooting for some time. It sounded immensely far away— like nothing so much as a clicking typewriter. Even while it held our attention it grew. The little trivial pricking of rifles deepened and became serious. Out in front now it was practically continuous—almost the roll of a snare-drum.

Don Petronilo was a little white. He called Apolinario and told him to harness the mules to the coach.

"If anything happens that we get the worst of it," he said lightly to Juan Vallejo, "call my woman and you and Reed go with her in the coach. Come on, Fernando—Juanito!" Silveyra and Juan Santillanes spurred out; the three vanished toward the Puerta.

We could see them now, hundreds of little black figures riding everywhere through the chaparral; the desert swarmed with them. Savage Indian yells reached us. A spent bullet droned overhead, then another; then one unspent, and then a whole flock singing fiercely. Thud! went the adobe walls as bits of clay flew. Peons and their women rushed from house to house, distracted with fear. A trooper, his face black with powder and hateful with killing and terror, galloped past, shouting that all was lost. . . .

Apolinario hurried out the mules with their harness on their backs, and began to hitch them to the coach. His hands trembled. He dropped a trace, picked it up, and dropped it again. He shook all over. All at once he threw the harness to the ground and took to his heels. Juan and I rushed forward. Just then a stray bullet took the off mule in the rump. Nervous already, the animals plunged wildly. The wagon tongue snapped with the report of a rifle. The mules raced madly north into the desert.

And then came the rout, a wild huddle of troopers all together, lashing their terrified horses. They passed us without stopping, without noticing, all blood and sweat and blackness. Don Tomas, Pablo Arriola, and after them little Gil Tomas, his horse staggering and falling dead right in front of us. Bullets whipped the wall on all sides of us.

"Come on, meester!" said Juan. "Let's go!" We began to run. As I panted up the steep opposite bank of the arroyo, I looked back. Gil Tomas was right behind me, with a red- and black-checked serape round his shoulders. Don Petronilo came in sight, shooting back over his shoulder, with Juan Santillanes at his side. In front raced Fernando Silveyra, bending low over his horse's neck. All around the hacienda was a ring of galloping, shooting, yelling men; and as far as the eye could reach, on every rise of the desert, came more.

CHAPTER XI

MEESTER'S FLIGHT

JUAN VALLEJO was already far ahead, running doggedly with his rifle in one hand. I shouted to him to turn off the high road, and he obeyed, without looking back. I followed. It was a straight path through the desert toward the mountains. The desert was as bald as a billiard table here. We could be seen for miles. My camera got between my legs. I dropped it. My overcoat became a terrible weight. I shook it off. We could see the *compañeros* fleeing wildly up the Santo Domingo road. Beyond them unexpectedly appeared a wave of galloping men—the flanking party from the south. The shooting broke out again—and then pursuers and pursued vanished around the corner of a little hill. Thank God the path was diverging from the road!

I ran on—ran and ran and ran, until I could run no more. Then I walked a few steps and ran again. I was sobbing instead of breathing. Awful cramps gripped my legs. Here there was more chaparral, more brush, and the foothills of the western mountains were near. But the entire length of the path was visible from behind. Juan Vallejo had reached the foothills, half a mile ahead. I saw him crawling up a little rise. Suddenly three armed horsemen swept in behind him, and raised a shout. He looked around, threw his rifle far into the brush, and fled for his life. They shot at him, but stopped to recover the rifle. He disappeared over the crest, and then they did, too.

I ran. I wondered what time it was. I wasn't very frightened. Everything still was so unreal, like a page out of Richard Harding Davis. It just seemed to me that if I didn't get away I wouldn't be doing my job well. I kept thinking to myself: "Well, this is certainly an experience. I'm going to have something to write about."

Then came yells and hoofs drumming in the rear. About a hundred yards behind ran little Gil Tomas, the ends of his gay serape flying out straight. And about a hundred yards behind him rode two black men with crossed bandoliers and rifles in their hands. They shot. Gil Tomas raised a ghastly little Indian face to me, and ran on. Again they shot. One bullet z-z-z-m-m-d by my head. The boy staggered, stopped, wheeled, and doubled suddenly into the chaparral. They turned after him. I saw the foremost horse's hoofs strike him. The *colorados* jerked their mounts to their haunches over him, shooting down again and again. . . .

I ran into the chaparral, topped a little hill, tripped on a mesquite root, fell, rolled down a sandy incline, and landed in a little arroyo. Dense mesquite covered the place. Before I could stir the *colorados* came plunging down the hillside. "There he goes!" they yelled, and, jumping their horses over the arroyo not ten feet from where I lay, galloped off into the desert. I suddenly fell asleep.

I couldn't have slept very long, for when I woke the sun was still in about the same place, and a few scattered shots could be heard way to the west, in the direction of Santo Domingo. I stared up through the brush tangle into the hot sky, where one great vulture slowly circled over me, wondering whether or not I was dead. Not twenty paces away a barefooted Indian with a rifle crouched on his motionless horse. He looked up at the vulture, and then searched the face of the desert. I lay still. I couldn't tell whether he was one of ours or not. After a little time he jogged slowly north over a hill and disappeared.

I waited about half an hour before crawling out of the arroyo. In the direction of the hacienda they were still shooting—making sure of the dead, I afterward learned. I couldn't see it. The little valley in which I was ran roughly east and west. I traveled westward, toward the sierra. But it was still too near the fatal path. I stooped low and ran up over the hill, without looking back. Beyond was another, higher, and then another still. Running over the hills, walking in the sheltered valleys, I bore steadily northwest, toward the always-nearing mountains. Soon there were no more sounds. The sun burned fiercely down, and the long ridges of desolate country wavered in the heat. High chaparral tore my clothes and face. Underfoot were cactuses, century plants, and the murderous *espadas*, whose long, interlaced spikes slashed my boots, drawing blood at every step; and beneath them sand and jagged stones. It was terrible going. The big still forms of Spanish bayonet, astonishingly like men, stood up all around the skyline. I stood stiffly for a moment on the top of a high hill, in a clump of them, looking back. The hacienda was already so far away that it was only a white blur in the immeasurable reaches of the desert. A thin line of dust moved from it toward the Puerta— the *colorados* taking back their dead to Mapimi.

Then my heart gave a jump. A man was coming silently up the valley. He had a green serape over one arm, and nothing on his head but a blood-clotted handkerchief. His bare legs were covered with blood from the *espadas*. He caught sight of me all of a sudden, and stood still; after a pause he beckoned. I went down to where he was; he never said a word, but led the way back down the valley. About a hundred yards farther he stopped and pointed. A dead horse sprawled in the sand, its stiff legs in the air; beside it lay a man, disemboweled by a knife or a sword—evidently a *colo-rado*, because his cartridge-belt was almost full. The man with the green serape produced a wicked-looking dagger, still ruddy with blood, fell on his knees, and began to dig among the *espadas*. I brought rocks. We cut a branch of mesquite and made a cleft cross out of it. And so we buried him.

"Where are you bound, *compañero?*" I asked.

"For the sierra," he answered. "And you?"

I pointed north, where I knew the Güercas' ranch lay.

"The Pelayo is over that way—eight leagues."

"What is the Pelayo?"

"Another hacienda. There are some of ours at the Pelayo, I think. . . ."

We parted with an "*adios.*"

For hours I went on, running over the hilltops, staggering through the cruel *espadas*, slipping down the steep sides of dried river beds. There was no water. I hadn't eaten or drunk. It was intensely hot.

About eleven I rounded the shoulder of a mountain and saw the small gray patch that was Bruquilla. Here passed the Camino Real, and the desert lay flat and open. A mile away a tiny horseman jogged along. He seemed to see me; he pulled up short and looked in my direction a long time. I stood perfectly motionless. Pretty soon he went on, getting smaller and smaller, until at last there was nothing but a little puff of dust. There was no other sign of life for miles and miles. I bent low and ran along the side of the road, where there was no dust. Half a league westward lay the

Güerca's house, hidden in the gigantic row of alamo trees that fringed its running brook. A long way off I could see a little red spot on the top of the low hill beside it; when I came nearer, I saw it was father Güereca, staring toward the east. He came running down when he saw me, clenching his hands.

"What has passed? What has passed? Is it true that the *colorados* have taken the Cadena?"

I told him briefly what had happened.

"And Longinos?" he cried, wrenching at my arm. "Have you seen Longinos?"

"No," I said. "The *compañeros* all retreated to Santo Domingo."

"You must not stay here," said the old man, trembling.

"Let me have some water—I can hardly speak."

"Yes, yes, drink. There is the brook. The *colorados* must not find you here." The old man looked around with anguish at the little rancho he had fought so hard to gain. "They would destroy us all."

Just then the old mother appeared in the doorway.

"Come here, Juan Reed," she cried. "Where is my boy? Why doesn't he come? Is he dead? Tell me the truth!"

"Oh, I think they all got away all right," I told her.

"And you! Have you eaten? Have you breakfasted?"

"I haven't had a drop of water since last night, nor any food. And I came all the way from La Cadena on foot."

"Poor little boy! Poor little boy!" she wailed, putting her arms around me. "Sit down now, and I will cook you something."

Old Güereca bit his lip in an agony of apprehension. Finally hospitality won.

"My house is at your orders," he muttered. "But hurry! Hurry! You must not be seen here! I will go up on the hill and watch for dust!"

I drank several quarts of water and ate four fried eggs and some cheese. The old man had returned and was fidgeting around.

"I sent all my children to Jarral Grande," he said. "We heard this morning. The whole valley is fleeing to the mountains. Are you ready?"

"Stay here," invited the Señora. "We will hide you from the *colorados* until Longinos comes home!"

Her husband screamed at her. "Are you mad? He mustn't be found here! Are you ready now? Come on then!"

I limped along down through a burnt, yellow corn-field. "Follow this path," said the old man, "through those two fields and the chaparral. It will take you to the highroad to the Pelayo. May you go well!" We shook hands, and a moment later I saw him shuffling back up the hill with flapping sandals.

I crossed an immense valley covered with mesquite as high as my head. Twice horsemen passed, probably only *pacificos*, but I took no chances. Beyond that valley lay another, about seven miles long. Now there were bare mountains all around, and ahead loomed a range of fantastic white, pink, and yellow hills. After about four hours, with stiff legs and bloody feet, a backache and a spinning head, I rounded these and came in sight of the alamo trees and low adobe walls of the Hacienda del Pelayo.

The peons gathered around, listening to my story.

"*Que carrai-i-i-i!*" they murmured. "But it is impossible to walk from La Cadena in one day! *Pobrecito!* You must be tired! Come now and eat. And to-night there will be a bed."

"My house is yours," said Don Felipe, the blacksmith. "But are you quite sure the *colorados* are not coming this way? The last time they paid us a visit" (he pointed to the blackened walls of the Casa Grande) "they killed four *pacificos* who refused to join them." He put his arm through mine. "Come now, *amigo*, and eat."

"If there were only some place to bathe first!"

At this they smiled and led me behind the hacienda, along a little stream overhung with willows, whose banks were the most vivid green. The water gushed out from under a high wall, and over that wall reared the gnarled branches of a giant alamo. We entered a little door; there they left me.

The ground inside sloped sharply up, and the wall—it was faded pink—followed the contour of the land. Sunk in the middle of the enclosure was a pool of crystal water. The bottom was white sand. At one end of the pool the water fountained up from a hole in the bottom. A faint steam rose from the surface. It was *hot* water.

There was a man already standing up to his neck in the water, a man with a circle shaved on the top of his head.

"Señor," he said, "are you a Catholic?"

MEESTER'S FLIGHT

"No."

"Thank God," he returned briefly. "We Catholics are liable to be intolerant. Are you a Mexican?"

"No, señor."

"It is well," he said, smiling sadly. "I am a priest and a Spaniard. I have been made to understand that I am not wanted in this beautiful land, señor. God is good. But He is better in Spain than He is in Mexico. . . ."

I let myself slowly down into the pellucid, hot depths. The pain and the soreness and the weariness fled shuddering up my body. I felt like a disembodied spirit. Floating there in the warm embrace of that marvelous pool, with the crooked gray branches of the alamo above our heads, we discussed philosophy. The fierce sky cooled slowly, and the rich sunlight climbed little by little up the pink wall.

Don Felipe insisted that I sleep in his house, in his bed. This bed consisted of an iron frame with loose wooden slats stretched across it. Over these was laid one tattered blanket. My clothing covered me. Don Felipe, his wife, his grown son and daughter, his two small infants, all of whom had been accustomed to use the bed, lay down upon the soft floor. There were also two sick persons in the room—a very old man covered with red spots, too far gone to speak, and a boy with extraordinarily swollen tonsils. Occasionally a centenarian hag entered and ministered unto the patients. Her method of treatment was simple. With the old man she merely heated a piece of iron at the candle and touched the spots. For the boy's case she made

95

a paste of corn-meal and lard, and gently rubbed his elbows with it, loudly saying prayers. This went on at intervals all night. Between treatments the babies would wake up at intervals and insist upon being nursed. . . . The door was shut early in the evening, and windows there were none.

Now all this hospitality meant a real sacrifice to Don Felipe, especially the meals, at which he unlocked a tin trunk and brought me with all reverence his precious sugar and coffee. He was, like all peons, incredibly poor and lavishly hospitable. The giving up of his bed was a mark of the highest honor, too. But when I tried to pay him in the morning he wouldn't hear of it.

"My house is youʀs," he repeated. " 'A stranger might be God,' as we say."

Finally I told him that I wanted him to buy me some tobacco, and he took the money. I knew then that it would go to the right place, for a Mexican can be trusted never to carry out a commission. He is delightfully irresponsible.

At six o'clock in the morning I set out for Santo Domingo in a two-wheeled cart driven by an old peon named Froilan Mendarez. We avoided the main road, jolting along by a mere track that led behind a range of hills. After we'd traveled for about an hour, I had an unpleasant thought.

"What if the *compañeros* fled beyond Santo Domingo and the *colorados* are there?"

"What indeed?" murmured Froilan, chirruping to the mule.

"But if they are, what'll we do?"

MEESTER'S FLIGHT

Froilan thought a minute. "We might say we were cousins to President Huerta," he suggested, without a smile. Froilan was a barefooted peon, his face and hands incredibly damaged by age and dirt; I was a ragged Gringo. . . .

We jogged on for several hours. At one place an armed man started out of the brush and hailed us. His lips were split and leathery with thirst. The *espadas* had slashed his legs terribly. He had escaped over the Sierra, climbing and slipping all night. We gave him all the water and food we had, and he went on toward the Pelayo.

Long after noon our cart topped the last desert rise, and we saw sleeping below us the long spread-out hacienda of Santo Domingo, with its clump of tall alamos like palm trees around the oasis-like spring. My heart was in my mouth as we drove down. In the big *ribota* court the peons were playing hand ball. Up from the spring moved the long line of water carriers. A fire sent up thin smoke among the trees.

We came upon an aged peon carrying fagots. "No," he said, "there had been no *colorados*. The Maderistas? Yes, they had come last night—hundreds of them, all running. But at dawn they had gone back to La Cadena to 'lift the fields' (bury the dead)."

From around the fire under the alamos came a great shout: "The meester! Here comes the meester! *Que tal, compañero?* How did you escape?" It was my old friends, the peddlers. They crowded around eagerly, questioning, shaking my hand, throwing their arms around me.

97

"Ah, but that was close! *Carramba*, but I was lucky! Did I know that Longinos Güereca was killed? Yes, but he shot six *colorados* before they got him. And Martinez also, and Nicanor, and Redondo."

I felt sick. Sick to think of so many useless deaths in such a petty fight. Blithe, beautiful Martinez; 'Gino Güereca, whom I had learned to love so much; Redondo, whose girl was even then on her way to Chihuahua to buy her wedding dress; and jolly Nicanor. It seems that when Redondo found that his flank had been turned his troop deserted him; so he galloped alone toward La Cadena, and was caught by three hundred *colorados*. They literally shot him to pieces. 'Gino, and Luis Martinez, and Nicanor, with five others, held the eastward side of the hacienda unaided until their cartridges were gone, and they were surrounded by a ring of shooting men. Then they died. The *colorados* carried off the Colonel's woman.

"But there's a man who's been through it all," said one of the peddlers. "He fought till his last cartridge was gone, and then cut his way through the enemy with a saber."

I looked around. Surrounded by a ring of gaping peons, his lifted arm illustrating the great deed, was —Apolinario! He caught sight of me, nodded coldly, as to one who has run from the fight, and went on with his recital.

All through the long afternoon Froilan and I played *ribota* with the peons. It was a drowsy, peaceful day. A gentle wind rustled the high branches of the great

98

trees, and the late sun, from behind the hill that is back of Santo Domingo, warmed with color their lofty tops.

It was a strange sunset. The sky became overcast with light cloud toward the end of the afternoon. First it turned pink, then scarlet, then of a sudden the whole firmament became a deep, bloody red.

An immense drunken man—an Indian about seven feet tall—staggered out in the open ground near the *ribota* court with a violin in his hand. He tucked it under his chin and sawed raggedly on the strings, staggering to and fro as he played. Then a little one-armed dwarf sprang out of the crowd of peons and began to dance. A dense throng made a circle around the two, roaring with mirth.

And just at that moment there appeared against the bloody sky, over the eastern hill, the broken, defeated men—on horseback and on foot, wounded and whole, weary, sick, disheartened, reeling and limping down to Santo Domingo. . . .

CHAPTER XII

ELIZABETTA

SO, against a crimson sky, the beaten, exhausted soldiers came down the hill. Some rode, their horses hanging weary heads—occasionally two on a horse. Others walked, with bloody bandages around their foreheads and arms. Cartridge-belts

99

were empty, rifles gone. Their hands and faces were foul with sweaty dirt and stained still with powder. Beyond the hill, across the twenty-mile arid waste that lay between us and La Cadena, they straggled. There were not more than fifty left, including the women—the rest had dispersed in the barren mountains and the folds of the desert—but they stretched out for miles; it took hours for them to arrive.

Don Petronilo came in front, with lowered face and folded arms, the reins hanging loose upon the neck of his swaying, stumbling horse. Right behind him came Juan Santillanes, gaunt and white, his face years older. Fernando Silveyra, all rags, dragged along at his saddle. As they waded the shallow stream they looked up and saw me. Don Petronilo weakly waved his hand; Fernando shouted, "Why, there's meester! How did you escape? We thought sure they had shot you."

"I ran a race with the goats," I answered. Juan gave a laugh. "Scared to death, eh?"

The horses thrust eager muzzles into the stream, sucking fiercely. Juan cruelly spurred across, and we fell into each other's arms. But Don Petronilo dismounted in the water, dully, as if in a dream, and, wading up to the tops of his boots, came to where I was.

He was weeping. His expression didn't change, but slow, big tears fell silently down his cheeks.

"The *colorados* captured his wife!" murmured Juan in my ear.

I was filled with pity for the man.

ELIZABETTA

"It is a terrible thing, *mi Coronel,*" I said gently, "to feel the responsibility for all these brave fellows who died. But it was not your fault."

"It is not that," he replied slowly, staring through tears at the pitiful company crawling down from the desert.

"I, too, had many friends who died in the battle," I went on. "But they died gloriously, fighting for their country."

"I do not weep for them," he said, twisting his hands together. "This day I have lost all that is dear to me. They took my woman who was mine, and my commission and all my papers, and all my money. But I am wrenched with grief when I think of my silver spurs inlaid with gold, which I bought only last year in Mapimi!" He turned away, overcome.

And now the peons began to come down from their houses, with pitying cries and loving offers. They threw their arms around the soldiers' necks, assisting the wounded, patting them shyly on the shoulders and calling them "brave." Desperately poor themselves, they offered food, and beds, and fodder for the horses, inviting them to stay at Santo Domingo until they should become well. I already had a place to sleep. Don Pedro, the chief goatherd, had given me his room and his bed in a gush of warm-hearted generosity, and had removed himself and his family to the kitchen. He did so without hope of recompense, for he thought I had no money. And now everywhere men, women and children left their houses to make way for the defeated and weary troops.

Fernando, Juan and I went over and begged some tobacco from the four peddlers camped under the trees beside the spring. They had made no sales for a week, and were almost starving, but they loaded us lavishly with *macuche*. We talked of the battle, lying there on our elbows watching the shattered remnants of the garrison top the hill.

"You have heard that 'Gino Güereca fell," said Fernando. "Well, I saw him. His big gray horse that he rode for the first time was terrified by the bridle and saddle. But once he came where the bullets were flying and the guns roaring, he steadied at once. Pure race, that horse. . . . His fathers must have been all warriors. Around 'Gino were four or five more heroes, with almost all their cartridges gone. They fought until on the front and on both sides double galloping lines of *colorados* closed in. 'Gino was standing beside his horse—suddenly a score of shots hit the animal all at once, and he sighed and fell over. The rest ceased firing in a sort of panic. 'We're lost!' they cried. 'Run while there is yet a chance!' 'Gino shook his smoking rifle at them. 'No,' he shouted. 'Give the *compañeros* time to get away!' Shortly after that they closed around him, and I never saw him until we buried his body this morning. . . . It was the devil's hell out there. The rifles were so hot you couldn't touch the barrels, and the whirling haze that belched out when they shot twisted everything like a mirage. . . ."

Juan broke in. "We rode straight out toward the Puerta when the retreat began, but almost immediately

we saw it was no use. The *colorados* broke over our
little handfuls of men like waves of the sea. Martinez
was just ahead. He never had a chance even to fire his
gun—and this was his first battle, too. They hit him
as he rode. . . . I thought how you and Martinez
loved each other. You used to talk together at night
so warmly, and never wished to leave each other to
sleep. . . ."

Now the tall, naked tops of the trees had dulled with
the passing of the light, and seemed to stand still
among the swarming stars in the deep dome overhead.
The peddlers had kindled their tiny fire; the low, contented murmur of their gossip floated to us. Open
doors of the peons' huts shed wavering candlelight.
Up from the river wound a silent line of black-robed
girls with water-jars on their heads. Women ground
their corn-meal with a monotonous stony scraping.
Dogs barked. Drumming hoofs marked the passing of
the *caballada* to the river. Along the ledge in front of
Don Pedro's house the warriors smoked and fought the
battle over again, stamping around and shouting
descriptive matter. "I took my rifle by the barrel
and smashed in his grinning face, just as——" some
one was narrating, with gestures. The peons squatted
around, breathlessly listening. . . . And still the
ghastly procession of the defeated straggled down the
road and across the river.

It was not yet quite dark. I wandered down to the
bank to watch them, in the vague hope of finding some
of my *compadres* who were still reported missing. And
it was there that I first saw Elizabetta.

There was nothing remarkable about her. I think I noticed her chiefly because she was one of the few women in that wretched company. She was a very dark-skinned Indian girl, about twenty-five years old, with the squat figure of her drudging race, pleasant features, hair hanging forward over her shoulders in two long plaits, and big, shining teeth when she smiled. I never did find out whether she had been just a peon woman working around La Cadena when the attack had come, or whether she was a *vieja*—a camp follower of the army.

Now she was trudging stolidly along in the dust behind Captain Felix Romero's horse—and had trudged so for thirty miles. He never spoke to her, never looked back, but rode on unconcernedly. Sometimes he would get tired of carrying his rifle and hand it back to her to carry, with a careless "Here! Take this!" I found out later that when they returned to La Cadena after the battle to bury the dead he had found her wandering aimlessly in the hacienda, apparently out of her mind; and that, needing a woman, he had ordered her to follow him. Which she did, unquestioningly, after the custom of her sex and country.

Captain Felix let his horse drink. Elizabetta halted, too, knelt and plunged her face into the water.

"Come on," ordered the Captain. *"Andale!"* She rose without a word and waded through the stream. In the same order they climbed the near bank, and there the Captain dismounted, held out his hand for the rifle she carried, and said, "Get me my supper!" Then

ELIZABETTA

he strolled away toward the houses where the rest of the soldiers sat.

Elizabetta fell upon her knees and gathered twigs for her fire. Soon there was a little pile burning. She called a small boy in the harsh, whining voice that all Mexican women have, "*Aie! chamaco!* Fetch me a little water and corn that I may feed my man!" And, rising upon her knees above the red glow of the flames, she shook down her long, straight black hair. She wore a sort of blouse of faded light blue rough cloth. There was dried blood on the breast of it.

"What a battle, señorita!" I said to her.

Her teeth flashed as she smiled, and yet there was a puzzling vacancy about her expression. Indians have mask-like faces. Under it I could see that she was desperately tired and even a little hysterical. But she spoke tranquilly enough.

"Perfectly," she said. "Are you the Gringo who ran so many miles with the *colorados* after you shooting?" And she laughed—catching her breath in the middle of it as if it hurt.

The *chamaco* shambled up with an earthen jar of water and an armful of corn-ears that he tumbled at her feet. Elizabetta unwound from her shawl the heavy little stone trough that Mexican women carry, and began mechanically husking the corn into it.

"I do not remember seeing you at La Cadena," I said. "Were you there long?"

"Too long," she answered simply, without raising her head. And then suddenly, "Oh, but this war is no game for women!" she cried.

Don Felix loomed up out of the dark, with a cigarette in his mouth.

"My dinner," he growled. "Is it *pronto?*"

"*Luego, luego!*" she answered. He went away again.

"Listen, señor, whoever you are!" said Elizabetta swiftly, looking up to me. "My lover was killed yesterday in the battle. This man is my man, but, by God and all the Saints, I can't sleep with him this night. Let me stay then with you!"

There wasn't a trace of coquetry in her voice. This blundering, childish spirit had found itself in a situation it couldn't bear, and had chosen the instinctive way out. I doubt if she even knew herself why the thought of this new man so revolted her, with her lover scarcely cold in the ground. I was nothing to her, nor she to me. That was all that mattered.

I assented, and together we left the fire, the Captain's neglected corn spilling from the stone trough. And then we met him a few feet into the darkness.

"My dinner!" he said impatiently. His voice changed. "Where are you going?"

"I'm going with this señor," Elizabetta answered nervously. "I'm going to stay with him——"

"You——" began Don Felix, gulping. "You are my woman. *Oiga,* señor, this is my woman here!"

"Yes," I said. "She is your woman. I have nothing to do with her. But she is very tired and not well, and I have offered her my bed for the night."

"This is very bad, señor!" exclaimed the Captain, in a tightening voice. "You are the guest of this

ELIZABETTA

Tropa and the Colonel's friend, but this is my woman and I want her——"

"Oh!" Elizabetta cried out. "Until the next time, señor!" She caught my arm and pulled me on.

We had been living in a nightmare of battle and death—all of us. I think everybody was a little dazed and excited. I know I was.

By this time the peons and soldiers had begun to gather around us, and as we went on the Captain's voice rose as he retailed his injustice to the crowd.

"I shall appeal to the Colonel," he was saying. "I shall tell the Colonel!" He passed us, going toward the Colonel's cuartel, with averted, mumbling face.

"*Oiga, mi Coronel!*" he cried. "This Gringo has taken away my woman. It is the grossest insult!"

"Well," returned the Colonel calmly, "if they both want to go, I guess there isn't anything we can do about it, eh?"

The news had traveled like light. A throng of small boys followed us close behind, shouting the joyful indelicacies they shout behind rustic wedding parties. We passed the ledge where the soldiers and the wounded sat, grinning and making rough, genial remarks as at a marriage. It was not coarse or suggestive, their banter; it was frank and happy. They were honestly glad for us.

As we approached Don Pedro's house we were aware of many candles within. He and his wife and daughter were busy with brooms, sweeping and resweeping the earthen floor, and sprinkling it with water. They had put new linen on the bed, and lit the rush candle before the table altar of the Virgin. Over the doorway hung a festoon of paper blossoms, faded relics of many a Christmas Eve celebration—for it was winter, and there were no real flowers.

Don Pedro was radiant with smiles. It made no difference who we were, or what our relation was. Here were a man and a maid, and to him it was a bridal.

"May you have a happy night," he said softly, and closed the door. The frugal Elizabetta immediately made the rounds of the room, extinguishing all the candles but one.

And then, outside, we heard music beginning to tune up. Some one had hired the village orchestra to serenade us. Late into the night they played steadily, right outside our door. In the next house we heard them moving chairs and tables out of the way; and just before I went to sleep they began to dance there, economically combining a serenade with a *baile*.

Without the least embarrassment, Elizabetta lay down beside me on the bed. Her hand reached for mine. She snuggled against my body for the comforting human warmth of it, murmured, "Until morning," and went to sleep. And calmly, sweetly, sleep came to me. . . .

When I woke in the morning she was gone. I opened my door and looked out. Morning had come dazzlingly, all blue and gold—a heaven of flame-trimmed big white clouds and windy sky, and the desert brazen and luminous. Under the ashy bare trees the peddlers' morning fire leaped horizontal in the wind. The black women, with wind-folded draperies, crossed the open ground to the river in single file, with red water-jars on their heads. Cocks crew, goats clamored for milking, and a hundred horses drummed up the dust as they were driven to water.

Elizabetta was squatted over a little fire near the corner of the house, patting *tortillas* for the Captain's breakfast. She smiled as I came up, and politely asked me if I had slept well. She was quite contented now; you knew from the way she sang over her work.

Presently the Captain came up in a surly manner and nodded briefly to me.

"I hope it's ready now," he grunted, taking the *tortillas* she gave him. "You take a long time to cook a little breakfast. *Carramba!* Why is there no coffee?" He moved off, munching. "Get ready," he flung back over his shoulder. "We go north in an hour."

"Are you going?" I asked curiously. Elizabetta looked at me with wide-open eyes.

"Of course I am going. *Seguro!* Is he not my man?" She looked after him admiringly. She was no longer revolted.

"He is my man," she said. "He is very handsome, and very brave. Why, in the battle the other day——"

Elizabetta had forgotten her lover.

PART TWO

FRANCISCO VILLA'

CHAPTER I

VILLA ACCEPTS A MEDAL

IT was while Villa was in Chihuahua City, two weeks before the advance on Torreon, that the artillery corps of his army decided to present him with a gold medal for personal heroism on the field.

In the audience hall of the Governor's palace in Chihuahua, a place of ceremonial, great luster chandeliers, heavy crimson portières, and gaudy American wallpaper, there is a throne for the governor. It is a gilded chair, with lion's claws for arms, placed upon a dais under a canopy of crimson velvet, surmounted by a heavy, gilded, wooden cap, which tapers up to a crown.

The officers of artillery, in smart blue uniforms faced with black velvet and gold, were solidly banked across one end of the audience hall, with flashing new swords and their gilt-braided hats stiffly held under their arms. From the door of that chamber, around the gallery, down the state staircase, across the grandiose inner court of the palace, and out through the imposing gates to the street, stood a double line of soldiers, with their rifles at present arms. Four regimental bands grouped in one wedged in the crowd. The people of the capital were massed in solid thousands on the Plaza de Armas before the palace.

INSURGENT MEXICO

"*Ya viene!*" "Here he comes!" "Viva Villa!" "Viva Madero!" "Villa, the Friend of the Poor!"

The roar began at the back of the crowd and swept like fire in heavy growing crescendo until it seemed to toss thousands of hats above their heads. The band in the courtyard struck up the Mexican national air, and Villa came walking down the street.

He was dressed in an old plain khaki uniform, with several buttons lacking. He hadn't recently shaved, wore no hat, and his hair had not been brushed. He walked a little pigeon-toed, humped over, with his hands in his trousers pockets. As he entered the aisle between the rigid lines of soldiers he seemed slightly embarrassed, and grinned and nodded to a *compadre* here and there in the ranks. At the foot of the grand staircase, Governor Chao and Secretary of State Terrazzas joined him in full-dress uniform. The band threw off all restraint, and, as Villa entered the audience chamber, at a signal from someone in the balcony of the palace, the great throng in the Plaza de Armas uncovered, and all the brilliant crowd of officers in the room saluted stiffly.

It was Napoleonic!

Villa hesitated for a minute, pulling his mustache and looking very uncomfortable, finally gravitated toward the throne, which he tested by shaking the arms, and then sat down, with the Governor on his right and the Secretary of State on his left.

Señor Bauche Alcalde stepped forward, raised his right hand to the exact position which Cicero took when denouncing Catiline, and pronounced a short discourse, indicting Villa for personal bravery on the field on six counts, which he mentioned in florid detail. He was followed by the Chief of Artillery, who said: "The army adores you. We will follow you wherever you lead. You can be what you desire in Mexico." Then three other officers spoke in the high-flung, extravagant periods necessary to Mexican oratory. They called him "The Friend of the Poor," "The Invincible General," "The Inspirer of Courage and Patriotism," "The Hope of the Indian Republic." And through it all Villa slouched on the throne, his mouth hanging open, his little shrewd eyes playing around the room. Once or twice he yawned, but for the most part he seemed to be speculating, with some intense interior amusement, like a small boy in church, what it was all about. He knew, of course, that it was the proper thing, and perhaps felt a slight vanity that all this conventional ceremonial was addressed to him. But it bored him just the same.

Finally, with an impressive gesture, Colonel Servin stepped forward with the small pasteboard box which held the medal. General Chao nudged Villa, who stood up. The officers applauded violently; the crowd outside cheered; the band in the court burst into a triumphant march.

Villa put out both hands eagerly, like a child for a new toy. He could hardly wait to open the box and see what was inside. An expectant hush fell upon everyone, even the crowd in the square. Villa looked at the medal, scratching his head, and, in a reverent silence, said clearly: "This is a hell of a little thing to give

a man for all that heroism you are talking about!"
And the bubble of Empire was pricked then and there
with a great shout of laughter.

They waited for him to speak—to make a conventional address of acceptance. But as he looked around
the room at those brilliant, educated men, who said
that they would die for Villa, the peon, and meant it,
and as he caught sight through the door of the ragged
soldiers, who had forgotten their rigidity and were
crowding eagerly into the corridor with eyes fixed
eagerly on the *compañero* that they loved, he realized
something of what the Revolution signified.

Puckering up his face, as he did always when he concentrated intensely, he leaned across the table in front
of him and poured out, in a voice so low that people
could hardly hear: "There is no word to speak. All I
can say is my heart is all to you." Then he nudged
Chao and sat down, spitting violently on the floor; and
Chao pronounced the classic discourse.

CHAPTER II

THE RISE OF A BANDIT

VILLA was an outlaw for twenty-two years.
When he was only a boy of sixteen, delivering
milk in the streets of Chihuahua, he killed a
government official and had to take to the mountains.
The story is that the official had violated his sister,
but it seems probable that Villa killed him on account

of his insufferable insolence. That in itself would not have outlawed him long in Mexico, where human life is cheap; but once a refugee he committed the unpardonable crime of stealing cattle from the rich *hacendados*. And from that time to the outbreak of the Madero revolution the Mexican government had a price on his head.

Villa was the son of ignorant peons. He had never been to school. He hadn't the slightest conception of the complexity of civilization, and when he finally came back to it, a mature man of extraordinary native shrewdness, he encountered the twentieth century with the naïve simplicity of a savage.

It is almost impossible to procure accurate information about his career as a bandit. There are accounts of outrages he committed in old files of local newspapers and government reports, but those sources are prejudiced, and his name became so prominent as a bandit that every train robbery and hold-up and murder in northern Mexico was attributed to Villa. But an immense body of popular legend grew up among the peons around his name. There are many traditional songs and ballads celebrating his exploits—you can hear the shepherds singing them around their fires in the mountains at night, repeating verses handed down by their fathers or composing others extemporaneously. For instance, they tell the story of how Villa, fired by the story of the misery of the peons on the Hacienda of Los Alamos, gathered a small army and descended upon the Big House, which he looted, and distributed the spoils among the poor people. He drove off thousands of cattle from the Terrazzas range and ran them across the border. He would suddenly descend upon a prosperous mine and seize the bullion. When he needed corn he captured a granary belonging to some rich man. He recruited almost openly in the villages far removed from the well-traveled roads and railways, organizing the outlaws of the mountains. Many of the present rebel soldiers used to belong to his band and several of the Constitutionalist generals, like Urbina. His range was confined mostly to southern Chihuahua and northern Durango, but it extended from Coahuila right across the Republic to the State of Sinaloa.

His reckless and romantic bravery is the subject of countless poems. They tell, for example, how one of his band named Reza was captured by the rurales and bribed to betray Villa. Villa heard of it and sent word into the city of Chihuahua that he was coming for Reza. In broad daylight he entered the city on horseback, took ice cream on the Plaza—the ballad is very explicit on this point—and rode up and down the streets until he found Reza strolling with his sweetheart in the Sunday crowd on the Paseo Bolivar, where he shot him and escaped. In time of famine he fed whole districts, and took care of entire villages evicted by the soldiers under Porfirio Diaz's outrageous land law. Everywhere he was known as The Friend of the Poor. He was the Mexican Robin Hood.

In all these years he learned to trust nobody. Often in his secret journeys across the country with one faithful companion he camped in some desolate spot

THE RISE OF A BANDIT

and dismissed his guide; then, leaving a fire burning, he rode all night to get away from the faithful companion. That is how Villa learned the art of war, and in the field to-day, when the army comes into camp at night, Villa flings the bridle of his horse to an orderly, takes a serape over his shoulder, and sets out for the hills alone. He never seems to sleep. In the dead of night he will appear somewhere along the line of out-, posts to see if the sentries are on the job; and in the morning he returns from a totally different direction. No one, not even the most trusted officer of his staff, knows the least of his plans until he is ready for action.

When Madero took the field in 1910, Villa was still an outlaw. Perhaps, as his enemies say, he saw a chance to whitewash himself; perhaps, as seems probable, he was inspired by the Revolution of the peons. Anyway, about three months after they rose in arms, Villa suddenly appeared in El Paso and put himself, his band, his knowledge of the country and all his fortune at the command of Madero. The vast wealth that people said he must have accumulated during his twenty years of robbery turned out to be 363 silver *pesos*, badly worn. Villa became a Captain in the Maderista army, and as such went to Mexico City with Madero and was made honorary general of the new *rurales*. He was attached to Huerta's army when it was sent north to put down the Orozco Revolution. Villa commanded the garrison of Parral, and defeated Orozco with an inferior force in the only decisive battle of the war.

119

Huerta put Villa in command of the advance, and let him and the veterans of Madero's army do the dangerous and dirty work while the old line Federal regiments lay back under the protection of their artillery. In Jimenez Huerta suddenly summoned Villa before a court-martial and charged him with insubordination—claiming to have wired an order to Villa in Parral, which order Villa said he never received. The court-martial lasted fifteen minutes, and Huerta's most powerful future antagonist was sentenced to be shot.

Alfonso Madero, who was on Huerta's staff, stayed the execution, but President Madero, forced to back up the orders of his commander in the field, imprisoned Villa in the Penitentiary of the capital. During all this time Villa never wavered in his loyalty to Madero —an unheard-of thing in Mexican history. For a long time he had passionately wanted an education. Now he wasted no time in regrets or political intrigue. He set himself with all his force to learn to read and write. Villa hadn't the slightest foundation to work upon. He spoke the crude Spanish of the very poor—what is called *pelado*. He knew nothing of the rudiments or philosophy of language; and he started out to learn those first, because he always must know the *why* of things. In nine months he could write a very fair hand and read the newspapers. It is interesting now to see him read, or, rather, hear him, for he has to drone the words aloud like a small child. Finally, the Madero government connived at his escape from prison, either to save Huerta's face because Villa's friends had demanded an investigation, or because Ma-

dero was convinced of his innocence and didn't dare
openly to release him.

From that time to the outbreak of the last revolution, Villa lived in El Paso, Texas, and it was from
there that he set out, in April, 1913, to conquer Mexico with four companions, three led horses, two pounds
of sugar and coffee, and a pound of salt.

There is a little story connected with that. He
hadn't money enough to buy horses, nor had any of
his companions. But he sent two of them to a local
livery stable to rent riding horses every day for a week.
They always paid carefully at the end of the ride, so
when they asked for eight horses the livery stable man
had no hesitation about trusting them with them. Six
months later, when Villa came triumphantly into
Juarez at the head of an army of four thousand men,
the first public act he committed was to send a man
with double the price of the horses to the owner of the
livery stable.

He recruited in the mountains near San Andres, and
so great was his popularity that within one month he
had raised an army of three thousand men; in two
months he had driven the Federal garrisons all over the
State of Chihuahua back into Chihuahua City; in six
months he had taken Torreon; and in seven and a half
Juarez had fallen to him, Mercado's Federal army had
evacuated Chihuahua, and Northern Mexico was almost free.

INSURGENT MEXICO

CHAPTER III

A PEON IN POLITICS

VILLA proclaimed himself military governor of the State of Chihuahua, and began the extraordinary experiment—extraordinary because he knew nothing about it—of creating a government for 300,000 people out of his head.

It has often been said that Villa succeeded because he had educated advisers. As a matter of fact, he was almost alone. What advisers he had spent most of their time answering his eager questions and doing what he told them. I used sometimes to go to the Governor's palace early in the morning and wait for him in the Governor's chamber. About eight o'clock Sylvestre Terrazzas, the Secretary of State, Sebastian Vargas, the State Treasurer, and Manuel Chao, then Interventor, would arrive, very bustling and busy, with huge piles of reports, suggestions and decrees which they had drawn up. Villa himself came in about eight-thirty, threw himself into a chair, and made them read out loud to him. Every minute he would interject a remark, correction or suggestion. Occasionally he waved his finger back and forward and said: "*No sirve.*" When they were all through he began rapidly and without a halt to outline the policy of the State of Chihuahua, legislative, financial, judicial, and even educational. When he came to a place that bothered him, he said: "How do they do that?" And then, after

122

A PEON IN POLITICS

it was carefully explained to him: "Why?" Most of
the acts and usages of government seemed to him extraordinarily unnecessary and snarled up. For example, his advisers proposed to finance the Revolution
by issuing State bonds bearing 30 or 40 per cent. interest. He said, "I can understand why the State
should pay something to people for the rent of their
money, but how is it just to pay the whole sum back
to them three or four times over?" He couldn't see
why rich men should be granted huge tracts of land
and poor men should not. The whole complex struc-
ture of civilization was new to him. You had to be a
philosopher to explain anything to Villa; and his advisers were only practical men.

There was the financial question. It came to Villa in
this way. He noticed, all of a sudden, that there was
no money in circulation. The farmers who produced
meat and vegetables refused to come into the city mar-
kets any more because no one had any money to buy
from them. The truth was that those possessing silver or Mexican bank-notes buried them in the ground.
Chihuahua not being a manufacturing center, and the
few factories there having closed down, there was nothing which could be exchanged for food. So, like a
blight, the paralysis of the production of food began
all at once and actual starvation stared at the town
populations. I remember hearing vaguely of several
highly elaborate plans for the relief of this condition
put forward by Villa's advisers. He himself said:
"Why, if all they need is money, let's print some." So

they inked up the printing press in the basement of the Governor's palace and ran off two million pesos on strong paper, stamped with the signatures of government officials, and with Villa's name printed across the middle in large letters. The counterfeit money, which afterward flooded El Paso, was distinguished from the original by the fact that the names of the officials were signed instead of stamped.

This first issue of currency was guaranteed by absolutely nothing but the name of Francisco Villa. It was issued chiefly to revive the petty internal commerce of the State so that the poor people could get food. And yet almost immediately it was bought by the banks of El Paso at 18 to 19 cents on the dollar because Villa guaranteed it.

Of course he knew nothing of the accepted ways of getting his money into circulation. He began to pay the army with it. On Christmas Day he called the poor people of Chihuahua together and gave them $15 apiece outright. Then he issued a short decree, ordering the acceptance of his money at par throughout the State. The succeeding Saturday the market-places of Chihuahua and the other nearby towns swarmed with farmers and with buyers. Villa issued another proclamation, fixing the price of beef at seven cents a pound, milk at five cents a quart, and bread at four cents a loaf. There was no famine in Chihuahua. But the big merchants, who had timidly reopened their stores for the first time since his entry into Chihuahua, placarded their goods with two sets of price marks— one for Mexican silver money and bank-bills, and the other for 'Villa money.' He stopped that by another decree, ordering sixty days' imprisonment for anybody who discriminated against his currency.

But still the silver and bank-bills refused to come out of the ground, and these Villa needed to buy arms and supplies for his army. So he simply proclaimed to the people that after the tenth of February Mexican silver and bank-bills would be regarded as counterfeit, and that before that time they could be exchanged for his own money at par in the State Treasury. But the large sums of the rich still eluded him. Most of the financiers declared that it was all a bluff, and held on. But lo! on the morning of February tenth, a decree was pasted up on the walls all over Chihuahua City, announcing that from that time on all Mexican silver and bank-notes were counterfeit and could not be exchanged for Villa money in the Treasury, and anyone attempting to pass them was liable to sixty days in the penitentiary. A great howl went up, not only from the capitalists, but from the shrewd misers of distant villages.

About two weeks after the issue of this decree, I was taking lunch with Villa in the house which he had confiscated from Manuel Gomeros and used as his official residence. A delegation of three peons in sandals arrived from a village in the Tarahumare to protest against the Counterfeit Decree.

"But, *mi General*," said the spokesman, "we did not hear of the decree until to-day. We have been using bank-bills and silver in our village. We had not seen your money, and we did not know. . . ."

"You have a good deal of money?" interrupted Villa suddenly.

"Yes, *mi General.*"

"Three or four or five thousand, perhaps?"

"More than that, *mi General.*"

"Señores," Villa squinted at them ferociously, "samples of my money reached your village within twenty-four hours after it was issued. You decided that my government would not last. You dug holes under your fireplaces and put the silver and bank-notes there. You knew of my first proclamation a day after it was posted up in the streets of Chihuahua, and you ignored it. The Counterfeit Decree you also knew as soon as it was issued. You thought there was always time to change if it became necessary. And then you got frightened, and you three, who have more money than anyone else in the village, got on your mules and rode down here. Señores, your money is counterfeit. You are poor men!"

"*Valgame dios!*" cried the oldest of the three, sweating profusely.

"But we are ruined, *mi General!*—I swear to you—We did not know—We would have accepted—There is no food in the village——"

The General in Chief meditated for a moment.

"I will give you one more chance," he said, "not for you, but for the poor people of your village who can buy nothing. Next Wednesday at noon bring all your money, every cent of it, to the Treasury, and I will see what can be done."

To the perspiring financiers who waited hat in hand

out in the hall, the news spread by word of mouth; and Wednesday at high noon one could not pass the Treasury door for the eager mob gathered there.

Villa's great passion was schools. He believed that land for the people and schools would settle every question of civilization. Schools were an obsession with him. Often I have heard him say: "When I passed such and such a street this morning I saw a lot of kids. Let's put a school there." Chihuahua has a population of under 40,000 people. At different times Villa established over fifty schools there. The great dream of his life has been to send his son to school in the United States, but at the opening of the term in February he had to abandon it because he didn't have money enough to pay for a half year's tuition.

No sooner had he taken over the government of Chihuahua than he put his army to work running the electric light plant, the street railways, the telephone, the water works and the Terrazzas flour mill. He delegated soldiers to administer the great haciendas which he had confiscated. He manned the slaughter-house with soldiers, and sold Terrazzas's beef to the people for the government. A thousand of them he put in the streets of the city as civil police, prohibiting on pain of death stealing, or the sale of liquor to the army. A soldier who got drunk was shot. He even tried to run the brewery with soldiers, but failed because he couldn't find an expert maltster. "The only thing to do with soldiers in time of peace," said Villa, "is to put them to work. An idle soldier is always thinking of war."

In the matter of the political enemies of the Revolution he was just as simple, just as effective. Two hours after he entered the Governor's palace the foreign consuls came in a body to ask his protection for 200 Federal soldiers who had been left as a police force at the request of the foreigners. Before answering them, Villa said suddenly: "Which is the Spanish consul?" Scobell, the British vice-consul, said: "I represent the Spaniards." "All right!" snapped Villa. "Tell them to begin to pack. Any Spaniard caught within the boundaries of this State after five days will be escorted to the nearest wall by a firing squad."

The consuls gave a gasp of horror. Scobell began a violent protest, but Villa cut him short.

"This is not a sudden determination on my part," he said; "I have been thinking about this since 1910. The Spaniards must go."

Letcher, the American consul, said: "General, I don't question your motives, but I think you are making a grave political mistake in expelling the Spaniards. The government at Washington will hesitate a long time before becoming friendly to a party which makes use of such barbarous measures."

"Señor Consul," answered Villa, "we Mexicans have had three hundred years of the Spaniards. They have not changed in character since the *Conquistadores*. They disrupted the Indian empire and enslaved the people. We did not ask them to mingle their blood with ours. Twice we drove them out of Mexico and allowed them to return with the same rights as Mexicans, and they used these rights to steal away our land, to make the people slaves, and to take up arms against the cause of liberty. They supported Porfirio Diaz. They were perniciously active in politics. It was the Spaniards who framed the plot that put Huerta in the palace. When Madero was murdered the Spaniards in every State in the Republic held banquets of rejoicing. They thrust on us the greatest superstition the world has ever known—the Catholic Church. They ought to be killed for that alone. I consider we are being very generous with them."

Scobell insisted vehemently that five days was too short a time, that he couldn't possibly reach all the Spaniards in the State by that time; so Villa extended the time to ten days.

The rich Mexicans who had oppressed the people and opposed the Revolution, he expelled promptly from the State and confiscated their vast holdings. By a simple stroke of the pen the 17,000,000 acres and innumerable business enterprises of the Terrazzas family became the property of the Constitutionalist government, as well as the great lands of the Creel family and the magnificent palaces which were their town houses. Remembering, however, how the Terrazzas exiles had once financed the Orozco Revolution, he imprisoned Don Luis Terrazzas, Jr., as a hostage in his own house in Chihuahua. Some particularly obnoxious political enemies were promptly executed in the penitentiary. The Revolution possesses a black book in which are set down the names, offenses, and property of

those who have oppressed and robbed the people. The
Germans, who had been particularly active politically,
the Englishmen and Americans, he does not yet dare to
molest. Their pages in the black book will be opened
when the Constitutionalist government is established in
Mexico City; and there, too, he will settle the account
of the Mexican people with the Catholic Church.

Villa knew that the reserve of the Banco Minero,
amounting to about $500,000 gold, was hidden some-
where in Chihuahua. Don Luis Terrazzas, Jr., was a director of that bank. When he refused to divulge the
hiding-place of the money, Villa and a squad of soldiers
took him out of his house one night, rode him on a
mule out into the desert, and strung him up to a tree
by the neck. He was cut down just in time to save
his life, and led Villa to an old forge in the Terrazzas
iron works, under which was discovered the reserve of
the Banco Minero. Terrazzas went back to prison
badly shaken, and Villa sent word to his father in El
Paso that he would release the son upon payment of
$500,000 ransom.

CHAPTER IV

THE HUMAN SIDE

VILLA has two wives, one a patient, simple woman
who was with him during all his years of out-
lawry, who lives in El Paso, and the other a
cat-like, slender young girl, who is the mistress of his

house in Chihuahua. He is perfectly open about it, though lately the educated, conventional Mexicans who have been gathering about him in ever-increasing numbers have tried to hush up the fact. Among the peons it is not only not unusual but customary to have more than one mate.

One hears a great many stories of Villa's violating women. I asked him if that were true. He pulled his mustache and stared at me for a minute with an inscrutable expression. "I never take the trouble to deny such stories," he said. "They say I am a bandit, too. Well, you know my history. But tell me; have you ever met a husband, father or brother of any woman that I have violated?" He paused: "Or even a witness?"

It is fascinating to watch him discover new ideas. Remember that he is absolutely ignorant of the troubles and confusions and readjustments of modern civilization. "Socialism," he said once, when I wanted to know what he thought of it: "Socialism—is it a thing? I only see it in books, and I do not read much." Once I asked him if women would vote in the new Republic. He was sprawled out on his bed, with his coat unbuttoned. "Why, I don't think so," he said, startled, suddenly sitting up. "What do you mean—vote? Do you mean elect a government and make laws?" I said I did and that women already were doing it in the United States. "Well," he said, scratching his head: "if they do it up there I don't see that they shouldn't do it down here." The idea seemed to amuse him enormously. He rolled it over and over in his mind, looking at me and away again. "It may be as you say," he said; "but I have never thought about it. Women seem to me to be things to protect, to love. They have no stern-ness of mind. They can't consider anything for its right or wrong. They are full of pity and softness. Why," he said, "a woman would not give an order to execute a traitor."

"I am not so sure of that, *mi General*," I said. "Women can be crueller and harder than men."

He stared at me, pulling his mustache. And then he began to grin. He looked slowly to where his wife was setting the table for lunch. "*Oiga*," he said, "come here. Listen. Last night I caught three traitors crossing the river to blow up the railroad. What shall I do with them? Shall I shoot them or not?"

Embarrassed, she seized his hand and kissed it. "Oh, I don't know anything about that," she said. "You know best."

"No," said Villa. "I leave it entirely to you. Those men were going to try to cut our communications be-tween Juarez and Chihuahua. They were traitors—Federals. What shall I do? Shall I shoot them or not?"

"Oh, well, shoot them," said Mrs. Villa.

Villa chuckled delightedly. "There is something in what you say," he remarked, and for days afterward went around asking the cook and the chambermaids whom they would like to have for President of Mexico.

THE HUMAN SIDE

He never missed a bull-fight, and every afternoon at four o'clock he was to be found at the cock-pit, where he fought his own birds with the happy enthusiasm of a small boy. In the evening he played faro in some gambling hall. Sometimes in the late morning he would send a fast courier after Luis Leon, the bull-fighter, and telephone personally to the slaughter-house, asking if they had any fierce bulls in the pen. They almost always did have, and we would all get on horseback and gallop through the streets about a mile to the big adobe corrals. Twenty cowboys cut the bull out of the herd, threw and tied him and cut off his sharp horns, and then Villa and Luis Leon and anybody else who wanted to would take the professional red capes and go down into the ring; Luis Leon with professional caution, Villa as stubborn and clumsy as the bull, slow on his feet, but swift as an animal with his body and arms. Villa would walk right up to the pawing, infuriated animal, and, with his double cape, slap him insolently across the face, and, for half an hour, would follow the greatest sport I ever saw. Sometimes the sawed-off horns of the bull would catch Villa in the seat of the trousers and propel him violently across the ring; then he would turn and grab the bull by the head and wrestle with him with the sweat streaming down his face until five or six *compañeros* seized the bull's tail and hauled him plowing and bellowing back.

Villa never drinks nor smokes, but he will outdance the most ardent *novio* in Mexico. When the order was given for the army to advance upon Torreon, Villa

stopped off at Camargo to be best man at the wedding
of one of his old *compadres*. He danced steadily without stopping, they said, all Monday night, all Tuesday, and all Tuesday night, arriving at the front on
Wednesday morning with blood-shot eyes and an air
of extreme lassitude.

CHAPTER V

THE FUNERAL OF ABRAM GONZALES

THE fact that Villa hates useless pomp and cere-
mony makes it more impressive when he does
appear on a public occasion. He has the knack
of absolutely expressing the strong feeling of the great
mass of the people. In February, exactly one year
after Abram Gonzales was murdered by the Federals
at Bachimba Cañon, Villa ordered a great funeral cere-
mony to be held in the City of Chihuahua. Two trains,
carrying the officers of the army, the consuls and repre-
sentatives of the foreign colony, left Chihuahua early
in the morning to take up the body of the dead Governor from its resting-place under a rude wooden cross
in the desert. Villa ordered Major Fierro, his Superintendent of Railroads, to get the trains ready—
but Fierro got drunk and forgot; and when Villa and
his brilliant staff arrived at the railway station the
next morning the regular passenger train to Juarez
was just leaving and there was no other equipment on
hand. Villa himself leaped on to the already moving

engine and compelled the engineer to back the train up to the station. Then he walked through the train, ordering the passengers out, and switched it in the direction of Bachimba. They had no sooner started than he summoned Fierro before him and discharged him from the superintendency of the railroads, appointing Calzado in his place, and ordered the latter to return at once to Chihuahua and be thoroughly informed about the railroads by the time he returned. At Bachimba Villa stood silently by the grave with the tears rolling down his cheeks. For Gonzales had been his close friend. Ten thousand people stood in the heat and dust at Chihuahua railway station when the funeral train arrived, and poured weeping through the narrow streets behind the army, at the head of which walked Villa beside the hearse. His automobile was waiting, but he angrily refused to ride, stumbling stubbornly along in the dirt of the streets with his eyes on the ground.

That night there was a *velada* in the Theater of the Heroes, an immense auditorium packed with emotional peons and their women. The ring of boxes was brilliant with officers in their full dress, and wedged behind them up the five high balconies were the ragged poor. Now, the *velada* is an entirely Mexican institution. First there comes a speech, then a "recitation" on the piano, then a speech, followed by a patriotic song rendered by a chorus of awkward little Indian girls from the public school with squeaky voices, another speech,

and a soprano solo from "Trovatore" by the wife of
some government official, still another speech, and so
on for at least five hours. Whenever there is a prominent funeral, or a national holiday, or a President's
anniversary, or, in fact, an occasion of the least importance, a *velada* must be held. It is the conventional
and respectable way of celebrating anything. Villa
sat in the left hand stage box and controlled the proceedings by tapping a little bell. The stage itself
was brilliantly hideous with black bunting, huge masses
of artificial flowers, abominable crayon portraits of
Madero, Piño Suarez and the dead Governor, and red,
white and green electric lights. At the foot of all this
was a very small, plain, black wooden box which held
the body of Abram Gonzales.

The *velada* proceeded in an orderly and exhausting
manner for about two hours. Local orators, trembling
with stage fright, mouthed the customary Castilian extravagant phrases, and little girls stepped on their
own feet and murdered Tosti's "Good-bye." Villa,
with his eyes riveted on that wooden box, never moved
nor spoke. At the proper time he mechanically tapped
the little bell, but after a while he couldn't stand it
any longer. A large fleshy Mexican was in the middle of Handel's "Largo" on the grand piano, when Villa
stood erect. He put his foot on the railing of the
box and leaped to the stage, knelt, and took up the
coffin in his arms. Handel's "Largo" petered out.
Silent astonishment paralyzed the audience. Holding
the black box tenderly in his arms as a mother with

her baby, not looking at anyone, Villa started down the steps of the stage and up the aisle. Instinctively, the house rose; and as he passed out through the swinging doors they followed on silently behind him. He strode down between the lines of waiting soldiers, his sword banging on the floor, across the dark square to the Governor's palace; and, with his own hands, put the coffin on the flower-banked table waiting for it in the audience hall. It had been arranged that four generals in turn should stand the death watch, each for two hours. Candles shed a dim light over the table and the surrounding floor, but the rest of the room was in darkness. A dense mass of silent, breathing people packed the doorway. Villa unbuckled his sword and threw it clattering into a corner. Then he took his rifle from the table and stood the first watch.

CHAPTER VI

VILLA AND CARRANZA

IT seems incredible to those who don't know him, that this remarkable figure, who has risen from obscurity to the most prominent position in Mexico in three years, should not covet the Presidency of the Republic. But that is in entire accordance with the simplicity of his character. When asked about it he answered as always with perfect directness, just in the way that you put it to him. He didn't quibble

over whether he could or could not be President of
Mexico. He said: "I am a fighter, not a statesman.
I am not educated enough to be President. I only
learned to read and write two years ago. How could
I, who never went to school, hope to be able to talk
with the foreign ambassadors and the cultivated gentlemen of the Congress? It would be bad for Mexico
if an uneducated man were to be President. There is
one thing that I will not do,—and that is to take a
position for which I am not fitted. There is only one
order of my Jefe (Carranza) which I would refuse
to obey,—if he would command me to be a President
or a Governor." On behalf of my paper I had to ask
him this question five or six times. Finally he became
exasperated. "I have told you many times," he said,
"that there is no possibility of my becoming President of Mexico. Are the newspapers trying to make
trouble between me and my Jefe? This is the last time
that I will answer that question. The next correspondent that asks me I will have him spanked and
sent to the border." For days afterward he went
around grumbling humorously about the *chatito* (pug-
nose) who kept asking him whether he wanted to be
President of Mexico. The idea seemed to amuse him.
Whenever I went to see him after that he used to say,
at the end of our talk: "Well, aren't you going to ask
me to-day whether I want to be President?"

He never referred to Carranza except as "my Jefe,"
and he obeyed implicitly the slightest order from "the

VILLA AND CARRANZA

First Chief of the Revolution." His loyalty to Carranza was perfectly obstinate. He seemed to think that in Carranza were embodied the entire ideals of the Revolution. This, in spite of the fact that many of his advisers tried to make him see that Carranza was essentially an aristocrat and a reformer, and that the people were fighting for more than reform.

Carranza's political program, as set forth in the plan of Guadelupe, carefully avoids any promise of settlement of the land question, except a vague endorsement of Madero's plan of San Luis Potosi, and it is evident that he does not intend to advocate any radical restoration of the land to the people until he becomes provisional president—and then to proceed very cautiously. In the meantime he seems to have left it to Villa's judgment, as well as all other details of the conduct of the Revolution in the north. But Villa, being a peon, and feeling with them, rather than consciously reasoning it out, that the land question is the real cause of the Revolution, acted with characteristic promptness and directness. No sooner had he settled the details of government of Chihuahua State, and appointed Chao his provisional governor, than he issued a proclamation, giving sixty-two and one-half acres out of the confiscated lands to every male citizen of the State, and declaring these lands inalienable for any cause for a period of ten years. In the State of Durango the same thing has happened and as other states are free of Federal garrisons, he will pursue the same policy.

CHAPTER VII

THE RULES OF WAR

ON the field, too, Villa had to invent an entirely original method of warfare, because he never had a chance to learn anything of accepted military strategy. In that he is without the possibility of any doubt the greatest leader Mexico has ever had. His method of fighting is astonishingly like Napoleon's. Secrecy, quickness of movement, the adaptation of his plans to the character of the country and of his soldiers,—the value of intimate relations with the rank and file, and of building up a tradition among the enemy that his army is invincible, and that he himself bears a charmed life,—these are his characteristics. He knew nothing of accepted European standards of strategy or of discipline. One of the troubles of the Mexican federal army is that its officers are thoroughly saturated with conventional military theory. The Mexican soldier is still mentally at the end of the eighteenth century. He is, above all, a loose, individual, guerrilla fighter. Red-tape simply paralyzes the machine. When Villa's army goes into battle he is not hampered by salutes, or rigid respect for officers, or trigonometrical calculations of the trajectories of projectiles, or theories of the percentage of hits in a thousand rounds of rifle fire, or the function of cavalry, infantry and artillery in any particular position, or rigid obedience to the secret knowledge of its superiors.

140

THE RULES OF WAR

It reminds one of the ragged Republican army that Napoleon led into Italy. It is probable that Villa doesn't know much about those things himself. But he does know that guerrilla fighters cannot be driven blindly in platoons around the field in perfect step, that men fighting individually and of their own free will are braver than long volleying rows in the trenches, lashed to it by officers with the flat of their swords. And where the fighting is fiercest—when a ragged mob of fierce brown men with hand bombs and rifles rush the bullet-swept streets of an ambushed town—Villa is among them, like any common soldier.

Up to his day, Mexican armies had always carried with them hundreds of the women and children of the soldiers; Villa was the first man to think of swift forced marches of bodies of cavalry, leaving their women behind. Up to his time no Mexican army had ever abandoned its base; it had always stuck closely to the railroad and the supply trains. But Villa struck terror into the enemy by abandoning his trains and throwing his entire effective army upon the field, as he did at Gomez Palacio. He invented in Mexico that most demoralizing form of battle—the night attack. When, after the fall of Torreon last September, he withdrew his entire army in the face of Orozco's advance from Mexico City and for five days unsuccessfully attacked Chihuahua, it was a terrible shock to the Federal General when he waked up one morning and found that Villa had sneaked around the city under cover of darkness, captured a freight train at Terrazzas and descended with his entire army upon the

141

comparatively undefended city of Juarez. It wasn't fair! Villa found that he hadn't enough trains to carry all his soldiers, even when he had ambushed and captured a Federal troop train, sent south by General Castro, the Federal commander in Juarez. So he telegraphed that gentleman as follows, signing the name of the Colonel in command of the troop train: "Engine broken down at Moctezuma. Send another engine and five cars." The unsuspecting Castro immediately dispatched a new train. Villa then telegraphed him: "Wires cut between here and Chihuahua. Large force of rebels approaching from south. What shall I do?" Castro replied: "Return at once." And Villa obeyed, telegraphing cheering messages at every station along the way. The Federal commander got wind of his coming about an hour before he arrived, and left, without informing his garrison, so that, outside of a small massacre, Villa took Juarez almost without a shot. And with the border so near he managed to smuggle across enough ammunition to equip his almost armless forces and a week later sallied out and routed the pursuing Federal forces with great slaughter at Tierra Blanca.

General Hugh L. Scott, in command of the American troops at Fort Bliss, sent Villa a little pamphlet containing the Rules of War adopted by the Hague Conference. He spent hours poring over it. It interested and amused him hugely. He said: "What is this Hague Conference? Was there a representative of Mexico there? Was there a representative of the Constitutionalists there? It seems to me a funny thing to make rules about war. It's not a game. What is the difference between civilized war and any other kind of war? If you and I are having a fight in a *cantina* we are not going to pull a little book out of our pockets and read over the rules. It says here that you must not use lead bullets; but I don't see why not. They do the work."

For a long time afterward he went around popping questions at his officers like this: "If an invading army takes a city of the enemy, what must you do with the women and children?"

As far as I could see, the Rules of War didn't make any difference in Villa's original method of fighting. The *colorados* he executed wherever he captured them; because, he said, they were peons like the Revolutionists and that no peon would volunteer against the cause of liberty unless he were bad. The Federal officers also he killed, because, he explained, they were educated men and ought to know better. But the Federal common soldiers he set at liberty because most of them were conscripts, and thought that they were fighting for the Patria. There is no case on record where he wantonly killed a man. Anyone who did so he promptly executed—except Fierro.

Fierro, the man who killed Benton, was known as "The Butcher" throughout the army. He was a great handsome animal, the best and cruellest rider and fighter, perhaps, in all the revolutionary forces. In his furious lust for blood Fierro used to shoot down a hundred prisoners with his own revolver, only stopping long enough to reload. He killed for the pure joy of it. During two weeks that I was in Chihuahua, Fierro killed fifteen inoffensive citizens in cold blood. But there was always a curious relationship between him and Villa. He was Villa's best friend; and Villa loved him like a son and always pardoned him.

But Villa, although he had never heard of the Rules of War, carried with his army the only field hospital of any effectiveness that any Mexican army has ever carried. It consisted of forty box-cars enameled inside, fitted with operating tables and all the latest appliances of surgery, and manned by more than sixty doctors and nurses. Every day during the battle shuttle trains full of the desperately wounded ran from the front to the base hospitals at Parral, Jimenez and Chihuahua. He took care of the Federal wounded just as carefully as of his own men. Ahead of his own supply train went another train, carrying two thousand sacks of flour, and also coffee, corn, sugar, and cigarettes to feed the entire starving population of the country around Durango City and Torreon.

The common soldiers adore him for his bravery and his coarse, blunt humor. Often I have seen him slouched on his cot in the little red caboose in which he always traveled, cracking jokes familiarly with twenty ragged privates sprawled on the floor, chairs and tables. When the army was entraining or detraining, Villa personally would be on hand in a dirty old suit, without a collar, kicking mules in the stomach and pushing horses in and out of the stock-cars. Getting thirsty all of a sudden, he would grab some soldier's canteen and drain it, in spite of the indignant protests of its owner; and then tell him to go over to the river and say that Pancho Villa said that he should fill it there.

CHAPTER VIII

THE DREAM OF PANCHO VILLA

IT might not be uninteresting to know the passionate dream—the vision which animates this ignorant fighter, "not educated enough to be President of Mexico." He told it to me once in these words: "When the new Republic is established there will never be any more army in Mexico. Armies are the greatest support of tyranny. There can be no dictator without an army.

"We will put the army to work. In all parts of the Republic we will establish military colonies composed of the veterans of the Revolution. The State will give them grants of agricultural lands and establish big industrial enterprises to give them work. Three days a week they will work and work hard, because honest work is more important than fighting, and only honest work makes good citizens. And the other three days they will receive military instruction and go out and teach all the people how to fight. Then, when the Patria is invaded, we will just have to telephone from the palace at Mexico City, and in half a day all the Mexican people will rise from their fields and factories, fully armed, equipped and organized to defend their children and their homes.

INSURGENT MEXICO

"My ambition is to live my life in one of those military colonies among my *compañeros* whom I love, who have suffered so long and so deeply with me. I think I would like the government to establish a leather factory there where we could make good saddles and bridles, because I know how to do that; and the rest of the time I would like to work on my little farm, raising cattle and corn. It would be fine, I think, to help make Mexico a happy place."

PART THREE

JIMENEZ AND POINTS WEST

CHAPTER I

DONA LUISA'S HOTEL

I WENT south from Chihuahua on a troop train bound for the advance near Escalon. Attached to the five freight cars, filled with horses and carrying soldiers on top, was a coach in which I was allowed to ride with two hundred noisy *pacificos*, male and female. It was gruesomely suggestive: car windows smashed, mirrors, lamps and plush seats torn out, and bullet holes after the manner of a frieze. The time of our departure was not fixed, and no one knew when the train would arrive. The railroad had just been repaired. In places where there had once been bridges we plunged into arroyos and snorted up the farther bank on a rickety new-laid track that bent and cracked under us. All day long the roadside was lined with immense distorted steel rails, torn up with a chain and a backing engine by the thorough Orozco last year. There was a rumor that Castillo's bandits were planning to blow us up with dynamite sometime during the afternoon. . . .

Peons with big straw sombreros and beautifully faded serapes, Indians in blue working clothes and cowhide sandals, and squat-faced women with black shawls around their heads, and squalling babies,—packed the

149

seats, aisles and platforms, singing, eating, spitting, chattering. Occasionally there staggered by a ragged man with a cap labeled "conductor" in tarnished gold letters, very drunk, embracing his friends and severely demanding the tickets and safe conducts of strangers. I introduced myself to him by a small present of United States currency. He said, "Señor, you may travel freely over the Republic henceforth without payment. Juan Algomero is at your orders." An officer smartly uniformed, with a sword at his side, was at the rear of the car. He was bound for the front, he said, to lay down his life for his country. His only baggage consisted of four wooden bird-cages full of meadow-larks. Farther to the rear two men sat across the aisle from each other, each with a white sack contain-ing something that moved and clucked. As soon as the train started these bags were opened to disgorge two large roosters, who wandered up and down the aisles eating crumbs and cigarette butts. The two owners immediately raised their voices. "Cock-fight, señores! Five pesos on this valiant and handsome rooster. Five pesos, señores!" The males at once deserted their seats and rushed clamoring toward the center of the car. Not one of them appeared to lack the necessary five dollars. In ten minutes the two promoters were kneeling in the middle of the aisle, throwing their birds. And, as we rattled along, sway-ing from side to side, swooping down into the gullies and laboring up the other bank, a whirling mass of feathers and flashing steel rolled up and down the aisle. That over, a one-legged youth stood up and played

"Whistling Rufus" on a tin flute. Someone had a leather bottle of *tequila,* of which we all took a swig. From the rear of the car came shouts of "*Vamonos a bailar!* Come on and dance!" And in a moment five couples, all men, of course, were madly two-stepping. A blind old peasant was assisted to climb upon his seat, where he quaveringly recited a long ballad about the heroic exploits of the great General Maclovio Herrera. Everybody was silently attentive and showered pennies into the old man's sombrero. Occasionally there floated back to us the singing of the soldiers on the box-cars in front and the sound of their shots as they caught sight of a coyote galloping through the mesquite. Then everybody in our car would make a rush for the windows, pulling at their revolvers, and shoot fast and furiously.

All the long afternoon we ambled slowly south, the western rays of the sun burning as they struck our faces. Every hour or so we stopped at some station, shot to pieces by one army or the other during the three years of Revolution; there the train would be besieged by vendors of cigarettes, pine-nuts, bottles of milk, *camotes,* and *tamales* rolled in corn-husks. Old women, gossiping, descended from the train, built themselves a little fire and boiled coffee. Squatting there, smoking their corn-husk cigarettes, they told one another interminable love stories.

It was late in the evening when we pulled into Jimenez. I shouldered through the entire population, come down to meet the train, passed between the flaring torches of the little row of candy booths, and went along the street, where drunken soldiers alternated with painted girls, walking arm in arm, to Doña Luisa's Station Hotel. It was locked. I pounded on the door and a little window opened at the side, showing an incredibly ancient woman's face, crowned with straggly white hair. This being squinted at me through a pair of steel spectacles and remarked, "Well, I guess you're all right!" Then there came a sound of bars being taken down, and the door swung open. Doña Luisa herself, a great bunch of keys at her belt, stood just inside. She held a large Chinaman by the ear, addressing him in fluent and profane Spanish. "*Chango!*" she said: "What do you mean by telling a guest at this hotel that there wasn't any more hot cakes? Why didn't you make some more? Now take your dirty little bundle and get out of here!" With a final wrench she released the squealing Oriental. "These damn heathen," she announced in English, "the nasty beggars! I don't take any lip from a dirty Chinaman who can live on a nickel's worth of rice a day!" Then she nodded apologetically toward the door. "There's so many damned drunken generals around to-day that I've got to keep the door locked. I don't want the —————— —————— Mexican ——————s in here!"

Doña Luisa is a small, dumpy American woman more than eighty years of age—a benevolent New-England-grandmother sort of person. For forty-five years she has been in Mexico, and thirty or more years ago, when her husband died, she began to keep the Station Hotel. War and peace make no difference to her. The American flag flies over the door and in her house she alone

DUELLO A LA FRIGADA

is boss. When Pascual Orozco took Jimenez, his men began a drunken reign of terror in the town. Orozco himself—Orozco the invincible, the fierce, who would as soon kill a person as not—came drunk to the Station Hotel with two of his officers and several women. Doña Luisa planted herself across the doorway—alone —and shook her fist in his face. "Pascual Orozco," she cried, "take your disreputable friends and go away from here. I'm keeping a decent hotel!" And Orozco went. . . .

CHAPTER II

DUELLO A LA FRIGADA

I WANDERED up the mile-long, incredibly dilapidated street that leads to the town. A streetcar came past, drawn by one galloping mule and bulging with slightly intoxicated soldiers. Open surreys full of officers with girls on their laps rolled along. Under the dusty, bare alamo trees each window held its señorita, with a blanket-wrapped *caballero* in attendance. There were no lights. The night was dry and cold and full of a subtle exotic excitement; guitars twanged, snatches of song and laughter and low voices, and shouts from distant streets, filled the darkness. Occasionally little companies of soldiers on foot came along, or a troop of horsemen in high sombreros and serapes jingled silently out of the blackness and faded away again, bound probably for the relief of guard.

In one quiet stretch of street near the bull-ring, where there are no houses, I noticed an automobile speeding from the town. At the same time a galloping horse came from the other direction, and just in front of me the headlights of the machine illumined the horse and his rider, a young officer in a Stetson hat. The automobile jarred to a grinding stop and a voice from it cried, *"Haltoie!"*

"Who speaks?" asked the horseman, pulling his mount to its haunches.

"I, Guzman!" and the other leaped to the ground and came intó the light, a coarse, fat Mexican, with a sword at his belt.

"Como le va, mi Capitan?" The officer flung himself from his horse. They embraced, patting each other on the back with both hands.

"Very well. And you? Where are you going?"

"To see Maria."

The captain laughed. "Don't do it," he said; "I'm going to see Maria myself, and if I see you there I shall certainly kill you."

"But I am going just the same. I am as quick with my pistol as you, señor."

"But you see," returned the other mildly, "we both cannot go!"

"Perfectly!"

"Oiga!" said the captain to his chauffeur. "Turn your car so as to throw the light evenly along the sidewalk. . . . And now we will walk thirty paces apart and stand with our backs turned until you count three.

Then the man who first puts a bullet through the other man's hat wins. . . ."

Both men drew immense revolvers and stood a moment in the light, spinning the chambers.

"*Listo!* Ready!" cried the horseman.

"Hurry it," said the captain. "It is a bad thing to balk love."

Back to back, they had already begun to pace the distance.

"One!" shouted the chauffeur.

"Two!"

But quick as a flash the fat man wheeled in the trembling, uncertain light, threw down his lifted arm, and a mighty roar went soaring slowly into the heavy night. The Stetson of the other man, whose back was still turned, took an odd little leap ten feet beyond him. He spun around, but the captain was already climbing into his machine.

"*Bueno!*" he said cheerfully. "I win. Until to-morrow then, *amigo!*" And the automobile gathered speed and disappeared down the street. The horseman slowly went to where his hat lay, picked it up and examined it. He stood a moment meditating, and then deliberately mounted his horse and he also went away. I had already started some time before. . . .

In the plaza the regimental band was playing "El Pagare," the song which started Orozco's Revolution. It was a parody of the original, referring to Madero's payment of his family's $750,000 war claims as soon as he became president, that spread like wildfire over the Republic, and had to be suppressed with police and soldiers. "El Pagare" is even now taboo in most revolutionary circles, and I have heard of men being shot for singing it; but in Jimenez at this time the utmost license prevailed. Moreover, the Mexicans, unlike the French, have absolutely no feeling for symbols. Bitterly antagonistic sides use the same flag; in the plaza of almost every town still stand eulogistic statues of Porfirio Diaz; even at officers' mess in the field I have drunk from glasses stamped with the likeness of the old dictator, while Federal army uniforms are plentiful in the ranks.

But "El Pagare" is a swinging, glorious tune, and under the hundreds of little electric light globes strung on the plaza a double procession marched gaily round and round. On the outside, in groups of four, went the men, mostly soldiers. On the inside, in the opposite direction, the girls walked arm in arm. As they passed they threw handfuls of confetti at one another. They never talked to one another, never stopped; but as a girl caught a man's fancy, he slipped a lover's note into her hand as she went by, and she answered with a smile if she liked him. Thus they met, and later the girl would manage to let the *caballero* know her address; this would lead to long talks at her window in the darkness, and then they would be lovers. It was a delicate business, this handing of notes. Every man carried a gun, and every man's girl was his jealously guarded property. It was a killing matter to hand a note to someone else's girl. The close-packed throng moved gaily on, thrilling to the music. . . . Beyond the plaza gaped the ruins of Marcos Russek's store, which these same men had looted less than two weeks before, and at one side the ancient pink cathedral towered among its fountains and great trees, with the iron and glass illuminated sign, "Santo Cristo de Burgos," shining above the door.

There, at the side of the plaza, I came upon a little group of five Americans huddled upon a bench. They were ragged beyond belief, all except a slender youth in leggings and a Federal officer's uniform, who wore a crownless Mexican hat. Feet protruded from their shoes, none had more than the remnants of socks, all were unshaven. One mere boy wore his arm in a sling made out of a torn blanket. They made room for me gladly, stood up, crowded around, cried how good it was to see another American among all these damned greasers.

"What are you fellows doing here?" I asked.

"We're soldiers of fortune!" said the boy with the wounded arm.

"Aw——!" interrupted another. "Soldiers of——!"

"Ye see it's this way," began the soldierly looking youth. "We've been fighting right along in the Brigada Zaragosa—was at the battle of Ojinaga and everything. And now comes an order from Villa to discharge all the Americans in the ranks and ship 'em back to the border. Ain't that a hell of a note?"

"Last night they gave us our honorable discharges and threw us out of the cuartel," said a one-legged man with red hair.

"And we ain't had any place to sleep and nothing to

eat——" broke in a little gray-eyed boy whom they
called the ·Major.

"Don't try and panhandle the guy!" rebuked the soldier indignantly. "Ain't we each going to get fifty Mex
in the morning?"

We adjourned for a short time to a nearby restaurant, and when we returned I asked them what they
were going to do.

"The old U. S. for mine," breathed a good-looking
black Irishman who hadn't spoken before. "I'm going
back to San Fran and drive a truck again. I'm sick of
greasers, bad food and bad fighting."

"I got two honorable discharges from the United
States army," announced the soldierly youth proudly.
"Served through the Spanish War, I did. I'm the only
soldier in this bunch." The others sneered and cursed
sullenly. "Guess I'll reënlist when I get over the border."

"Not for mine," said the one-legged man. "I'm
wanted for two murder charges—I didn't do it, swear
to God I didn't—it was a frame-up. But a poor guy
hasn't got a chance in the United States. When they
ain't framing up some fake charge against me, they
jail me for a 'vag.' I'm all right though," he went
on earnestly. "I'm a hard-working man, only I can't
get no job."

The Major raised his hard little face and cruel eyes.
"I got out of a reform school in Wisconsin," he said,
"and I guess there's some cops waiting for me in El
Paso. I always wanted to kill somebody with a gun,
and I done it at Ojinaga, and I ain't got a bellyful

yet. They told us we could stay if we signed Mex citizenship papers; I guess I'll sign to-morrow morning."

"The hell you will," cried the others. "That's a rotten thing to do. Suppose we get Intervention and you have to shoot against your own people. You won't catch me signing myself away to be a greaser."

"That's easy fixed," said the Major. "When I go back to the States I leave my name here. I'm going to stay down here till I get enough of a stake to go back to Georgia and start a child-labor factory."

The other boy had suddenly burst into tears. "I got my arm shot through in Ojinaga," he sobbed, "and now they're turning me loose without any money, and I can't work. When I get to El Paso the cops 'll jail me and I'll have to write my dad to come and take me home to California. I run away from there last year," he explained.

"Look here, Major," I advised, "you'd better not stay down here if Villa wants Americans out of the ranks. Being a Mexican citizen won't help you if Intervention comes."

"Perhaps you're right," agreed the Major thoughtfully. "Aw, quit your bawling, Jack! I guess I'll beat it over to Galveston and get on a South American boat. They say there's a revolution started in Peru."

The soldier was about thirty, the Irishman twenty-five, and the three others somewhere between sixteen and eighteen.

"What did you fellows come down here for?" I asked.

INSURGENT MEXICO

"Excitement!" answered the soldier and the Irishman, grinning. The three boys looked at me with eager, earnest faces, drawn with hunger and hardship.

"Loot!" they said simultaneously. I cast an eye at their dilapidated garments, at the throngs of tattered volunteers parading around the plaza, who hadn't been paid for three months, and restrained a violent impulse to shout with mirth. Soon I left them, hard, cold misfits in a passionate country, despising the cause for which they were fighting, sneering at the gaiety of the irrepressible Mexicans. And as I went away I said, "By the way; what company did you fellows belong to? What did you call yourselves?"

The red-haired youth answered, "The Foreign Legion!" he said.

I want to say right here that I saw few soldiers of fortune except one—and he was a dry-as-dust scientist studying the action of high explosives in field-guns—who would not have been tramps in their own country.

It was late night when I finally got back to the hotel. Doña Luisa went ahead to see to my room, and I stopped a moment in the bar. Two or three soldiers, evidently officers, were drinking there—one pretty far gone. He was a pock-marked man with a trace of black mustache; his eyes couldn't seem to focus. But when he saw me he began to sing a pleasant little song:

Yo tengo un pistole
Con manago de marfil
Para matar todos los Gringos
Qui viennen por ferrocarril!

160

SAVED BY A WRIST-WATCH

(I have a pistol with a marble handle
(With which to kill all the Americans who come by
    railroad!)

I thought it diplomatic to leave, because you can
never tell what a Mexican will do when he's drunk. His
temperament is much too complicated.

Doña Luisa was in my room when I got there. With
a mysterious finger to her lips she shut the door and
produced from beneath her skirt a last year's copy of
the *Saturday Evening Post*, in an incredible state of
dissolution. "I got it out of the safe for you," she
said. "The damn thing's worth more than anything
in the house. I've been offered fifteen dollars for it by
Americans going out to the mines. You see we haven't
had any American magazines in a year now."

CHAPTER III

SAVED BY A WRIST-WATCH

AFTER that what could I do but read the
precious magazine, although I had read it before. I lit the lamp, undressed, and got into
bed. Just then came an unsteady step on the gallery
outside and my door was flung violently open. Framed
in it stood the pock-marked officer who had been drinking in the bar. In one hand he carried a big revolver.
For a moment he stood blinking at me malevolently,
then stepped inside and closed the door with a bang.

161

"I am Lieutenant Antonio Montoya, at your orders," he said. "I heard there was a Gringo in this hotel and I have come to kill you."

"Sit down," said I politely. I saw he was drunkenly in earnest. He took off his hat, bowed politely and drew up a chair. Then he produced another revolver from beneath his coat and laid them both on the table. They were loaded.

"Would you like a cigarette?" I offered him the package. He took one, waved it in thanks, and lit it at the lamp. Then he picked up the guns and pointed them both at me. His fingers tightened slowly on the triggers, but relaxed again. I was too far gone to do anything but just wait.

"My only difficulty," said he, lowering his weapons, "is to determine which revolver I shall use."

"Pardon me," I quavered, "but they both appear a little obsolete. That Colt forty-five is certainly an 1895 model, and as for the Smith and Wesson, between ourselves it is only a toy."

"True," he answered, looking at them a little ruefully. "If I had only thought I would have brought my new automatic. My apologies, señor." He sighed and again directed the barrels at my chest, with an expression of calm happiness. "However, since it is so, we must make the best of it." I got ready to jump, to duck, to scream. Suddenly his eye fell upon the table, where my two-dollar wrist-watch was lying.

"What is that?" he asked.

"A watch!" Eagerly I demonstrated how to fasten it on. Unconsciously the pistols slowly lowered. With parted lips and absorbed attention he watched it delightedly, as a child watches the operation of some new mechanical toy.

"Ah," he breathed. *"Que esta bonita!* How pretty!"

"It is yours," said I, unstrapping it and offering it to him. He looked at the watch, then at me, slowly brightening and glowing with surprised joy. Into his outstretched hand I placed it. Reverently, carefully, he adjusted the thing to his hairy wrist. Then he rose, beaming down upon me. The revolvers fell unnoticed to the floor. Lieutenant Antonio Montoya threw his arms around me.

"Ah, *compadre!*" he cried emotionally.

The next day I met him at Valiente Adiana's store in the town. We sat amicably in the back room drinking native *aguardiente*, while Lieutenant Montoya, my best friend in the entire Constitutionalist army, told me of the hardships and perils of the campaign. For three weeks now Maclovio Herrera's brigade had lain at Jimenez under arms, waiting the emergency call for the advance on Torreon.

"This morning," said Antonio, "the Constitutionalist spies intercepted a telegram from the Federal commander in Zacatecas City to General Velasco in Torreon. He said that upon mature judgment he had decided that Zacatecas was an easier place to attack than to defend. Therefore he reported that his plan of campaign was this. Upon the approach of the Constitutionalist forces he intended to evacuate the city and then take it again."

"Antonio," I said, "I am going a long journey across the desert to-morrow. I am going to drive to Magistral. I need a *mozo*. I will pay three dollars a week."

" *'Sta bueno!*" cried Lieutenant Montoya. "Whatever you wish, so that I can go with my *amigo!*"

"But you are on active service," said I. "How can you leave your regiment?"

"Oh, that's all right," answered Antonio. "I won't say anything about it to my colonel. They don't need me. Why, they've got five thousand other men here."

CHAPTER IV

SYMBOLS OF MEXICO

IN the early dawn, when yet the low gray houses and the dusty trees were stiff with cold, we laid a bull-whip on the backs of our two mules and rattled down the uneven streets of Jimenez and out into the open country. A few soldiers, wrapped to the eyes in their serapes, dozed beside their lanterns. There was a drunken officer sleeping in the gutter.

We drove an ancient buggy, whose broken pole was mended with wire. The harness was made of bits of old iron, rawhide and rope. Antonio and I sat side by side upon the seat, and at our feet dozed a dark, serious-minded youth named Primitivo Aguilar. Primitivo had been hired to open and shut gates, to tie up the harness when it broke, and to keep watch over wagon and mules at night, because bandits were reported to infest the roads.

The country became a vast fertile plain, cut up by irrigating ditches which were overshadowed by long lines of great alamo trees, leafless and gray as ashes. Like a furnace door, the white-hot sun blazed upon us, and the far-stretched barren fields reeked a thin mist. A cloud of white dust moved with us and around us. By the church of the Hacienda San Pedro we stopped and dickered with an aged peon for a sack of corn and straw for the mules. Farther along was an exquisite low building of pink plaster, set back from the road in a grove of green willows. "That?" said Antonio. "Oh, that is nothing but a flour mill." We had lunch in the long whitewashed, dirt-floored room of a peon's house at another great hacienda, whose name I forget, but which I know had once belonged to Luis Terrazzas and was now the confiscated property of the Constitutionalist government. And that night we made camp beside an irrigation ditch miles from any house, in the middle of the bandit territory.

After a dinner of chopped-up meat and peppers, *tortillas*, beans and black coffee, Antonio and I gave Primitivo his instructions. He was to keep watch beside the fire with Antonio's revolver and, if he heard anything, was to wake us. But on no account was he to go to sleep. If he did we would kill him. Primitivo said, "*Si, señor*," very gravely, opened his eyes wide, and gripped the pistol. Antonio and I rolled up in our blankets by the fire.

I must have gone to sleep at once, because when I

was wakened by Antonio's rising, my watch showed only half an hour later. From the place where Primitivo had been placed on guard came a series of hearty snores. The lieutenant walked over to him.

"Primitivo!" he said.

No answer.

"Primitivo, you fool!" Our sentinel stirred in his sleep and turned over with noises indicative of comfort.

"Primitivo!" shouted Antonio, violently kicking him.

He gave absolutely no response.

Antonio drew back and launched a kick at his back that lifted him several feet into the air. With a start Primitivo woke. He started up alertly, waving the revolver.

"*Quien vive?*" cried Primitivo.

The next day took us out of the lowlands. We entered the desert, winding over a series of rolling plains, sandy and covered with black mesquite and here and there an occasional cactus. Now we began to see beside the road those sinister little wooden crosses that the country people erect on the spot where some man died a violent death. Around the horizon barren purple mountains hemmed us in. To the right, across a vast dry valley, a white and green and gray hacienda stood like a city. An hour later we passed the first of those great fortified square ranchos that one comes across once a day lost in the folds of this tremendous country. Night gathered straight above in the cloudless zenith, while all the skyline still was luminous with

166

clear light, and then the day snuffed out, and stars burst out in the dome of heaven like a rocket. Antonio and Primitivo, in that queer harsh Mexican harmony which sounds like nothing so much as a fiddle with frazzled strings, sang *"Esperanza"* as we jogged along. It grew cold. For leagues and leagues around was a blasted land, a country of death. It was hours since we had passed a house.

Antonio claimed to know of a water-hole somewhere vaguely ahead. But toward midnight, which was black and without moon, we discovered that the road upon which we were traveling suddenly petered out in a dense mesquite thicket. Somewhere we had turned off the *Camino Real*. It was late and the mules were worn out. There seemed nothing for it but a "dry camp," for so far as we knew there was no water anywhere near.

Now we had unharnessed the mules and fed them, and were lighting our fire, when somewhere in the dense thicket of chaparral stealthy footsteps sounded. They moved a space and then were still. Our little blaze of greasewood crackled fiercely, lighting up a leaping, glowing radius of about ten feet. Beyond that all was black. Primitivo made one backward leap into the shelter of the wagon; Antonio drew his revolver, and we froze beside the fire. The sound came again.

"Who lives?" said Antonio. There was a little shuffling noise out in the brush, and then a voice.

"What party are you?" it asked hesitantly.

"Maderistas," answered Antonio. "Pass!"

"It is safe for *pacificos?*" queried the invisible one.

"On my word," I cried. "Come out that we may see you."

At that very moment two vague shapes materialized on the edge of the firelight glow, almost without a sound—two peons, we saw as soon as they came close, wrapped tightly in their torn blankets. One was an old, wrinkled, bent man wearing homemade sandals, his trousers hanging in rags upon his shrunken legs; the other a very tall, barefooted youth, with a face so pure and so simple as to almost verge upon idiocy. Friendly, warm as sunlight, eagerly curious as children, they came forward, holding out their hands. We shook hands with each of them in turn, greeting them with elaborate Mexican courtesy.

"Good evening, friend. How are you?"

"Very well, *gracias*. And you?"

"Well, *gracias*. And how are all your people?"

"Well, thanks. And yours?"

"Well, thanks. What have you of new here?"

"*Nada*. Nothing. And you?"

"Nothing. Sit down."

"Oh, thanks, but I am well standing."

"Sit down. Sit down."

"A thousand thanks. Excuse us for a moment."

They smiled and faded away once more into the thicket. In a minute they reappeared, with great armfuls of dried mesquite branches for our fire.

"We are *rancheros*," said the elder, bowing. "We keep a few goats, and our houses are at your orders, and our corrals for your mules, and our small stock of corn. Our *ranchitos* are very near here in the

168

mesquite. We are very poor men, but we hope you will do us the honor of accepting our hospitality." It was an occasion for tact.

"A thousand times many thanks," said Antonio politely, "but we are, unfortunately, in great haste and must leave early. We would not like to disturb your household at that hour."

They protested that their families and their houses were entirely ours, to be used as we saw fit with the greatest delight on their part. I do not remember how we finally managed to evade the invitation without wounding them, but I do recall that it took half an hour of courteous talking. For we knew, in the first place, that we would be unable to leave for hours in the morning if we accepted, because Mexican manners are that haste to leave a house signifies dissatisfaction with the entertainment; and then, too, one could not pay for one's lodging, but would have to bestow a handsome present upon the hosts—which we could none of us afford.

At first they politely refused our invitation to dine, but after much urging we finally persuaded them to accept a few *tortillas* and *chile*. It was ludicrous and pitiful to see how wretchedly hungry they were, and how they attempted to conceal it from us.

After dinner, when they had brought us a bucket of water out of sheer kindly thoughtfulness, they stood for a while by our fire, smoking our cigarettes and holding out their hands to the blaze. I remember how their serapes hung from their shoulders, open in front so the grateful warmth could reach their thin bodies

169

—and how gnarled and ancient were the old man's outstretched hands, and how the ruddy light glowed upon the other's throat, and kindled fires in his big eyes. Around them stretched the desert, held off only by our fire, ready to spring in upon us when it should die. Above the great stars would not dim. Coyotes wailed somewhere out beyond the firelight like demons in pain. I suddenly conceived these two human beings as symbols of Mexico—courteous, loving, patient, poor, so long slaves, so full of dreams, so soon to be free.

"When we saw your wagon coming here," said the old man, smiling, "our hearts sank within us. We thought you were soldiers, come, perhaps, to take away our last few goats. So many soldiers have come in the last few years—so many. It is mostly the Federals—the Maderistas do not come unless they are hungry themselves. Poor Maderistas!"

"Ay," said the young man, "my brother that I loved very much died in the eleven days' fighting around Torreon. Thousands have died in Mexico, and still more thousands shall fall. Three years—it is long for war in a land. Too long!" The old man murmured, "*Valgame Dios!*" and shook his head. "But there shall come a day——"

"It is said," remarked the old man quaveringly, "that the United States of the North covets our country—that Gringo soldiers will come and take away my goats in the end. . . ."

"That is a lie," exclaimed the other, animated. "It is the rich Americanos who want to rob us, just as the rich Mexicans want to rob us. It is the rich all over the world who want to rob the poor."

The old man shivered and drew his wasted body nearer to the fire. "I have often wondered," said he mildly, "why the rich, having so much, want so much. The poor, who have nothing, want so very little. Just a few goats. . . ."

His *compadre* lifted his chin like a noble, smiling gently. "I have never been out of this little country here—not even to Jimenez," he said. "But they tell me that there are many rich lands to the north and south and east. But this is my land and I love it. For the years of me, and my father and my grandfather, the rich men have gathered the corn and held it in their clenched fists before our mouths. And only blood will make them open their hands to their brothers."

The fire died down. At his post slept the alert Primitivo. Antonio stared into the embers, a faint glorified smile upon his mouth, his eyes shining like stars.

"*Adio!*" he said suddenly, as one who sees a vision. "When we get into Mexico City what a *baile* shall be held! How drunk I shall get! . . ."

PART FOUR

A PEOPLE IN ARMS

CHAPTER I

"ON TO TORREON!"

A T Yermo there is nothing but leagues and leagues of sandy desert, sparsely covered with scrubby mesquite and dwarf cactus, stretching away on the west to jagged, tawny mountains, and on the east to a quivering skyline of plain. A battered water-tank, with too little dirty alkali water, a demolished railway station shot to pieces by Orozco's cannon two years before, and a switch track compose the town. There is no water to speak of for forty miles. There is no grass for animals. For three months in the spring bitter, parching winds drive the yellow dust across it.

Along the single track in the middle of the desert lay ten enormous trains, pillars of fire by night and of black smoke by day, stretching back northward farther than the eye could reach. Around them, in the chaparral, camped nine thousand men without shelter, each man's horse tied to the mesquite beside him, where hung his one serape and red strips of drying meat. From fifty cars horses and mules were being unloaded. Covered with sweat and dust, a ragged trooper plunged into a cattle-car among the flying hoofs, swung himself upon a horse's back, and jabbed his spurs deep in, with

175

a yell. Then came a terrific drumming of frightened animals, and suddenly a horse shot violently from the open door, usually backward, and the car belched flying masses of horses and mules. Picking themselves up, they fled in terror, snorting through wide nostrils at the smell of the open. Then the wide, watchful circle of troopers turned *vaqueros* lifted the great coils of their lassoes through the choking dust, and the running animals swirled round and round upon one another in a panic. Officers, orderlies, generals with their staffs, soldiers with halters, hunting for their mounts, galloped and ran past in inextricable confusion. Bucking mules were being harnessed to the caissons. Troopers who had arrived on the last trains wandered about looking for their brigades. Way ahead some men were shooting at a rabbit. From the tops of the box-cars and the flat-cars, where they were camped by hundreds, the *soldaderas* and their half-naked swarms of children looked down, screaming shrill advice and asking everybody in general if they had happened to see Juan Moñeros, or Jesus Hernandez, or whatever the name of their man happened to be. . . . One man trailing a rifle wandered along shouting that he had had nothing to eat for two days and he couldn't find his woman who made his *tortillas* for him, and he opined that she had deserted him to go with some ——— of another brigade. . . . The women on the roofs of the cars said, "*Valgame Dios!*" and shrugged their shoulders; then they dropped him down some three-days-old *tortillas*, and asked him, for the love he bore Our Lady of Guadelupe, to lend them a cigarette. A clamorous, dirty throng stormed the engine of our train, screaming for water. When the engineer stood them off with a revolver, telling them there was plenty of water in the water-train, they broke away and aimlessly scattered, while a fresh throng took their places. Around the twelve immense tank-cars, a fighting mass of men and animals struggled for a place at the little faucets ceaselessly pouring. Above the place a mighty cloud of dust, seven miles long and a mile wide, towered up into the still, hot air, and, with the black smoke of the engines, struck wonder and terror into the Federal outposts fifty miles away on the mountains back of Mapimi.

When Villa left Chihuahua for Torreon, he closed the telegraph wires to the north, stopped train service to Juarez, and forbade on pain of death that anyone should carry or send news of his departure to the United States. His object was to take the Federals by surprise, and it worked beautifully. No one, not even Villa's staff, knew when he would leave Chihuahua; the army had delayed there so long that we all believed it would delay another two weeks. And then Saturday morning we woke to find the telegraph and railway cut, and three huge trains, carrying the Brigada Gonzalez-Ortega, already gone. The Zaragosa left the next day, and Villa's own troops the following morning. Moving with the swiftness that always characterizes him, Villa had his entire army concentrated at Yermo the day afterward, without the Federals knowing that he had left Chihuahua.

There was a mob around the portable field telegraph

that had been rigged up in the ruined station. Inside, the instrument was clicking. Soldiers and officers indiscriminately choked up the windows and the door, and every once in a while the operator would shout something in Spanish and a perfect roar of laughter would go up. It seemed that the telegraph had accidentally tapped a wire that had not been destroyed by the Federals—a wire that connected with the Federal military wire from Mapimi to Torreon.

"Listen!" cried the operator. "Colonel Argumedo in command of the *cabecillos colorados* in Mapimi is telegraphing to General Velasco in Torreon. He says that he sees smoke and a big dust cloud to the north, and thinks that some rebel troops are moving south from Escalon!"

Night came, with a cloudy sky and a rising wind that began to lift the dust. Along the miles and miles of trains, the fires of the *soldaderas* flared from the tops of the freight-cars. Out into the desert so far that finally they were mere pin-points of flame stretched the innumerable camp-fires of the army, half obscured by the thick, billowing dust. The storm completely concealed us from Federal watchers. "Even God," remarked Major Leyva, "even God is on the side of Francisco Villa!" We sat at dinner in our converted box-car, with young, great-limbed, expressionless General Maximo Garcia and his brother, the even huger red-faced Benito Garcia, and little Major Manuel Acosta, with the beautiful manners of his race. Garcia had long been holding the advance at Escalon. He and his brothers—one of whom, José Garcia, the idol of the army, had been killed in battle—but a short four years ago were wealthy *hacendados*, owners of immense tracts of land. They had come out with Madero. . . . I remember that he brought us a jug of whisky, and refused to discuss the Revolution, declaring that he was fighting for better whisky! As I write this comes a report that he is dead from a bullet wound received in the battle of Sacramento. . . .

Out in the dust storm, on a flat-car immediately ahead of ours, some soldiers lay around their fire with their heads in their women's laps, singing "The Cockroach," which tells in hundreds of satirical verses what the Constitutionalists would do when they captured Juarez and Chihuahua from Mercado and Orozco.

Above the wind one was aware of the immense sullen murmur of the host, and occasionally some sentry challenged in a falsetto howl: "*Quien vive?*" And the answer: "*Chiapas!*" "*Que gente?*" "*Chao!*" . . . Through the night sounded the eerie whistle of the ten locomotives at intervals as they signaled back and forth to one another.

CHAPTER II

THE ARMY AT YERMO

AT dawn next morning General Torribio Ortega came to the car for breakfast—a lean, dark Mexican, who is called "The Honorable" and "The Most Brave" by the soldiers. He is by far the most simple-hearted and disinterested soldier in Mexico.

He never kills his prisoners. He has refused to take a cent from the Revolution beyond his meager salary. Villa respects and trusts him perhaps beyond all his Generals. Ortega was a poor man, a cowboy. He sat there, with his elbows on the table, forgetting his breakfast, his big eyes flashing, smiling his gentle, crooked smile, and told us why he was fighting.

"I am not an educated man," he said. "But I know that to fight is the last thing for any people. Only when things get too bad to stand, eh? And, if we are going to kill our brothers, something fine must come out of it, eh? You in the United States do not know what we have seen, we Mexicans! We have looked on at the robbing of our people, the simple, poor people, for thirty-five years, eh? We have seen the *rurales* and the soldiers of Porfirio Diaz shoot down our brothers and our fathers, and justice denied to them. We have seen our little fields taken away from us, and all of us sold into slavery, eh? We have longed for our homes and for schools to teach us, and they have laughed at us. All we have ever wanted was to be let alone to live and to work and make our country great, and we are tired—tired and sick of being cheated. . . ."

Outside in the dust, that whirled along under a sky of driving clouds, long lines of soldiers on horseback stood in the obscurity, while their officers passed along in front, peering closely at cartridge-belts and rifles.

"Geronimo," said a Captain to one trooper, "go back to the ammunition train and fill up the gaps in your *cartouchera*. You fool, you've been wasting your cartridges shooting coyotes !"

Across the desert westward toward the distant mountains rode strings of cavalry, the first to the front. About a thousand went, in ten different lines, diverging like wheel spokes; the jingle of their spurs ringing, their red-white-and-green flags floating straight out, crossed bandoliers gleaming dully, rifles flopping across their saddles, heavy, high sombreros and many-colored blankets. Behind each company plodded ten or twelve women on foot, carrying cooking utensils on their heads and backs, and perhaps a pack mule loaded with sacks of corn. And as they passed the cars they shouted back to their friends on the trains.

"*Poco tiempo California!*" cried one.

"Oh! there's a *colorado* for you !" yelled another. "I'll bet you were with Salazar in Orozco's Revolution. Nobody ever said '*Poco tiempo California*' except Salazar when he was drunk !"

The other man looked sheepish. "Well, maybe I was," he admitted. "But wait till I get a shot at my old *compañeros*. I'll show you whether I'm a Maderista or not !"

A little Indian in the rear cried: "I know how much of a Maderista you are, Luisito. At the first taking of Torreon, Villa gave you the choice of turning your coat or getting a *cabronasso* or *balasso* through the head !" And, joshing and singing, they jogged southwest, became small, and finally faded into the dust.

Villa himself stood leaning against a car, hands in his

181

pockets. He wore an old slouch hat, a dirty shirt without a collar, and a badly frayed and shiny brown suit. All over the dusty plain in front of him men and horses had sprung up like magic. There was an immense confusion of saddling and bridling—a cracked blowing of tin bugles. The Brigada Zaragosa was getting ready to leave camp—a flanking column of two thousand men who were to ride southeast and attack Tlahualilo and Sacramento. Villa, it seemed, had just arrived at Yermo. He had stopped off Monday night at Camargo to attend the wedding of a *compadre*. His face was drawn into lines of fatigue.

"*Carramba!*" he was saying with a grin; "we started dancing Monday evening, danced all night, all the next day, and last night, too! What a *baile!* And what *muchachas!* The girls of Camargo and Santa Rosalia are the most beautiful in Mexico! I am worn out—*rendido!* It was harder work than twenty battles. . . ."

Then he listened to the report of some staff officer who dashed up on horseback, gave a concise order without hesitating, and the officer rode off. He told Señor Calzado, General Manager of the Railroad, in what order the trains should proceed south. He indicated to Señor Uro, the Quartermaster-general, what supplies should be distributed from the troop trains. To Señor Munoz, Director of the Telegraph, he gave the name of a Federal captain surrounded by Urbina's men a week before and killed with all his men in the hills near La Cadena, and ordered him to tap the Federal wire and send a message to General Velasco in Torreon purporting to be a report from this Captain from Conejos, and asking for orders. . . . He seemed to know and order everything.

We had lunch with General Eugenio Aguirre Benavides, the quiet, cross-eyed little commander of the Zaragosa Brigade, a member of one of the cultivated Mexican families that gathered around Madero in the first Revolution; with Raul Madero, brother of the murdered President, second in command of the Brigade, who is a graduate of an American University, and looks like a Wall Street bond salesman; with Colonel Guerra, who went through Cornell, and Major Leyva, Ortega's nephew, a historic full-back on the Notre Dame football team. . . .

In a great circle, ready for action, the artillery was parked, with caissons open and mules corralled in the center. Colonel Servin, commander of the guns, sat perched high up on an immense bay horse, a ridiculous tiny figure, not more than five feet tall. He was waving his hand and shouting a greeting across to General Angeles, Carranza's Secretary of War—a tall, gaunt man, bareheaded, in a brown sweater, with a war map of Mexico hanging from his shoulder; who straddled a small burro. In the thick dust-clouds, sweating men labored. The five American artillery men had squatted down in the lee of a cannon, smoking. They hailed me with a shout:

"Say, bo! What in hell did we ever get into this mess for? Nothing to eat since last night—work twelve hours—say, take our pictures, will you?"

There passed by with a friendly nod the little Cockney soldier that had served with Kitchener, and then the Canadian Captain Treston, bawling for his interpreter, so that he could give his men some orders about the machine guns; and Captain Marinelli, the fat Italian soldier of fortune, pouring an interminable and unintelligible mixture of French, Spanish and Italian into the ear of a bored Mexican officer. Fierro rode by, cruelly roweling his horse with the bloody mouth— Fierro, the handsome, cruel and insolent—The Butcher they called him, because he killed defenseless prisoners with his revolver, and shot down his own men without provocation.

Late in the afternoon the Brigada Zaragosa rode away southeast over the desert, and another night came down.

The wind rose steadily in the darkness, growing colder and colder. Looking up at the sky, which had been ablaze with polished stars, I saw that all was dark with cloud. Through the roaring whirls of dust a thousand thin lines of sparks from the fires streamed southward. The coaling of the engines' fire boxes made sudden glares along the miles of trains. At first we thought we heard the sound of big guns in the distance. But all at once, unexpectedly, the sky split dazzlingly open from horizon to horizon, thunder fell like a blow, and the rain came level and thick as a flood. For a moment the human hum of the army was silenced. All the fires disappeared at once. And then came a vast shout of anger and laughter and discomfiture from the soldiers out on the plain, and the most amazing wail of misery from the women that I have ever heard. The two sounds only lasted a minute. The men wrapped themselves in their serapes and sank down in the shelter of the chaparral; and the hundreds of women and children exposed to the cold and the rain on the flat-cars and the tops of the box-cars silently and with Indian stoicism settled down to wait for dawn. In General Maclovio Herrera's car ahead was drunken laughter and singing to a guitar. . . .

Daybreak came with a sound of all the bugles in the world blowing; and looking out of the car door I saw the desert for miles boiling with armed men saddling and mounting. A hot sun popped over the western mountains, burning in a clear sky. For a moment the ground poured up billowing steam, and then there was dust again, and a thirsty land. There might never have been rain. A hundred breakfast fires smoked from the car-tops, and the women stood turning their dresses slowly in the sun, chattering and joking. Hundreds of little naked babies danced around, while their mothers lifted up their little clothes to the heat. A thousand joyous troopers shouted to each other that the advance was beginning; away off to the left some regiment had given away to joy, and was shooting into the air. Six more long trains had come in during the night, and all the engines were whistling signals. I went forward to get on the first train out, and as I passed the car of Trinidad Rodriguez, a harsh, feminine voice cried: "Hey, kid! Come in and get some breakfast." Leaning out of the door were Beatrice and Carmen, two noted Juarez women that had been

brought to the front by the Rodriguez brothers. I
went in and sat down at the table with about twelve
men, several of them doctors in the hospital train, one
French artillery captain, and an assortment of Mexican officers and privates. It was an ordinary freight
box-car like all the private cars, with windows cut in
the walls, partitions built to shut out the Chinese cook
in the kitchen, and bunks arranged across sides and
end. Breakfast consisted of heaping platters of red
meat with *chile*, bowls of *frijoles*, stacks of cold flour
tortillas, and six bottles of Monopole Champagne. Carmen's complexion was bad, and she was a little stupid
from the gastronomic combination, but Beatrice's
white, colorless face and red hair cut Buster Brown
fashion fairly radiated a sort of malicious glee. She
was a Mexican, but talked Tenderloin English without
an accent. Jumping up from the table, she danced
around it, pulling the men's hair. "Hello, you damned
Gringo," she laughed at me. "What are you doing
here? You're going to get a bullet in you if you don't
get careful!"

A morose young Mexican, already a little drunk,
snapped at her furiously in Spanish: "Don't you talk
to him! Do you understand? I'll tell Trinidad how
you asked the Gringo in to breakfast, and he'll have
you shot!"

Beatrice threw back her head and roared. "Did
you hear what he said? He thinks he owns me, because he once stayed with me in Juarez! . . . My
God!" she went on. "How funny it seems to travel on
the railroad and not have to buy a ticket!"

FIRST BLOOD

"Look here, Beatrice," I asked her; "we may not have such an easy time of it down there. What will you do if we get licked?"

"Who, me?" she cried. "Why, I guess it won't take me long to get friends in the Federal army. I'm a good mixer!"

"What is she saying? What do you say?" asked the others in Spanish.

With the most perfect insolence Beatrice translated for them. And in the midst of the uproar that followed I left. . . .

CHAPTER III

FIRST BLOOD

THE water train pulled out first. I rode on the cow-catcher of the engine, which was already occupied by the permanent home of two women and five children. They had built a little fire of mesquite twigs on the narrow iron platform, and were baking *tortillas* there; over their heads, against the windy roar of the boiler, fluttered a little line of wash. . . .

It was a brilliant day, hot sunshine alternating with big white clouds. In two thick columns, one on each side of the train, the army was already moving south. As far as the eye could reach, a mighty double cloud of dust floated over them; and little straggling groups of mounted men jogged along, with every now and then a big Mexican flag. Between slowly moved the trains;

the pillars of black smoke from their engines, at regular intervals, growing smaller, until over the northern horizon only a dirty mist appeared.

I went down into the caboose to get a drink of water, and there I found the conductor of the train lying in his bunk reading the Bible. He was so interested and amused that he didn't notice me for a minute. When he did he cried delightedly: "*Oiga,* I have found a great story about a chap called Samson who was *muy hombre*—a good deal of a man—and his woman. She was a Spaniard, I guess, from the mean trick she played on him. He started out being a good Revolutionist, a Maderista, and she made him a *pelon!*"

Pelon means literally "cropped head," and is the slang term for a Federal soldier, because the Federal army is largely recruited from the prisons.

Our advance guard, with a telegraph field operator, had gone on to Conejos the night before, and they met the train in great excitement. The first blood of the campaign had been spilt; a few *colorados* scouting northward from Bermejillo had been surprised and killed just behind the shoulder of the big mountain which lies to the east. The telegrapher also had news. He had again tapped the Federal wire, and sent to the Federal commander in Torreon, signing the dead Captain's name and asking for orders, since a large force of rebels seemed to be approaching from the north. General Velasco replied that the Captain should hold Conejos and throw out outposts to the north, to try and discover how large the force was. At the same time the telegrapher had heard a message

FIRST BLOOD

from Argumedo, in command at Mapimi, saying that the entire north of Mexico was coming down on Torreon, together with the Gringo army!

Conejos was just like Yermo, except that there was no water tank. A thousand men, with white-bearded old General Rosalio Hernandez riding ahead, went out almost at once, and the repair train followed them a few miles to a place where the Federals had burned two railroad bridges a few months before. Out beyond the last little bivouac of the immense army spread around us, the desert slept silently in the heat waves. There was no wind. The men gathered with their women on the flat-cars, guitars came out, and all night hundreds of singing voices came from the trains.

The next morning I went to see Villa in his car. This was a red caboose with chintz curtains on the windows, the famous little caboose which Villa has used in all his journeys since the fall of Juarez. It was divided by partitions into two rooms—the kitchen and the General's bedroom. This tiny room, ten by twenty feet, was the heart of the Constitutionalist army. There were held all the councils of war, and there was scarcely room enough for the fifteen Generals who met there. In these councils the vital immediate questions of the campaign were discussed, the Generals decided what was to be done,—and then Villa gave his orders to suit himself. It was painted a dirty gray. On the walls were tacked photographs of showy ladies in theatrical poses, a large picture of Carranza, one of Fierro, and a picture of Villa himself. Two double-width wooden bunks

189

folded up against the wall, in one of which Villa and
General Angeles slept, and in the other José Rodriguez
and Doctor Raschbaum, Villa's personal physician.
That was all. . . .

"*Que desea, amigo?* What do you want?" said Villa,
sitting on the end of the bunk in blue underclothes. The
troopers who lounged around the place lazily made way
for me.

"I want a horse, *mi General.*"

"*Ca-r-r-r-ai-i,* our friend here wants a horse!" grinned
Villa sarcastically amid a burst of laughter from the
others. "Why, you correspondents will be wanting an
automobile next! *Oiga,* señor reporter, do you know
that about a thousand men in my army have no horses?
Here's the train. What do you want a horse for?"

"So I can ride with the advance."

"No," he smiled. "There are too many *balassos*—
too many bullets flying in the advance. . . ."

He was hurrying into his clothes as he talked, and
gulping coffee from the side of a dirty tin coffee-pot.
Somebody handed him his gold-handled sword.

"No!" he said contemptuously. "This is to be a
fight, not a parade. Give me my rifle!"

He stood at the door of his caboose for a moment,
thoughtfully looking at the long lines of mounted
men, picturesque in their crossed cartridge-belts and
varied equipment. Then he gave a few quick orders
and mounted his big stallion.

"*Vamonos!*" cried Villa. The bugles brayed and a
subdued silver clicking ringing sounded as the companies wheeled and trotted southward in the dust. . . .

ON THE CANNON-CAR

And so the army disappeared. During the day we thought we heard cannonading from the southwest, where Urbina was reported to be coming down from the mountains to attack Mapimi. And late in the afternoon news came of the capture of Bermejillo, and a courier from Benavides said that he had taken Tlahualilo.

We were in a fever of impatience to be off. About sundown Señor Calzado remarked that the repair train would leave in an hour, so I grabbed a blanket and walked a mile up the line of trains to it.

CHAPTER IV

ON THE CANNON-CAR

THE first car of the repair train was a steel-encased flat-car, upon which was mounted the famous Constitutionalist cannon "El Niño," with an open caisson full of shells behind it. Behind that was an armored car full of soldiers, then a car of steel rails, and four loaded with railroad ties. The engine came next, the engineer and fireman hung with cartridge-belts, their rifles handy. Then followed two or three box-cars full of soldiers and their women. It was a dangerous business. A large force of Federals were known to be in Mapimi, and the country swarmed with their outposts. Our army was already far ahead, except for five hundred men who guarded the trains at Conejos. If the enemy could capture or wreck the repair train the army would be cut off without water, food or ammunition. In the darkness we moved out. I sat upon the breech of "El Niño," chatting with Captain Diaz, the commander of the gun, as he oiled the breech lock of his beloved cannon and curled his vertical mustachios. In the armored recess behind the gun, where the Captain slept, I heard a curious, subdued rustling noise.

"What's that?"

"Eh?" cried he nervously. "Oh, nothing, nothing!"

Just then there emerged a young Indian girl with a bottle in her hand. She couldn't have been more than seventeen, very lovely. The Captain shot a glance at me, and suddenly whirled around.

"What are you doing here?" he cried furiously to her. "Why are you coming out here?"

"I thought you said you wanted a drink," she began.

I perceived that I was one too many, and excused myself. They hardly noticed me. But as I was climbing over the back of the car I couldn't help stopping and listening. They had gone back to the recess, and she was weeping.

"Didn't I tell you," stormed the Captain, "not to show yourself when there are strangers here? I will not have every man in Mexico looking at you. . . ."

I stood on the roof of the rocking steel car as we nosed slowly along. Lying on their bellies on the extreme front platform, two men with lanterns examined each foot of the track for wires that might mean mines planted under us. Beneath my feet the soldiers and their women were having dinner around fires built on

192

the floor. Smoke and laughter poured out of the loop-
holes. . . . There were other fires aft, brown-faced,
ragged people squatting at them, on the car-tops.
Overhead the sky blazed stars, without a cloud. It was
cold. After an hour of riding we came to a piece of
broken track. The train stopped with a jar, the
engine whistled, and a score of torches and lanterns
jerked past. Men came running. The flares clustered
bobbing together as the foremen examined the damage.
A fire sprang up in the brush, and then another. Soldiers of the train guard straggled by, dragging their
rifles, and formed impenetrable walls around the fires.
Iron tools clanged, and the "Wai-hoy!" of men shoving
rails off the flat-car. A Chinese dragon of workmen
passed with a rail on their shoulders, then others with
ties. Four hundred men swarmed upon the broken
spot, working with extraordinary energy and good humor, until the shouts of gangs setting rails and ties,
and the rattle of sledges on spikes, made a continuous
roar. It was an old destruction, probably a year old,
made when these same Constitutionalists were retreating north in the face of Mercado's Federal army, and
we had it all fixed in an hour. Then on again. Sometimes it was a bridge burned out, sometimes a hundred
yards of track twisted into grape vines by a chain and
a backing engine. We advanced slowly. At one big
bridge that it would take two hours to prepare, I built
by myself a little fire in order to get warm. Calzado
came past, and hailed me. "We've got a hand-car up
ahead," he said, "and we're going along down and see
the dead men. Want to come?"

"What dead men?"

"Why, this morning an outpost of eighty *rurales* was sent scouting north from Bermejillo. We heard about it over the wire and informed Benavides on the left. He sent a troop to take them in the rear, and drove them north in a running fight for fifteen miles until they smashed up against our main body and not one got out alive. They're scattered along the whole way just where they fell."

In a moment we were speeding south on the handcar. At our right hand and our left rode two silent, shadowy figures on horseback—cavalry guards, with rifles ready under their arms. Soon the flares and fires of the train were left behind, and we were enveloped and smothered in the vast silence of the desert.

"Yes," said Calzado, "the *rurales* are brave. They are *muy hombres*. *Rurales* are the best fighters Diaz and Huerta ever had. They never desert to the Revolution. They always remain loyal to the established government. Because they are police."

It was bitter cold. None of us talked much.

"We go ahead of the train at night," said the soldier at my left, "so that if there are any dynamite bombs underneath——"

"We could discover them and dig them out and put water in them, *carramba!*" said another sarcastically. The rest laughed. I began to think of that, and it made me shiver. The dead silence of the desert seemed an expectant hush. One couldn't see ten feet from the track.

"*Oiga!*" shouted one of the horsemen. "It was just

here that one lay." The brakes ground and we tumbled off and down the steep embankment, our lanterns jerking ahead. Something lay huddled around the foot of a telegraph pole—something infinitely small and shabby, like a pile of old clothes. The *rurale* was upon his back, twisted sideways from his hips. He had been stripped of everything of value by the thrifty rebels—shoes, hat, underclothing. They had left him his ragged jacket with the tarnished silver braid, because there were seven bullet holes in it; and his trousers, soaked with blood. He had evidently been much bigger when alive—the dead shrink so. A wild red beard made the pallor of his face grotesque, until you noticed that under it and the dirt, and the long lines of sweat of his terrible fight and hard riding, his mouth was gently and serenely open as if he slept. His brains had been blown out.

"*Carrai!*" said one guard. "There was a shot for the dirty goat! Right through the head!"

The others laughed. "Why, you don't think they shot him there in the fight, do you, *pendeco?*" cried his companion. "No, they *always* go around and make sure afterward——"

"Hurry up! I've found the other," shouted a voice off in the darkness.

We could reconstruct this man's last struggle. He had dropped off his horse, wounded—for there was blood on the ground—into a little dry arroyo. We could even see where his horse had stood while he pumped shells into his Mauser with feverish hands, and blazed away, first to the rear, where the pursuers came

running with Indian yells, and then at the hundreds
and hundreds of bloodthirsty horsemen pouring down
from the north, with the Demon Pancho Villa at their
head. He must have fought a long time, perhaps until
they ringed him round with living flame—for we found
hundreds of empty cartridges. And then, when the
last shot was spent, he made a dash eastward, hit at
every step; hid for a moment under the little railroad
bridge, and ran out upon the open desert, where he
fell. There were twenty bullet holes in him. They
had stripped him of all save his underclothes. He lay
sprawled in an attitude of desperate action, muscles
tense, one fist clenched and spread across the dust as if
he were dealing a blow; the fiercest exultant grin on his
face. Strong, savage, until one looked closer and saw
the subtle touch of weakness that death stamps on life
—the delicate expression of idiocy over it all. They
had shot him through the head three times—how exasperated they must have been!

Crawling south through the cold night once more.
. . . A few miles and then a bridge dynamited, or a
strip of track wrecked. The stop, the dancing torches,
the great bonfires leaping up from the desert, and the
four hundred wild men pouring furiously out and falling upon their work. . . . Villa had given orders to
hurry. . . .

About two o'clock in the morning I came upon two
soldaderas squatting around a fire, and asked them if
they could give me *tortillas* and coffee. One was an
old, gray-haired Indian woman with a perpetual grin,

the other a slight girl not more than twenty years old, who was nursing a four-months baby at her breast. They were perched at the extreme tip of a flat-car, their fire built upon a pile of sand, as the train jolted and swayed along. Around them, backed against them, feet sticking out between them, was a great, inconglomerate mass of sleeping, snoring humans. The rest of the train was by this time dark; this was the only patch of light and warmth in the night. As I munched my *tortilla* and the old woman lifted a burning coal in her fingers to light her corn-husk cigarette, wondering where her Pablo's brigade was this night; and the girl nursed her child, crooning to it, her blue-enameled ear-rings twinkling,—we talked.

"Ah! it is a life for us *viejas*," said the girl. "*Adio*, but we follow our men out in the campaign, and then do not know from hour to hour whether they live or die. I remember well when Filadelfo called to me one morning in the little morning before it was light—we lived in Pachuca—and said: 'Come! we are going out to fight because the good Pancho Madero has been murdered this day!' We had only been loving each other eight months, too, and the first baby was not born. . . . We had all believed that peace was in Mexico for good. Filadelfo saddled the burro, and we rode out through the streets just as light was coming, and into the fields where the farmers were not yet at work. And I said: 'Why must I come?' And he answered: 'Shall I starve, then? Who shall make my *tortillas* for me but my woman?' It took us three months to get north, and I was sick and the baby was born in a desert just

197

like this place, and died there because we could not get water. That was when Villa was going north after he had taken Torreon."

The old woman broke in: "Yes, and all that is true. When we go so far and suffer so much for our men, we are cruelly treated by the stupid animals of Generals. I am from San Luis Potosi, and my man was in the artillery of the Federacion when Mercado came north. All the way to Chihuahua we traveled, the old fool of a Mercado grumbling about transporting the *viejas*. And then he ordered his army to go north and attack Villa in Juarez, and he forbade the women to go. Is that the way you are going to do, *desgraciado?* I said to myself. And when he evacuated Chihuahua and ran away with my man to Ojinaga, I just stayed right in Chihuahua and got a man in the Maderista army when it came in. A nice handsome young fellow, too,—much better than Juan. I'm not a woman to stand being put upon."

"How much are the *tortillas* and coffee?" I asked.

They looked at each other, startled. Evidently they had thought me one of the penniless soldiers crowded on the train.

"What you would like," said the young woman faintly. I gave them a peso.

The old woman exploded in a torrent of prayer. "God, his sainted Mother, the Blessed Niño and Our Lady of Guadelupe have sent this stranger to us tonight! Here we had not a centavo to buy coffee and flour with. . . ."

I suddenly noticed that the light of our fire had

198

paled, and looked up in amazement to find it was dawn. Just then a man came running along the train from up front, shouting something unintelligible, while laughter and shouts burst out in his wake. The sleepers raised their curious heads and wanted to know what was the matter. In a moment our inanimate car was alive. The man passed, still yelling something about "*padre*," his face exultant with some tremendous joke.

"What is it?" I asked.

"Oh!" cried the old woman. "His woman on the car ahead has just had a baby!"

Just in front of us lay Bermejillo, its pink and blue and white plastered adobe houses as delicate and ethereal as a village of porcelain. To the east, across a still, dustless desert, a little file of sharp-cut horsemen, with a red-white-and-green flag over them, were riding into town. . . .

CHAPTER V

AT THE GATES OF GOMEZ

WE had taken Bermejillo the afternoon before, —the army breaking into a furious gallop five kilometers north of the town and pouring through it at top speed, driving the unprepared garrison in a rout southward,—a running fight that lasted five miles, as far as the Hacienda of Santa Clara, —and killing a hundred and six *colorados*. Within a the pillars of black smoke from their engines, at regular intervals, growing smaller, until over the northern horizon only a dirty mist appeared.

I went down into the caboose to get a drink of water, and there I found the conductor of the train lying in his bunk reading the Bible. He was so interested and amused that he didn't notice me for a minute. When he did he cried delightedly: "*Oiga*, I have found a great story about a chap called Samson who was *muy hombre*—a good deal of a man—and his woman. She was a Spaniard, I guess, from the mean trick she played on him. He started out being a good Revolutionist, a Maderista, and she made him a *pelon!*"

Pelon means literally "cropped head," and is the slang term for a Federal soldier, because the Federal army is largely recruited from the prisons.

Our advance guard, with a telegraph field operator, had gone on to Conejos the night before, and they met the train in great excitement. The first blood of the campaign had been spilt; a few *colorados* scouting northward from Bermejillo had been surprised and killed just behind the shoulder of the big mountain which lies to the east. The telegrapher also had news. He had again tapped the Federal wire, and sent to the Federal commander in Torreon, signing the dead Captain's name and asking for orders, since a large force of rebels seemed to be approaching from the north. General Velasco replied that the Captain should hold Conejos and throw out outposts to the north, to try and discover how large the force was. At the same time the telegrapher had heard a message belt around his waist. For a moment he remained there, absolutely expressionless, his small, hard eyes boring into me. I thought he did not recognize me, when all at once his harsh, sudden voice shot out: "That's not the camera you had! Where's the other one?"

I was about to reply when he interrupted: "I know. You left it behind you in La Cadena. Did you run very fast?"

"Yes, *mi General.*"

"And you've come down to Torreon to run again?"

"When I began to run from La Cadena," I remarked, nettled, "Don Petronilo and the troops were already a mile away."

He didn't answer, but came haltingly down the steps of the car, while a roar of laughter went up from the soldiers. Coming up to me he put a hand over my shoulder and gave me a little tap on the back. "I'm glad to see you, *compañero*," he said. . . .

Across the desert the wounded had begun to straggle in from the battle of Tlahualilo to the hospital train, which lay far up near the front of the line of trains. On the flat barren plain, as far as I could see, there were only three living things in sight: a limping, hatless man, with his head tied up in a bloody cloth; another staggering beside his staggering horse; and a mule mounted by two bandaged figures far behind them. And in the still hot night we could hear from our car groans and screams. . . .

Late Sunday morning we were again on "El Niño" at the head of the repair train, moving slowly down the track abreast of the army. "El Chavalito," another cannon mounted on a flat-car, was coupled behind, then came two armored cars, and the work-cars. This time there were no women. The army wore a different air, winding along in two immense serpents each side of us—there was little laughter or shouting. We were close now, only eighteen miles from Gomez Palacio, and no one knew what the Federals planned to do. It seemed incredible that they would let us get so close without making one stand. Immediately south of Bermejillo we entered a new land. To the desert succeeded fields bordered with irrigation ditches, along which grew immense green alamos, towering pillars of freshness after the baked desolation we had just passed through. Here were cotton-fields, the white tufts unpicked and rotting on their stalks; corn-fields with sparse green blades just showing. Along the big ditches flowed swift, deep water in the shade. Birds sang, and the barren western mountains marched steadily nearer as we went south. It was summer—hot, moist summer, such as we have at home. A deserted cotton-gin lay on our left, hundreds of white bales tumbled in the sun, and dazzling heaps of cotton-seed left just as the workmen had piled it months before. . . .

At Santa Clara the massed columns of the army halted and began to defile to left and right, thin lines of troops jogging out under the checkered sun and shade of the great trees, until six thousand men were spread in one long single front, to the right over fields and through ditches, beyond the last cultivated field, across the desert to the very base of the mountains; to the left over the roll of the flat world. The bugles blared faintly and near, and the army moved forward in a mighty line across the whole country. Above them lifted a five-mile-wide golden dust-glory. Flags flapped. In the center, level with them, came the cannon-car, and beside that Villa rode with his staff. At the little villages along the way the big-hatted, white-bloused *pacificos* stood in silent wonder, watching this strange host pass. An old man drove his goats homeward. The foaming wave of troopers broke upon him, yelling with pure mischief, and all the goats ran in different directions. A mile of army shouted with laughter,—the dust rolled up from their thousand hoofs, and they passed. At the village of Brittingham the great line halted, while Villa and his staff galloped up to the peons watching from their little mound.

"*Oyez!*" said Villa. "Have any troops passed through here lately?"

"*Si*, señor!" answered several men at once. "Some of Don Carlo Argumedo's *gente* went by yesterday pretty fast."

"Hum," Villa meditated. "Have you seen that bandit Pancho Villa around here?"

"No, señor!" they chorused.

"Well, he's the fellow I'm looking for. If I catch that *diablo* it will go hard with him!"

"We wish you all success!' cried the *pacificos*, politely.

"You never saw him, did you?"

"No, God forbid!" they said fervently.

"Well!" grinned Villa. "In the future when people ask if you know him you will have to admit the shameful fact! I am Pancho Villa!" And with that he spurred away, and all the army followed. . . .

CHAPTER VI

THE COMPAÑEROS REAPPEAR

SUCH had been the surprise of the Federals, and they had fled in such a hurry, that for many miles the railroad was intact. But toward afternoon we began to find little bridges burned and still smoking, and telegraph poles cut down with an axe— badly and hastily done bits of destruction that were easily repaired. But the army had got far ahead, and by nightfall, about eight miles from Gomez Palacio, we reached the place where eight solid miles of torn-up track began. There was no food on our train. We had only a blanket apiece; and it was cold. In the flare of torches and fires, the repair gang fell upon their work. Shouts and hammering steel, and the thud of falling ties. . . . It was a black night, with a few dim stars. We had settled down around one fire, talking and drowsing, when suddenly a new sound smote the air—a sound heavier than hammers, and deeper than the wind. It shocked—and was still. Then came a steady roll, as of distant drums, and then shock! shock! The hammers fell, voices were silent, we were frozen. Somewhere ahead, out of sight, in the darkness—so still it was that the air carried every sound—Villa and the army had flung themselves upon Gomez Palacio, and the battle had begun. It deepened steadily and slowly, until the booffs of cannon fell echoing upon each other, and the rifle fire rippled like steel rain.

"*Andale!*" screamed a hoarse voice from the roof of the cannon-car. "What are you doing? Get at that track! Pancho Villa is waiting for the trains!"

And, with a yell, four hundred raging maniacs flung themselves upon the break. . . .

I remember how we besought the Colonel in command to let us go to the front. He would not. Orders were strict that no one should leave the trains. We pled with him, offered him money, almost got on our knees to him. Finally he relented a little.

"At three o'clock," he said, "I'll give you the sign and countersign and let you go."

We curled miserably about a little fire of our own, trying to sleep, trying at least to get warm. Around us and ahead the flares and the men danced along the ruined track; and every hour or so the train would creep forward a hundred feet and stop again. It was not hard to repair—the rails were intact. A wrecker had been hitched to the right-hand rail and the ties twisted, splintered, torn from their bed. Always the monotonous and disturbing furious sound of battle filtered out of the blackness ahead. It was so tiresome, so much the *same*, that sound; and yet I could not sleep. . . .

INSURGENT MEXICO

About midnight one of our outposts galloped from the rear of the trains to report that a large body of horsemen had been challenged coming from the north, who said they were Urbina's *gente* from Mapimi. The Colonel didn't know of any body of troops that were to pass at that time of night. In a minute everything was a fury of preparation. Twenty-five armed and mounted men galloped like mad to the rear, with orders to stop the newcomers for fifteen minutes,—if they were Constitutionalists, by order of the Colonel; if not, by holding them off as long as possible. The workmen were hurried back to the train and given their rifles. The fires were put out, the flares,—all but ten, —extinguished. Our guard of two hundred slipped silently into the thick brush, loading their rifles as they went. On either side of the track the Colonel and five of his men took up their posts, unarmed, with torches held high over their heads. And then, out of the thick blackness, the head of the column appeared. It was made up of different men from the well-clothed, well-equipped, well-fed soldiers of Villa's army. These were ragged, gaunt people, wrapped in faded, tattered serapes, without shoes on their feet, crowned with the heavy, picturesque sombreros of the back-country. Lasso ropes hung coiled at their saddles. Their mounts were the lean, hard, half-savage ponies of the Durango mountains. They rode sullenly, contemptuous of us. They neither knew the countersign nor cared to know it. And as they rode, whole files sang the monotonous, extemporaneous ballads that the peons compose and sing to themselves as they guard the cattle at night on the great upland plains of the north.

And, suddenly, as I stood at the head of the line of flares, a passing horse was jerked to his haunches, and a voice I knew cried: "Hey! Meester!" The enfolding serape was cast high in the air, the man fell from his horse, and in a moment I was clasped in the arms of Isidro Amaya. Behind him burst forth a chorus of shouts: "*Que tal!* Meester! O Juanito, how glad we are to see you! Where have you been? They said you were killed in La Cadena! Did you run fast from the *colorados? Mucha susto,* eh?" They threw themselves to the ground, clustering around, fifty men reaching at once to pat me on the back; all my dearest friends in Mexico—the *compañeros* of La Tropa and the Cadena!

The long file of men, blocked in the darkness, raised a chorus of shouts: "Move on! *Vamonos!* What's the matter? Hurry up! We can't stay here all night!" And the others yelled back: "Here's meester! Here's the Gringo we were telling you about who danced the *jota* in La Zarca! Who was in La Cadena!" And then the others crowded forward too.

There were twelve hundred of them. Silently, sullenly, eagerly, sniffing the battle ahead, they defiled between the double line of high-held torches. And every tenth man I had known before. As they passed the Colonel shouted to them: "What is the countersign? Turn your hats up in front! Do you know the countersign?" Hoarsely, exasperatedly, he bawled at them. Serenely and insolently they rode by, without paying the least attention to him. "To hell with the countersign!" they hooted, laughing at him. "We don't need any countersign! They'll know well enough which side we're on when we begin to fight!"

For hours, it seemed, they jogged past, fading into the darkness, their horses with nervous heads turned to catch the sound of the guns, the men with glowing eyes fixed on the darkness ahead—rode into battle with their ancient Springfield rifles that had seen service for three years, with their meager ten rounds of ammunition. And when they had all gone the battle seemed to brighten and quicken with new life. . . .

CHAPTER VII

THE BLOODY DAWN

THE steady noise of battle filled all the night. Ahead torches danced, rails clanged, sledges drummed on the spikes, the men of the repair gang shouted in the frenzy of their toil. It was after twelve. Since the trains had reached the beginning of the torn track we had made half a mile. Now and then a straggler from the main body came down the line of trains, shuffled into the light with his heavy Mauser awry across his shoulders, and faded into the darkness toward the debauch of sound in the direction of Gomez Palacio. The soldiers of our guard, squatting about their little fires in the fields, relaxed their

THE BLOODY DAWN

tense expectancy; three of them were singing a little marching song, which began:

I don't want to be a Porfirista,
I don't want to be an Orozquista,
But I want to be a volunteer in the army Maderista!

Curious and excited, we hurried up and down the trains, asking people what they knew, what they thought. I had never heard a real killing-sound before, and it made me frantic with curiosity and nervousness. We were like dogs in a yard when a dogfight is going on outside. Finally the spell snapped and I found myself desperately tired. I fell into a dead sleep on a little ledge under the lip of the cannon, where the laborers tossed their wrenches and sledge-hammers and crowbars when the train moved forward a hundred feet, and piled on themselves with shouts and horseplay.

In the coldness of before dawn I woke with the Colonel's hand on my shoulder.

"You can go now," he said. "The sign is 'Zaragosa' and the countersign 'Guerrero.' Our soldiers will be recognized by their hats pinned up in front. May you go well!"

It was bitter cold. We threw our blankets around us, serape fashion, and trudged down past the fury of the repair gang as they hammered at it under the leaping flares—past the five armed men slouching around their fire on the frontier of the dark.

"Are you off to the battle, *compañeros?*" cried one of the gang. "Look out for the bullets!" At that they all laughed. The sentries cried, "*Adios!* Don't kill them all! Leave a few *pelones* for us!"

Beyond the last torch, where the torn track was wrenched and tumbled about on the uprooted roadbed, a shadowy figure waited for us.

"*Vamonos* together," he said, peering at us. "In the dark three are an army." We stumbled along over the broken track, silently, just able to make him out with our eyes. He was a little dumpy soldier with a rifle and a half-empty cartridge-belt over his breast. He said that he had just brought a wounded man from the front to the hospital train and was on his way back.

"Feel this," he said, holding out his arm. It was drenched. We could see nothing.

"Blood," he continued unemotionally. "His blood. He was my *compadre* in the Brigada Gonzales-Ortega. We went in this night down there and so many, so many—— We were cut in half."

It was the first we had heard, or thought, of wounded men. All of a sudden we heard the battle. It had been going on steadily all the time, but we had forgotten—the sound was so monstrous, so monotonous. Far rifle fire came like the ripping of strong canvas, the cannon shocked like pile-drivers. We were only six miles away now.

Out of the darkness loomed a little knot of men— four of them—carrying something heavy and inert in a blanket slung between. Our guide threw up his rifle and challenged, and his answer was a retching groan from the blanket.

"*Oiga compadre*," lisped one of the bearers huskily. "Where, for the love of the Virgin, is the hospital train?"

"About a league——"

"*Valgame Dios!* How can we. . . ."

"Water! Have you any water?"

They stood with the blanket taut between them, and something fell from it, drip, drip, drip, on the ties.

That awful voice within screamed once, "To drink!" and fell away to a shuddering moan. We handed our canteens to the bearers—and silently, bestially, they drained them. The wounded man they forgot. Then, sullen, they pitched on. . . .

Others appeared, singly, or in little groups. They were simply vague shapes staggering in the night, like drunkards, like men incredibly tired. One dragged between two walkers, his arms around their shoulders. A mere boy reeled along with the limp body of his father on his back. A horse passed with his nose to the ground, two bodies flopping sideways across the saddle, and a man walking behind and beating the horse on the rump, cursing shrilly. He passed, and we could hear his falsetto fading dissonantly in the distance. Some groaned, with the ugly, deadened groan of uttermost pain; one man, slouched in the saddle of a mule, screamed mechanically every time the mule took a step. Under two tall cotton-wood trees beside an irrigation ditch a little fire glowed. Three sleepers with empty cartridge-belts sprawled snoring on the uneven ground; beside the fire sat a man holding with both hands his leg straight out to the warmth. It was a perfectly good leg as far as the ankle—there it ended in a ragged, oozing mess of trousers and shattered flesh. The man simply sat looking at it. He didn't even stir as we came near, and yet his chest rose and fell with calm breathing, and his mouth was slightly open as if he were day-dreaming. By the side of the ditch knelt another. A soft lead bullet had entered his hand between the two middle fingers and then spread until it hollowed out a bloody cave inside. He had wrapped a rag around a little piece of stick and was unconcernedly dipping it in the water and gouging out the wound.

Soon we were near the battle. In the east, across the vast level country, a faint gray light appeared. The noble alamo trees, towering thickly in massy lines along the ditches to the west, burst into showers of bird-song. It was getting warm, and there came the tranquil smell of earth and grass and growing corn—a calm summer dawn. Into this the noise of battle broke like something insane. The hysterical chatter of rifle fire, that seemed to carry a continuous undertone of screaming—although when you listened for it it was gone. The nervous, deadly stab—stab—stab—stab of the machine guns, like some gigantic woodpecker. The cannon booming like great bells, and the whistle of their shells. Boom—Pi-i-i-e-e-a-uuu! And that most terrible of all the sounds of war, shrapnel exploding. Crash—Whee-e-eaaa!!

The great hot sun swam up in the east through a faint smoke from the fertile land, and over the eastern barrens the heat-waves began to wiggle. It caught the startlingly green tops of the lofty alamos fringing the ditch that paralleled the railroad on our right. The trees ended there, and beyond, the whole rampart of bare mountains, piled range on range, grew rosy. We were now in scorched desert again, thickly covered with dusty mesquite. Except for another line of alamos straggling across from east to west, close to the city, there were no trees in all the plain but two or three scattered ones to the right. So close we were, barely two miles from Gomez Palacio, that we could look down the torn track right into the town. We could see the black round water-tank, and back of that the roundhouse, and across the track from them both the low adobe walls of the Brittingham Corral. The smokestacks and buildings and trees of La Esperanza soap factory rose clear and still, like a little city, to the left. Almost directly to the right of the railroad track, it seemed, the stark, stony peak of the Cerro de la Pila mounted steeply to the stone reservoir that crowned it, and sloped off westward in a series of smaller peaks, a spiny ridge a mile long. Most of Gomez lay behind the shoulder of the Cerro, and at its western end the villas and gardens of Lerdo made a vivid patch of green in the desert. The great brown mountains on the west made a mighty sweep around behind the two cities, and then fell away south again in folds on folds of gaunt desolation. And directly south from Gomez, stretched along the base of this range, lay Torreon, the richest city of northern Mexico.

INSURGENT MEXICO

The shooting never ceased, but it seemed to be subdued to a subordinate place in a fantastic and disordered world. Up the track in the hot morning light straggled a river of wounded men, shattered, bleeding, bound up in rotting and bloody bandages, inconceivably weary. They passed us, and one even fell and lay motionless nearby in the dust—and we didn't care. Soldiers with their cartridges gone wandered aimlessly out of the chaparral, dragging their rifles, and plunged into the brush again on the other side of the railroad, black with powder, streaked with sweat, their eyes vacantly on the ground. The thin, subtle dust rose in lazy clouds at every footstep, and hung there, parching throat and eyes. A little company of horsemen jogged out of the thicket and drew up on the track, looking toward town. One man got down from his saddle and squatted beside us.

"It was terrible," he said suddenly. *"Carramba!* We went in there last night on foot. They were inside the water-tank, with holes cut in the iron for rifles. We had to walk up and poke our guns through the holes and we killed them all—a death trap! And then the Corral! They had two sets of loopholes, one for the men kneeling down and the other for the men standing up. Three thousand *rurales* in there—and they had five machine guns to sweep the road. And the roundhouse, with three rows of trenches outside and subterranean passages so they could crawl under and shoot us in the back. . . . Our bombs wouldn't work, and what could we do with rifles? *Madre de Dios!* But we were so quick—we took them by surprise. We captured the roundhouse and the water-tank. And then this morning thousands came—thousands—reinforcements from Torreon—and their artillery—and they drove us back again. They walked up to the water-tank and poked their rifles through the holes and killed all of us—the sons of the devils!"

We could see the place as he spoke and hear the hellish roar and shriek, and yet no one moved, and there wasn't a sign of the shooting—not even smoke, except when a shrapnel shell burst yelling down in the first row of trees a mile ahead and vomited a puff of white. The cracking rip of rifle fire and the staccato machine guns and even the hammering cannon didn't reveal themselves at all. The flat, dusty plain, the trees and chimneys of Gomez, and the stony hill, lay quietly in the heat. From the alamos off to the right came the careless song of birds. One had the impression that his senses were lying. It was an incredible dream, through which the grotesque procession of wounded filtered like ghosts in the dust.

CHAPTER VIII

THE ARTILLERY COMES UP

OVER to the right, along the base of the line of trees, heavy dust billowed up, men shouted, whips snapped, and there was a rumble and a jangling of chains. We plunged into a little path that wound among the chaparral and emerged upon a tiny

215

village, lost in the brush near the ditch. It was strikingly like a Chinese or Central American village: five or six adobe huts thatched with mud and twigs. It was called San Ramon, and there a little struggling knot of men swayed about every door, clamoring for coffee and *tortillas*, and waving fiat money. The *pacificos* squatted in their tiny corrals, selling *macuche* at exorbitant prices; their women sweated over the fire, hammering *tortillas* and pouring villainous black coffee. All around, in the open spaces, lay sleepers like the dead, and men with bloody arms and heads, tossing and groaning. Presently an officer galloped up, streaked with sweat, and screamed, "Get up, you fools! *Pendecos!* Wake up and get back to your companies! We're going to attack!" A few stirred and stumbled, cursing, to their weary feet—the others still slept. "*Hijos de la*——!" snapped the officer, and spurred his horse upon them, trampling, kicking. . . . The ground boiled men scrambling out of the way and yelling. They yawned, stretched, still half asleep, and sifted off slowly toward the front in an aimless way. . . . The wounded only dragged themselves listlessly to the shade of the brush.

Along the side of the ditch went a sort of wagon track, and up this the Constitutionalist artillery were arriving. One could see the gray heads of the straining mules, and the big hats of their drivers, and the circling whips—the rest was masked in dust. Slower than the army, they had been marching all night. Past us rumbled the carriages and caissons, the long, heavy guns yellow with dust. The drivers and gunners were in fine good humor. One, an American, whose features were absolutely indistinguishable in the all-mantling mud of sweat and earth, shouted to know if they were in time, or if the town had fallen.

I answered in Spanish that there were lots of *colorados* yet to kill, and a cheer ran along the line.

"Now we'll show them something," cried a big Indian on a mule. "If we could get into their cursed town without guns, what can we do with them?"

The alamos ended just beyond San Ramon, and under the last trees Villa, General Angeles, and the staff sat on horseback at the bank of the ditch. Beyond that the ditch ran naked across the naked plain into the town, where it took water from the river. Villa was dressed in an old brown suit, without a collar, and an ancient felt hat. He was covered with dirt, and had been riding up and down the lines all night; but he bore no trace of fatigue.

When he saw us he called out, "Hello, *muchachos!* Well, how do you like it?"

"Fine, *mi General!*"

We were worn out and very dirty. The sight of us amused him profoundly; he never could take the correspondents seriously, anyway, and it seemed to him very droll that an American periodical would be willing to spend so much money just to get the news.

"Good," he said with a grin. "I'm glad you like it, because you're going to get all you want."

The first gun had now come opposite the staff and unlimbered, the gunners ripping off the canvas covers and tilting up the heavy caisson. The captain of the battery screwed on the telescopic sight and the crank of the raising-lever spun. The brass butts of heavy shells shone in gleaming rows; two men staggered under the weight of one, and rested it on the ground while the captain regulated the shrapnel timer. The breech-lock crashed shut, and we ran far back. Cra-boom-shock! A soaring whistling Pi-i-i-e-e-eeuu! flew high after the shell, and then a tiny white smoke flowered at the foot of the Cerro de la Pila—and, minutes after, a far detonation. About a hundred yards apart, all along in front of the gun, picturesque ragged men stared motionless through their field-glasses. They burst into a chorus of yells, "Too low! Too far to the right! Their guns are all along the ridge! Time it about fifteen seconds later!" Down front the rifle fire had frittered away to ragged sputtering and the machine guns were silent. Everybody was watching the artillery duel. It was about five-thirty in the morning, and already very hot. In the fields behind sounded the parched chirp of crickets; the lofty fresh tops of the alamos rustled in a high languid breeze; birds began to sing again.

Another gun wheeled into line, and the breech-block of the first clacked again. There came the snap of the trigger, but no roar. The gunners wrenched open the breech and hurled the smoking brass projectile on the grass. Bad shell. I saw General Angeles in his faded brown sweater, hatless, peering through the sight and cranking up the range. Villa was spurring his reluctant horse up to the caisson. Cra—boom—shock!

THE ARTILLERY COMES UP

Pi-i-i-e-e-eeuu! The other gun this time. We saw the shell burst higher up the stony hill this time. And then four booms floated to us, and, simultaneously, the enemy's shells, which had been exploding desultorily over the line of trees nearest the city, marched out into the open desert and leaped toward us in four tremendous explosions, each nearer. More guns had wheeled into line; others filed off to the right along a diagonal of trees, and a long line of heavy trucks, plunging mules, and cursing, shouting men choked up the dusty road to the rear. The unlimbered mules jingled back and the drivers threw themselves, exhausted, under the nearest chaparral.

The Federal shrapnel, well fired and excellently timed, was bursting now only a few hundred yards in front of our line, and the minute boom of their guns was almost incessant. Crash—Wheeeeaa! Over our heads, snapping viciously in the leafy trees, sang the rain of lead. Our guns replied spasmodically. The home-made shells, fashioned on converted mining machinery in Chihuahua, were not reliable. Galloped past stout Captain Marinelli, the Italian soldier of fortune, steering as near the newspapermen as possible, with a serious, Napoleonic look on his face. He glanced once or twice at the camera man, smiling graciously, but the latter coldly looked away. With a workmanlike flourish he ordered the wheeling of his gun into position and sighted it himself. Just then a shell burst deafeningly about a hundred yards in front. The Federals were getting the range. Marinelli bounded away from his cannon, mounted his horse, limbered up and came galloping dramatically back with his gun rumbling along at a dead run behind. None of the other guns had retreated. Pulling up his foaming charger in front of the camera man, he flung himself to the ground and took a position.

"Now," he said, "you can take my picture!"

"Go to hell," said the camera man, and a great shout of laughter went up along the line.

The high cracked note of a bugle thrilled through the racking roar. Immediately mules dragging their jangling limbers appeared, and shouting men. The caissons snapped shut.

"Going down front," shouted Colonel Servin. "Not hitting. Too far away here. . . ."

And the long-halted line snapped taut and wound out into the open desert, under the bursting shells.

CHAPTER IX

BATTLE

WE returned along the winding path through the mesquite, crossed the torn-up track, and struck out across the dusty plain southeastward. Looking back along the railroad I could see smoke and the round front of the first train miles away; and in front of it throngs of active little dots swarming on the right of way, distorted like things seen in a wavy mirror. We strode along in a haze of thin dust. The giant mesquite dwindled until it scarcely reached to our knees. To the right the tall hill and the chimneys of the town swam tranquilly in the hot sun; rifle fire had almost ceased for the moment, and only dazzling bursts of thick white smoke marked our occasional shells along the ridge. We could see our drab guns rocking down the plain, spreading along the first line of alamos, where the searching fingers of the enemy's shrapnel probed continually. Little bodies of horsemen moved here and there over the desert, and stragglers on foot, trailing their rifles.

An old peon, stooped with age and dressed in rags, crouched in the low shrub gathering mesquite twigs.

"Say, friend," we asked him, "is there any way we can get in close to see the fighting?"

He straightened up and stared at us.

"If you had been here as long as I have," said he, "you wouldn't care about seeing the fighting. *Carramba!* I have seen them take Torreon seven times in three years. Sometimes they attack from Gomez Palacio and sometimes from the mountains. But it is always the same—war. There is something interesting in it for the young, but for us old people, we are tired of war." He paused and stared out over the plain. "Do you see this dry ditch? Well, if you will get down in it and follow along it will lead you into the town." And then, as an afterthought, he added incuriously, "What party do you belong to?"

"The Constitutionalists."

"So. First it was the Maderistas, and then the Orozquistas, and now the—what did you call them? I am very old, and I have not long to live; but this

war—it seems to me that all it accomplishes is to let
us go hungry. Go with God, señores." And he bent
again to his slow task, while we descended into the
arroyo. It was a disused irrigation ditch running a
little south of west, its bottom covered with dusty
weeds, and the end of its straight length hidden from
us by a sort of mirage that looked like a glaring pool
of water. Stooped a little, so as to be hidden from the
outside, we walked along, it seemed, for hours, the
cracked bottom and dusty sides of the ditch reflecting
the fierce heat upon us until we were faint with it.
Once horsemen passed quite near on our right, their
big iron spurs ringing; we crouched down until they
passed, for we didn't want to take any chances. Down
in the ditch the artillery fire sounded very faint and
far away, but once I cautiously lifted my head above
the bank and discovered that we were very near the
first line of trees. Shells were bursting along it, and
I could even see the belch of furious haze hurling out
from the mouths of our cannon, and feel the surf of
sound-waves hit me like a blow when they fired. We
were a good quarter of a mile in front of our artillery, and evidently making for the water-tank on the
very edge of the town. As we stooped again the shells
passing overhead whined sharply and suddenly across
the arc of sky and were cut off abruptly until the sullen echoless booff! of their explosion. There ahead,
where the railroad trestle of the main line crossed the
arroyo, huddled a little pile of bodies—evidently left
from the first attack. Hardly one was bloody; their
heads and hearts were pierced with the clean, tiny holes

of steel Mauser bullets. They lay limply, with the unearthly calm, lean faces of the dead. Someone, perhaps their own thrifty *compañeros*, had stripped them of arms, shoes, hats and serviceable clothing. One sleeping soldier, squatting on the edge of the heap with his rifle across his knees, snored deeply. Flies covered him—the dead hummed with them. But the sun had not yet affected them. Another soldier leaned against the townward bank of the ditch, his feet resting on a corpse, banging methodically away at something he saw. Under the shadow of the trestle four men sat playing cards. They played listlessly, without talking, their eyes red with lack of sleep. The heat was frightful. Occasionally a stray bullet came by screaming, "Where—is-s-s-z—ye!" This strange company took our appearance as a matter of course. The sharpshooter doubled up out of range and carefully put another cartridge-clip in his rifle.

"You haven't got another drop of water in that canteen, have you?" he asked. "*Adio!* we haven't eaten or drunk since yesterday!" He guzzled the water, furtively watching the card players lest they, too, should be thirsty. "They say that we are to attack the water-tank and the Corral again when the artillery is in position to support us. Chi-*hua*hua *hombre!* but it was *duro* in the night! They slaughtered us in the streets there. . . ." He wiped his mouth on the back of his hand and began firing again. We lay beside him and looked over. We were about two hundred yards from the deadly water-tank. Across the track and the wide street beyond lay the brown mud-walls of the

Brittingham Corral, innocent looking enough now, with
only black dots to show the double line of loop-holes.

"There are the machine guns," said our friend. "See
them, those slim barrels peeping over the edge?" We
couldn't make them out. Water-tank, Corral and town
lay sleeping in the heat. Dust hovered still in the air,
making a thin haze. About fifty yards in front of us
was a shallow exposed ditch, evidently once a Federal
trench, for the dirt had been piled on our side. Two
hundred drab, dusty soldiers lay in it now, facing
townward—the Constitutionalist infantry. They were
sprawled on the ground, in all attitudes of weariness;
some sleeping on their backs, facing up to the hot sun;
others wearily transferring the dirt with their scooped
hands from rear to front. Before them they had piled
up irregular heaps of rocks. Now infantry, in the
Constitutionalist army, is simply cavalry without
horses; all Villa's soldiers are mounted except the artillery, and those for whom horses cannot be procured.

Of a sudden the artillery in our rear boomed all together, and over our heads a dozen shells screamed toward the Cerro.

"That is the signal," said the man at our side. He
clambered down into the ditch and kicked the sleeper.
"Come on," he yelled. "Wake up. We're going to
attack the *pelones*." The snorer groaned and opened
his eyes slowly. He yawned and picked up his rifle
without a word. The card players began to squabble
about their winnings. A violent dispute broke out as
to who owned the pack of cards. Grumbling and still

arguing, they stumbled out and followed the sharp-shooter up over the edge of the ditch.

Rifle fire rang along the edge of the trench in front. The sleepers flopped over on their stomachs behind their little shelters—their elbows worked vigorously pumping the guns. The hollow steel water-tank resounded to the rain of thumping bullets; chips of adobe flew from the wall of the Corral. Instantly the wall bristled with shining barrels and the two awoke crackling with hidden vicious firing. Bullets roofed the heavens with whistling steel—drummed the smoking dust up until a yellow curtain of whirling cloud veiled us from the houses and the tank. We could see our friend running low along the ground, the sleepy man following, standing erect, still rubbing his eyes. Behind strung out the gamblers, squabbling yet. Somewhere in the rear a bugle blew. The sharpshooter running in front stopped suddenly, swaying, as if he had run against a solid wall. His left leg doubled under him and he sank crazily to one knee in the exposed flat, whipping up his rifle with a yell.

"—— —— the dirty monkeys!" he screamed, firing rapidly into the dust. "I'll show the ——! The cropped heads! The jail-birds!" He shook his head impatiently, like a dog with a hurt ear. Blood drops flew from it. Bellowing with rage, he shot the rest of his clip, and then slumped to the ground and thrashed to and fro for a minute. The others passed him with scarcely a look. Now the trench was boiling with men scrambling to their feet, like worms when you turn over a log. The rifle fire rattled shrilly. From behind us came running feet, and men in sandals, with blankets over their shoulders, came falling and slipping down the ditch, and scrambling up the other side—hundreds of them, it seemed. . . .

They almost hid from us the front, but through the dust and the spaces between running logs we could see the soldiers in the trench leap their barricade like a breaking wave. And then the impenetrable dust shut down and the fierce stabbing needle of the machine guns sewed the mighty jumble of sounds together. A glimpse through a rift in the cloud torn by a sudden hot gust of wind—we could see the first brown line of men reeling altogether like drunkards, and the machine guns over the wall spitting sharp, dull red in the sunshine. Then a man came running back out of it, the sweat streaming down his face, without a gun. He ran fast, half sliding, half falling, down into our ditch and up the other side. Other dim forms loomed up in the dust ahead.

"What is it? How is it going?" I cried.

He answered nothing, but ran on. Suddenly and terribly the monstrous crash and scream of shrapnel burst from the turmoil ahead. The enemy's artillery! Mechanically I listened for our guns. Except for an occasional boom they were silent. Our home-made shells were failing again. Two more shrapnel shells. Out of the dust-cloud men came running back—singly, in pairs, in groups, a stampeding mob. They fell over us, around us—drowned us in a human flood, shouting "To the alamos! To the trains! The Federation is coming!" We struggled up among them and ran, too, straight up the railroad track. . . . Behind us roared the shells searching in the dust, and the tearing musketry. And then we noticed that all the wide roadway ahead was filled with galloping horsemen, yelling shrill Indian cries and waving their rifles—the main column! We stood to one side as they whirled past, about five hundred of them—watched them stoop in their saddles and begin to shoot. The drumming of their horses' hoofs was like thunder.

"Better not go in there! It's too hot!" cried one of the infantry with a grin.

"Well, I'll bet I'm hotter," answered a horseman, and we all laughed. We walked tranquilly back along the railroad track, while the firing behind wound up to a continuous roar. A group of peons—*pacíficos*—in tall sombreros, blankets and white cotton blouses, stood along here with folded arms, looking down the track toward town.

"Look out there, friends," joshed a soldier. "Don't stand there. You'll get hit."

The peons looked at each other and grinned feebly. "But, señor," said one, "this is where we always stand when there is a battle."

A little farther along I came upon an officer—a German—wandering along, leading his horse by the bridle. "I cannot ride him any more," he said to me earnestly. "He is quite too tired. I am afraid he will die if he does not sleep." The horse, a big chestnut stallion, stumbled and swayed as he walked. Enormous tears trickled from his half-shut eyes and rolled down his nose. . . .

I was dead tired, reeling from lack of sleep and food

and the terrible heat of the sun. About half a mile out I looked back and saw the enemy's shrapnel poking into the line of trees more frequently than ever. They seemed to have thoroughly got the range. And just then I saw the gray line of guns, limbered to their mules, begin to crawl out from the trees toward the rear at four or five different points. Our artillery had been shelled out of their positions. . . . I threw myself down to rest in the shade of a big mesquite bush.

Almost immediately a change seemed to come in the sound of the rifle fire, as if half of it had been suddenly cut off. At the same time twenty bugles shrilled. Rising, I noticed a line of running horsemen fleeing up the track, shouting something. More followed, galloping, at the place where the railroad passed beyond the trees on its way into town. The cavalry had been repulsed. All at once the whole plain squirmed with men, mounted and on foot, all running rearward. One man threw away his blanket, another his rifle. They thickened over the hot desert, stamping up the dust, until the flat was crowded with them. Right in front of me a horseman burst out of the brush, shouting, "The Federals are coming! To the trains! They are right behind!" The entire Constitutionalist army was routed! I caught up my blanket and took to my heels. A little way farther on I came upon a cannon abandoned in the desert, traces cut, mules gone. Underfoot were guns, cartridge-belts and dozens of serapes. It was a rout. Coming to an open space, I saw ahead a large crowd of fleeing soldiers, without rifles. Suddenly three men on horseback swept across in front of them, waving their arms and yelling. "Go back!" they cried. "They aren't coming out! Go back for the love of God!" Two I didn't recognize. The other was Villa.

CHAPTER X

BETWEEN ATTACKS

A BOUT a mile back the flight was stopped. I met the soldiers coming back, with the relieved expression of men who have feared an unknown danger and been suddenly set free from it. That was always Villa's power—he could explain things to the great mass of ordinary people in a way that they immediately understood. The Federals, as usual, had failed to take advantage of their opportunity to inflict a lasting defeat upon the Constitutionalists. Perhaps they feared an ambush like the one Villa had arranged at Mapula, when the victorious Federals sallied out to pursue Villa's fleeing army after the first attack on Chihuahua, and were repulsed with heavy slaughter. Anyway, they did not come out. The men came straggling back, hunting in the mesquite for their guns and blankets, and for other people's guns and blankets. You could hear them shouting and joking all over the plain. "*Oija!* Where are you going with that rifle? That's my water-bag! I dropped my serape right here by this bush, and now it's gone!"

"O Juan," cried one man to another, "I always told you I could beat you running!"

"But you didn't, *compadre*. I was a hundred meters ahead, flying through the air like a cannon ball! . . ."

The truth was that after riding twelve hours the day before, fighting all night, and all morning in the blazing sun, under the frightful strain of charging an intrenched force in the face of artillery and machine guns, without food, water or sleep, the army's nerve had suddenly given way. But from the time that they returned after the flight the ultimate result was never in doubt. The psychological crisis was past. . . .

Now the rifle fire had altogether ceased, and even cannon shots from the enemy were few and far between. At the ditch under the first line of trees our men entrenched themselves; the artillery had withdrawn to the second line of trees—a mile back; and under the grateful shade the men threw themselves heavily down and slept. The strain had snapped. As the sun rose toward noon the desert, hill and town throbbed silently in the intense heat. Sometimes an exchange of shots far to the right or left told where the outposts were exchanging compliments. But even that soon stopped. In the cotton and cornfields to the north, among the sprouting green things, insects chirped. The birds sang no more because of the heat. It was breathless. The leaves stirred in no wind.

Here and there little fires smoked, where the soldiers rolled *tortillas* from the scanty flour they had brought in their saddle-bags—and those who didn't have any swarmed around, begging a crumb. Everybody simply and generously divided the food. I was hailed from a dozen fires with "Hey, *compañero*, have you break-

fasted? Here is a piece of my *tortilla*. Come and eat!"
Rows of men lay flat on their stomachs along the irrigation ditch, scooping up the dirty water in their
palms. Three or four miles back we could see the cannon-car and the first two trains, opposite the big ranch
of El Verjel, with the tireless repair gang hard at it
in the hot sun. The provision train had not come up
yet. . . .

Little Colonel Servin came by, perched on an immense bay horse, still dapper and fresh after the terrible work of the night.

"I don't know what we shall do yet," he said. "Only
the General knows that, and he never tells. But we
shall not assault again until the Brigada Zaragosa returns. Benavides has had a hard battle over there at
Sacramento—two hundred and fifty of ours killed, they
say. And the General has sent for General Robles and
General Contreras, who have been attacking from the
south, to bring up all their men and join him here. . . .
They say, though, that we are going to deliver a night
attack next, so that their artillery won't be effective.
. . ." He galloped on.

About midday thin columns of sluggish, dirty smoke
began to rise from several points in the town, and toward afternoon a slow, hot wind brought to us the
faintly sickening smell of crude oil mingled with
scorched human flesh. The Federals were burning piles
of the dead. . . .

We walked back to the trains and stormed General
Benavides' private car in the Brigada Zaragosa train.
The major in charge had them cook us something to

eat in the General's kitchen. We ate ravenously, and afterward went over along the line of trees and slept for hours. Late in the afternoon we started once more for the front. Hundreds of soldiers and peons of the neighborhood, ravenously hungry, prowled around the trains, hoping to pick up discarded food, or slops, or anything at all to eat. They were ashamed of themselves, however, and affected a sauntering indolence when we passed. I remember that we sat for a while talking with some soldiers on the top of a box-car, when a boy, criss-crossed with cartridge-belts and lugging a huge rifle, came past beneath, his eyes searching the ground. A stale *tortilla*, half rotting, crunched into the dirt by many passing feet, caught his attention. He pounced upon it and bit a piece out. Then he looked up and saw us. "As if I were dying of hunger!" he said scornfully and tossed it away with contempt. . . .

Down in the shade of the alamos, across the ditch from San Ramon, the Canadian Captain Treston was bivouacked with his machine gun battery. The guns and their heavy tripods were unloaded from the mules, and all around lay the unlimbered field-pieces, their animals grazing in the rich green fields, the men squatted around their fires or lying stretched out on the bank of the ditch. Treston waved an ashy *tortilla* he was munching and bawled, "Say, Reed! Please come here and interpret for me! I can't find my interpreters, and if we go into action I'll be in a hell of a fix! You see I don't know the damn language, and when I came down here Villa hired two interpreters to go around with me all the time. And I can't ever find the sons-of-guns; they always go off and leave me in a hole!"

I took part of the proffered delicacy and asked him if he thought there was any chance of going into action.

"I think we'll go in to-night as soon as it's dark," he answered. "Do you want to go along with the machine guns and interpret?" I said I did.

A ragged man near the fire, whom I had never seen before, rose and came across smiling.

"I thought when I looked at you that you seemed to be an *hombre* who hadn't tasted tobacco for a while. Will you take half my cigarette?" Before I could protest he produced a lop-sided brown cigarette and tore it across in two pieces. . . .

The sun went gloriously down behind the notched purple mountains in front of us, and for a minute a clear fan of quivering light poured up the high arc of stainless sky. The birds awoke in the trees; leaves rustled. The fertile land exhaled a pearly mist. A dozen ragged soldiers, lying close together, began to improvise the air and words of a song about the battle of Torreon—a new ballad was being born. . . . Other singing came to us through the still, cool dusk. I felt my whole feeling going out to these gentle, simple people—so lovable they were. . . .

It was just after I had been to the ditch for a drink that Treston said casually: "By the way, one of our men found this floating in the ditch a little while ago. I can't read Spanish, so I didn't know what the word meant. You see the water from these ditches all comes from the river inside the town, so I thought it might be a Federal paper." I took it from his hand. It was a little folded white piece of wet paper, like the corner and front of a package. In large black letters was printed on the front, "*ARSENICO*," and in smaller type, "*Cuidado! Veneno!*" "Arsenic. Beware! Poison!"

"Look here," I demanded, sitting up suddenly. "Have there been any sick people around here this evening?"

"That's funny you're asking," he said. "A good many of the men have had bad cramps in the stomach, and I don't feel altogether well. Just before you came a mule suddenly keeled over and died in that next field, and a horse across the ditch. Fatigue or sunstroke, probably. . . ."

Fortunately the ditch carried a large body of swiftly running water, so the danger was not great. I explained to him that the Federals had poisoned the ditch.

"My God," said Treston. "Perhaps that is what they were trying to tell me. About twenty people have come up to me and said something about *envenenado*. What does that mean?"

"That's what it means," I answered. "Where can we get about a quart of strong coffee?" We found a great can of it at the nearest fire and felt better.

"O yes, we knew," said the men. "That is why we watered the animals at the other ditch. We heard long ago. They say that ten horses are dead down in front, and that many men are rolling very sick on the ground."

BETWEEN ATTACKS

An officer on horseback rode by, shouting that we were all to go back to El Verjel and camp there beside the trains for the night; that the general had said that everyone but the advance guards were to get a good night's sleep out of the zone of fire, and that the commissary train had come up and was just behind the hospital train. Bugles sounded, and the men struggled up off the ground, catching mules, fastening their harness on amid shouting and braying and jingling, saddling horses and limbering guns. Treston got on his pony and I walked along beside him. So there was to be no night attack then. It was now almost dark. Across the ditch we fell in with the shadowy forms of a company of soldiers trotting northward, all muffling blankets and big hats and ringing spurs. They hailed me. "Hey, *compañero*, where's your horse?" I admitted I had none. "Jump up behind me then," chimed in five or six altogether. One pulled up right beside me and I mounted with him. We jogged on through the mesquite and across a dim, lovely field. Someone began to sing and two more joined in. A round, full moon bubbled up in the clear night.

"*Oiga*, how do you say '*mula*' in English?" asked my horseman.

"G—— d—— stubborn-fathead-mule," I told him. And for days after entire strangers would stop me and ask me, with roars of laughter, how the Americans said "*mula*." . . .

Around the ranch of El Verjel the army was encamped. We rode into a field dotted with fires, where aimless soldiers wandered around in the dark, shouting

235

to know where the Brigada Gonzales-Ortega was, or
Jose Rodriguez's *gente*, or the *amitrailladoras*. Townward the artillery was unlimbering in a wide, alert half-
circle, guns pointing south. To the east, the camp of
Benavides' Brigada Zaragosa, just arrived from Sacramento, made an immense glow in the sky. From the
direction of the provision train a long ant-like file of
men bore sacks of flour, coffee, and packages of cigarettes. . . . A hundred different singing choruses
swelled up into the night. . . .

It comes to my mind with particular vividness how I
saw a poor poisoned horse suddenly double up and fall,
thrashing; how we passed a man bent to the ground in
the darkness, vomiting violently; how, after I had
rolled up on the ground in my blankets, terrible cramps
suddenly wrenched me, and I crawled out a way into
the brush and didn't have the strength to crawl back.
In fact, until gray dawn, I "rolled very sick on the
ground."

CHAPTER XI

AN OUTPOST IN ACTION

TUESDAY, early in the morning, the army was in
motion again toward the front, straggling
down the track and across the field. Four hundred raging demons sweated and hammered at the
ruined track; the foremost train had made half a mile
in the night. Horses were plenty that morning, and I
bought one, saddle and all, for seventy-five pesos—

AN OUTPOST IN ACTION

about fifteen dollars in gold. Trotting down by San Ramon, I fell in with two wild-looking horsemen, in high sombreros, with little printed pictures of Our Lady of Guadelupe sewed on the crowns. They said they were going out to an outpost upon the extreme right wing, near the mountains above Lerdo, where their company was posted to hold a hill. Why should I want to come with them? Who was I, anyway? I showed them my pass, signed by Francisco Villa. They were still hostile. "Francisco Villa is nothing to us," they said. "And how do we know whether this is his name, written by him? We are of the Brigada Juarez, Calixto Contreras' *gente*." But after a short consultation the taller grunted, "Come."

We left the protection of the trees, striking out diagonally across the ramparted cotton-fields, due west, straight for a steep, high hill that already quivered in the heat. Between us and the suburbs of Gomez Palacio stretched a barren, flat plain, covered with low mesquite and cut by dry irrigation ditches. The Cerro de la Pila, with its murderous concealed artillery, lay perfectly quiet, except that up one side of it, so clear was the air, we could make out a little knot of figures dragging what looked like a cannon. Just outside of the nearest houses some horsemen were riding around; we immediately struck north, making a wide détour, carefully on the watch, for this intermediate ground was overrun by pickets and scouting parties. About a mile beyond, almost along the foot of the hill, ran the high road from the north to Lerdo. We reconnoitered this carefully from the brush. A peasant passed whistling, driving a flock of goats. On the very edge of this road, under a bush, was an earthen jar full of milk. Without the least hesitation the first soldier drew his revolver and shot. The jar split into a hundred pieces —milk spurting everywhere.

"Poisoned," he said briefly. "The first company stationed over here drank some of that stuff. Four died." We rode on.

Up on the hill crest a few black figures squatted, their rifles tilted against their knees. My companions waved to them, and we turned north along the bank of a little river that unrolled a narrow strip of green grass in the midst of desolation. The outpost was camped on both sides of the water, in a sort of meadow. I asked where the colonel was, and finally found him stretched out in the shade of a tent that he had made by hanging his serape over a bush.

"Get down from your horse, friend," he said. "I am glad to welcome you here. My house" (pointing quizzically to the roof of his tent) "is at your disposal. Here are cigarettes. There is meat cooking on the fire." Upon the meadow, fully saddled, grazed the horses of the troop, about fifty of them. The men sprawled on the grass in the shade of the mesquite, chatting and playing cards. This was a different breed of men from the well-armed, well-mounted, comparatively disciplined troops of Villa's army. They were simply peons who had risen in arms, like my friends of La Tropa—a tough, happy race of mountaineers and cowboys, among whom were many who had been bandits in the old days. Unpaid, ill-clad, undisciplined—

their officers merely the bravest among them—armed only with aged Springfields and a handful of cartridges apiece, they had fought almost continuously for three years. For four months they, and the irregular troops of such guerrilla chiefs as Urbina and Robles, had held the advance around Torreon, fighting almost daily with Federal outposts and suffering all the hardships of the campaign, while the main army garrisoned Chihuahua and Juarez. These ragged men were the bravest soldiers in Villa's army.

I had lain there about fifteen minutes, watching the beef sizzle in the flames and satisfying the eager curiosity of a crowd as to my curious profession, when there was a sound of galloping, and a voice, "They're coming out of Lerdo! To horse!"

Half a hundred men reluctantly, and in a leisurely manner, made for their horses. The colonel rose, yawning. He stretched.

"―――― ―――― the animals of Federals!" he growled. "They stay on our minds all the time. You never have time to think of more pleasant things. It's a shame they won't let us even eat our dinner!"

We were mounted soon, trotting down the bank of the stream. Far in front sounded the pin-pricking rifles. Instinctively, without order, we broke into a gallop; through the streets of a little village, where the *pacificos* stood on the roofs of their houses, looking off to the south, little bundles of their belongings beside them so they could flee if the battle went against us, for the Federals cruelly punish villages which have harbored the enemy. Beyond lay the stony little hill. We got off our horses, and throwing the reins over their heads, climbed on foot. About a dozen men already lay there, shooting spasmodically in the direction of the green bank of trees behind which lay Lerdo. Unseen scattering shots ripped from the blank desert between. About half a mile away small brown figures dodged around in the brush. A thin dust-cloud showed where another detachment was marching slowly north in their rear.

"We already got one sure, and another one in the leg," said a soldier, spitting.

"How many do you make them out?" asked the colonel.

"About two hundred."

The Colonel stood bolt upright, carelessly looking out over the sunny plain. Immediately a roll of shots swept along their front. A bullet chirped overhead. Already the men had gone to work, unordered. Each soldier picked out a smooth place to lie and piled up a little heap of stones in front to shield him. They lay down grunting, loosening their belts and taking off their coats to be perfectly comfortable; then they began slowly and methodically to shoot.

"There goes another," announced the Colonel. "Yours, Pedro."

"Not Pedro's at all," interrupted another man fretfully. "I got him."

"O the devil you did," snapped Pedro. They quarreled. . . .

AN OUTPOST IN ACTION

The firing from the desert was now pretty general, and we could see the Federals slipping toward us under the protection of every bush and arroyo. Our men fired slowly and carefully, aiming a long time before they pulled the trigger, for the months with scanty ammunition around Torreon had made them economical. But now every hill and bush along our line held a little knot of sharpshooters, and looking back on the wide flats and fields between the hill and the railroad, I saw innumerable single horsemen and squads of them spurring through the brush. In ten minutes we would have five hundred men with us.

The rifle fire along the line swelled and deepened until there was a solid mile of it. The Federals had stopped; now the dust-clouds began slowly to move backward in the direction of Lerdo. The fire from the desert slackened. And then, from nowhere, we suddenly saw the broad-winged vultures sailing, serene and motionless, in the blue. . . .

The Colonel, his men and I democratically ate lunch in the shade of the village houses. Our meat was, of course, scorched, so we had to do the best we could with jerked beef and *piñole,* which seems to be cinnamon and bran, ground fine. I never enjoyed a meal so. . . . And when I left the men made up a double handful of cigarettes as a present.

Said the Colonel: "*Amigo,* I am sorry that we had not time for a talk together. There are many things I want to ask you about your country—whether it is

true, for example, that in your cities men have entirely
lost the use of their legs and don't ride horseback in
the streets, but are borne about in automobiles. I
had a brother once who worked on the railroad track
near Kansas City, and he told me wonderful things.
But a man called him 'greaser' one day and shot him
without that my brother did anything to him. Why is
it your people don't like Mexicans? I like many Americans. I like you. Here is a gift for you." He unbuckled one of his huge iron spurs, inlaid with silver,
and gave it to me. "But we never had any time here
for talk. These —— always annoy us, and then we
have to get up and kill a few of them before we can
have a moment's peace. . . ."

Under the alamo trees I found one of the photographers and a moving-picture man. They were lying
flat on their backs near a fire, around which squatted
twenty soldiers, gorging ravenously flour *tortillas*, meat
and coffee. One proudly displayed a silver wrist-watch.

"That used to be my watch," explained the photographer. "You see we hadn't had anything to eat
for two days, and when we came past here these boys
called us and gave us the most magnificent feed I have
ever tasted. After that I just couldn't help giving
them a present!"

The soldiers had accepted the gift communally and
were agreeing that each should wear it for two hours;
from then on until the end of life. . . .

CHAPTER XII

CONTRERAS' MEN ASSAULT

WEDNESDAY my friend the photographer and I were wandering across a field when Villa came by on his horse. He looked tired, dirty, but happy. Reining up in front of us, the motions of his body as easy and graceful as a wolf's, he grinned and said, "Well, boys, how is it going now?"

We answered that we were perfectly contented.

"I haven't time to worry about you, so you must be careful not to go into danger. It is bad—the wounded. Hundreds. They are brave, those *muchachos;* the bravest people in the world. But," he continued delightedly, "you must go and see the hospital train. There is something fine for you to write your papers about. . . ."

And truly it was a magnificent thing to see. The hospital train lay right behind the work train now. Forty box-cars, enameled inside, stenciled on the side with a big blue cross and the legend, "Servicio Sanitario," handled the wounded as they came from the front. They were fitted inside with the latest surgical appliances and manned by sixty competent American and Mexican doctors. Every night shuttle trains carried the seriously hurt back to the base hospitals at Chihuahua and Parral.

We went down through San Ramon and beyond the end of the line of trees out across the desert. It was

243

already stinging hot. In front a snake of rifle fire unfolded along the line, and then a machine gun, "spat—spat—spat!" As we emerged into the open a lone Mauser began cracking down to the right somewhere. We.paid no attention to it at first, but pretty soon we noticed that there was a little plumping sound on the ground around us—puffs of dust flew up every few minutes.

"By God," said the photographer. "Some beggar's sniping at us."

Instinctively we both sprinted. The rifle shots came faster. It was a long distance across the plain. After a little we reduced it to a jog-trot. Finally we walked along, with the dust spurting up as before, and a feeling that, after all, it wouldn't do any good to run. Then we forgot it. . . .

Half an hour later we crept through the brush a quarter of a mile from the outskirts of Gomez and came upon a tiny ranch of six or eight adobe huts, with a street running between. In the lee of one of the houses lounged and sprawled about sixty of Contreras' ragged fighters. They were playing cards and talking lazily. Down the street, just around the corner, which pointed straight as a die toward the Federal positions, a storm of bullets swept continually, whipping up the dust. These men had been on duty at the front all night. The countersign had been "no hats," and they were bareheaded in the broiling sun. They had had no sleep and no food, and there wasn't any water for half a mile.

"There is a Federal cuartel up ahead there that is

firing," explainèd a boy about twelve years old. "We've got orders to attack when the artillery comes."

An old man squatting against the wall asked me where I came from. I said New York.

"Well," he said, "I don't know anything about New York, but I'll bet you don't see such fine cattle going through the streets as you see in the streets of Jiminez."

"You don't see any cattle in the streets of New York," I said.

He looked at me incredulously. "What, no cattle? You mean to tell me that they don't drive cattle through the streets up there? Or sheep?"

I said they didn't. He looked at me as if he thought I was a great liar; then he cast his eyes on the ground and thought deeply.

"Well," he pronounced finally, "then I don't want to go there! . . ."

Two skylarking boys started a game of tag; in a minute twenty full-grown men were chasing each other around in great glee. The card players had one short deck of torn cards, and at least eight people were trying to play some game and arguing about the rules at the top of their voices, or perhaps there weren't enough cards to go around. Four or five had crawled into the shade of the house, singing satirical love songs. All this time the steady infernal din up ahead never relented, and the bullets spattered in the dust like rain drops. Occasionally one of the men would slouch over, poke his rifle around the corner and fire. . . .

We stayed there about half an hour. Then two gray

cannons came rocketing out of the brush behind and
wheeled into position in a dry ditch seventy-five yards
away on the left.

"I guess we're going in a minute," said the boy.

At that moment three men galloped up from the rear,
evidently officers. They were entirely exposed to rifle
fire over the roofs of the huts, but jerked up their
horses with the shots yelling all around, contemptuous
of them. The first to speak was Fierro, the superb
great animal of a man who had murdered Benton.

He sneered down at the ragged soldiers from his
saddle. "Well, this is a fine-looking crowd to take a
city with," he said. "But we've got nobody else down
here. Go in when you hear the bugle." Pulling cruelly
on the bit, so that his big horse reared straight up and
whirled on his hind legs, Fierro galloped off rearward,
saying as he went, "Useless, those simple fools of Contreras——"

"Death to the Butcher!" said a man furiously.
"That murderer killed my *compadre* in the streets of
Durango—for no crime or insult! My *compadre* was
very drunk, walking in front of the theater. He asked
Fierro what time it was, and Fierro said, You ——!
How dare you speak to me before I speak to you
first——"

But the bugle was blowing, and up they got, grabbing their guns. The tag game tried to stop, but
couldn't. Furious card players were accusing each
other of stealing the deck.

"*Oiga*, Fidencio!" cried one soldier. "I'll bet you

my saddle I come back and you don't! This morning I won a nice bridle from Juan——"

"All right! *Muy bien!* My new pinto horse. . . ."

Laughing, joking, rollicking, they swept out of the shelter of the houses into the rain of steel. They scuttled awkwardly up the street, like little brown animals unused to running. Billowing dust veiled them and a hell of noise. . . .

CHAPTER XIII

A NIGHT ATTACK

TWO or three of us had a sort of camp beside the ditch far up along the alamos. Our car, with its food supply, clothes and blankets, was still twenty miles back. Most of the time we went without meals. When we could manage to beg a few cans of sardines or some flour from the commissary train we were lucky. Wednesday one of the crowd had managed to get hold of tinned salmon, coffee, crackers and a big package of cigarettes; and as we cooked dinner Mexican after Mexican, passing on his way to the front, dismounted and joined us. After the most elaborate exchange of courtesies, in which we had to persuade our guest to eat hugely of the dinner we had painfully foraged for ourselves, and he had to comply out of politeness, he would mount and ride away without gratitude, though full of friendliness.

We stretched out on the bank in the golden twilight, smoking. The first train, headed by a flat-car upon

247

which was mounted the cannon "El Niño," had now reached a point opposite the end of the second line of trees—scarcely a mile from town. As far as you could see ahead of her, the repair gang toiled on the track. All at-once there came a terrific boom, and a little puff of smoke lifted from the front of the train. Far cheering scattered among the trees and fields. "El Niño," the darling of the army, had got within range at last. Now the Federals would sit up and take notice. She was a three-inch gun—the largest we had. . . . Later we found out that an exploratory engine had sallied forth from the Gomez roundhouse, and that a shot from "El Niño" had hit her square in the middle of the boiler and blown her up. . . .

We were to attack that night, they said, and long after dark I got on my horse, Bucephalus, and rode down front. The sign was "Herrera" and the countersign "Chihuahua number four." So as to be sure of recognition as one of "ours," the command was to pin your hat up behind. Everywhere the strictest orders had been sent out that no fires should be lit in the "zone of fire," and that anyone striking a match until the battle began should be shot by the sentries.

Bucephalus and I jogged slowly along in the moonless and absolutely silent night. Nowhere was there a light or a stir all over the vast plain before Gomez, except the far hammering of the tireless repair gang working on the track. In the town itself the electric lights shone brightly, and even a street car bound for Lerdo lost itself behind the Cerro de la Pila.

Then I heard a tiny murmuring of human voices in

the. darkness near the ditch ahead—evidently an outpost.

"*Quien vive!*" came a shout. And before I had a
chance to answer, BANG! He fired. The bullet went
past my head. *Biou!*

"No, no, you fool," drawled an exasperated voice.
"Don't shoot as soon as you challenge! Wait until he
gives the wrong answer! Listen to me, now." This
time the formality was satisfactory to both sides and
the officer said, "*Pase Usted!*" But I could hear the
original sentry growling, "Well, I don't see what
difference it makes. I never hit anybody when I
shoot. . . ."

Feeling my way carefully through the darkness, I
stumbled into the rancho of San Ramon. I knew that
the *pacificos* had all fled, so it surprised me to see light
shining around the chinks of a door. I was thirsty and
didn't care to trust the ditch. I called. A woman appeared, with a little brood of four babies clinging to her
skirts. She brought water, and all of a sudden burst
out with, "O señor, do you know where the guns of the
Brigada Zaragosa are? My man is there, and I haven't
seen him for seven days."

"Then you are not a *pacifico!*"

"Truly I am not," she returned indignantly, pointing to her children. "We belong to the artillery."

Down front the army lay stretched along the ditch
at the foot of the first line of trees. In absolute darkness they whispered to each other, waiting until the
word of Villa to the advance guard a quarter of a mile
ahead should precipitate the first rifle shots.

"Where are your rifles?" I asked.

"This brigade is to use no rifles to-night," answered a voice. "Over on the left, where they are to attack the intrenchments, there are rifles. But we must capture the Brittingham Corral to-night, and rifles are no good. We are Contreras' men, the Brigada Juarez. See, we have orders to walk up to the walls and throw these bombs inside!" He held out the bomb. It was made of a short stick of dynamite sewed in a strip of cowhide, with a fuse stuck in one end. He went on: "General Robles' *gente* are over there on the right. They, too, have *granados*, but rifles also. They are going to assault the Cerro de la Pila. . . ."

And now down the warm, still night came suddenly the sound of heavy firing from the direction of Lerdo, where Maclovio Herrera was going in with his brigade. Almost simultaneously from dead ahead rifle fire awoke sputtering. A man came down the line with a lighted cigar glowing like a firefly in the hollow of his hands.

"Light your cigarettes from this," he said, "and don't set fire to your fuses until you're right up under the wall."

"Captain, *carramba!* It's going to be very, very *duro!* How shall we know the right time?"

Another voice, deep, rough, spoke up in the dark.

"I'll tell you. Just come along with me."

A whispered, smothered shout of "Viva Villa!" burst from them. On foot, holding a lighted cigar in one hand—for he never smoked—and a bomb in the other, the General climbed the bank of the ditch and plunged into the brush, the others pouring after him. . . .

A NIGHT ATTACK

All along the line now the rifle fire roared, though
down behind the trees I could see nothing of the attack.
The artillery was silent, the troops being too close together in the dark to permit the use of shrapnel by
either side. I rode back and over to the right, where I
climbed my horse up the steep ditch bank. From there
I could see the dancing tiny fires of the guns at Lerdo,
and scattered spurts like a string of jewels all along
our front. Over to the extreme left a new and deeper
noise told where Benavides was making a demonstration
against Torreon proper with quick-firing guns. I stood
tensely awaiting the attack.

It came with the force of an explosion. In the direction of the Brittingham Corral, which I could not see,
the syncopated rhythm of four machine guns and a
continuous inhuman blast of volleying rifles made the
previous noise seem like the deepest silence. A quick
glare reddened the heaven above, and then the shock-
ing detonations of dynamite. I could imagine the yelling savages sweeping up the street against that wither-
ing flame, wavering, pausing, struggling on again, with
Villa just in front, talking to them back over his shoulder, as he always did. Now more furious firing over to
the right indicated that the attack against the Cerro
de la Pila had reached the foot of the hill. And all at
once on the far end of the ridge toward Lerdo, there
were flashes. Maclovio must have taken Lerdo! Lo!
All at once appeared a magical sight. Up the steep
slope of the Cerro, around three sides of it, slowly rose
a ring of fierce light. It was the steady flame of rifle
fire from the attackers. The summit, too, streamed

fire, which intensified as the ring converged toward it, raggeder now. A bright glare burst from the top— then another. A second later arrived the dreadful reports of cannon. They were opening upon the little line of climbing men with artillery! But still they rose upon the black hill. The ring of flame was broken now in many places, but it never faltered. So until it seemed to merge with the venomous spitting blaze at the summit. Then all at once it seemed to wither completely, and little single fireflies kept dropping down the slope—all that were left. And when I thought that all was lost, and marveled at the useless heroism of these peons who walked up a hill in the face of artillery, behold! The ring of flame was creeping slowly upward again. . . . That night they attacked the Cerro seven times on foot, and at every attack seven-eighths of them were killed. . . . All this time the infernal roaring and the play of red light over the Corral did not stop. Occasionally there seemed to come a lull, but it recommenced only more terribly. They assaulted the Corral eight times. . . . The morning that I entered Gomez, although the Federals had been steadily burning bodies for three days, they were so thick in the wide space before the Brittingham Corral that I could hardly ride through on horseback, and around the Cerro were seven distinct ridges of rebel dead. . . .

The wounded began creeping through the plain obscurely in the dense darkness. Their cries and groans could be distinctly heard, though the battle noise drowned every other sound—you could even hear the rustle of the bushes as they crept through, and their dragging feet on the sand. A horseman passed along the path below me, cursing furiously that he must leave the battle because his arm was broken, and weeping between curses. Then came a footman, who sat at the foot of my bank and nursed a hand, talking without cessation about all sorts of things to keep from a nervous breakdown.

"How brave we Mexicans are," he said drolly. "Killing each other like this! . . ."

I soon went back to camp, sick with boredom. A battle is the most boring thing in the world if it lasts any length of time. It is all the same. . . . And in the morning I went to get the news at headquarters. We had captured Lerdo, but the Cerro, the Corral and the cuartel were still the enemy's. All that slaughter for nothing!

CHAPTER XIV

THE FALL OF GOMEZ PALACIO

E L NINO" was now within half a mile of the town, and the workmen of the repair gang labored on the last stretch of track under heavy shrapnel fire. The two cannon on the front of the trains bore all the brunt of their artillery, and bravely did they return the fire—so well, in fact, that after one Federal shell had killed ten workmen, "El Niño's" captain put two guns on the Cerro out of action. So the

Federals left the trains alone and turned their attention to shelling Herrera out of Lerdo.

The Constitutionalist army was terribly shattered. In the four days' fighting about a thousand men had been killed and almost two thousand more wounded. Even the excellent hospital train was inadequate to handle the wounded. Out on the wide plain where we were the faint smell of dead bodies pervaded everything. In Gomez it must have been horrible. Thursday the smoke from twenty funeral pyres stained the sky. But Villa was more determined than ever. Gomez must be taken, and quickly. He didn't have ammunition or supplies enough for a siege, and, moreover, his name was a legend already with the enemy—wherever Pancho Villa appeared in battle, they had begun to believe it lost. And the effect on his own troops was most important, too. So he scheduled another night attack.

"The track is all repaired," reported Calzado, Superintendent of the Railways.

"Good," said Villa. "Bring up all the trains from the rear to-night, because we're going into Gomez in the morning!"

Night fell; breathless, silent night, with a sound of frogs along the ditches. Across the front of the town the soldiers lay waiting for the word to attack. Wounded, worn out, nervously broken, they straggled to the front, keyed up to the last notch of desperation. This night they would not be repulsed. They would take the town or die where they stood. And as nine o'clock approached, the hour at which the attack had been set, the tension became dangerous.

THE FALL OF GOMEZ PALACIO

Nine o'clock came and passed—not a sound or movement. For some reason the order was withheld. Ten o'clock. Suddenly off to the right a volley burst from the town. All along our line awoke the answer, but after a few more volleys the Federal fire altogether ceased. From the town came other, more mysterious sounds. The electric lights went out and in the darkness there was a subtle stir and movement, indefinable. At length the order was given to advance, but as our men crept forward in the dark the front rank suddenly gave a yell, and the truth spread through the ranks and out into the country, in one triumphant shout. Gomez Palacio had been evacuated! With a great babble of voices the army poured into the town. A few scattered shots sounded where our troops caught some of the Federals looting—for the Federal army had gutted the whole town before it left. And then our army began to loot. Their shouts and drunken singing and the sounds of smashing doors reached us out on the plain. Little tongues of flame flickered up where the soldiers were burning some house that had been a fort of Federals. But the looting of the rebels was confined, as it almost always is, to food, and drink, and clothes to cover them. They disturbed no private house.

The chiefs of the army winked at this. A specific order was issued by Villa stating that whatever any soldier picked up was his and could not be taken from him by an officer. Now up to this time there was not much of stealing in the army—at least so far as we were concerned. But the morning of the entry into

Gomez a curious change had come over the psychology
of the soldiers. I woke at our camp beside the ditch
to find my horse gone. Bucephalus had been stolen in
the night and I never saw him again. During breakfast several troopers dropped in to share our meal—
when they had gone we missed a knife and a revolver.
The truth was that everybody was looting from everybody else. So I, too, stole what I needed. There was a
great gray mule grazing in the field near by, with a
rope around his neck. I put my saddle on him and
rode down toward the front. He was a noble animal—
worth at least four times as much as Bucephalus, as
I soon discovered. Everybody I met coveted that mule.
One trooper marching along with two rifles hailed me.
"*Oija, compañero,* where did you get that mule?"

"I found him in a field," said I unwisely.

"It is just as I thought," he exclaimed. "That is my
mule! Get off and give him to me at once!"

"And is this your saddle?" I asked.

"By the Mother of God, it is!"

"Then you lie about the mule, for the saddle is my
own." I rode on, leaving him yelling in the road. A
short distance farther on an old peon walking along
suddenly ran up and threw his arms around the animal's neck.

"Ah, at last! My beautiful mule which I lost! My
Juanito!" I shook him off in spite of his entreaties
that at least I should pay him fifty pesos as compen-
sation for his mule. In town a cavalryman rode across
in front of me, demanding his mule at once. He was
rather ugly and had a revolver. I got away by saying

that I was a captain of artillery and that the mule belonged to my battery. Every few feet some owner of that mule sprang up and asked me how dared I ride his own dear Panchito, or Pedrito, or Tomasito! At last one came out of a cuartel with a written order from his Colonel, who had seen the mule from his window. I showed them my pass signed by Francisco Villa. That was enough. . . .

Across the wide desert, where the Constitutionalists had fought so long, the army was winding in from every direction, in long snake-like columns, dust hanging over them. And along the track, as far as the eye could reach, came. the trains, one after another, blowing triumphant whistles, crowded with thousands of women and soldiers cheering. Within the city, dawn had brought absolute quiet and order. With the entrance of Villa and his staff the looting had absolutely ceased and the soldiers again respected other people's property. A thousand were hard at work gathering up the bodies and carrying them to the edge of the city, where they were set on fire. Five hundred more policed the town. The first order issued was that any soldier caught drinking should be shot.

In the third train was our car—the private box-car fitted up for the correspondents, photographers and moving-picture men. At last we had our bunks, our blankets, and Fong, our beloved Chinese cook. The car was switched up near in the railway station—in the very front rank of trains. And as we gathered in its grateful interior, hot, dusty and worn out, the Federals

in Torreon dropped a few shrapnel shells right close
beside us. I was standing in the door of the car at the
time and heard the boom of cannon, but paid no particular attention to it. Suddenly I noticed a small object in the air like an exaggerated beetle, trailing a
little spiral of black smoke behind it. It passed the
door of the car with a zzzzzing noise and about forty
feet beyond burst with a frightful Crash—Whee-e-e-
eeaa!! among the trees of a park where a company of
cavalry and their women were camping. A hundred
men leaped for their plunging horses in a panic and
galloped frantically toward the rear, the women streaming after them. Two women had been killed, it seemed,
and a horse. Blankets, food, rifles—all were discarded
in the panic. Pow! Another burst on the other side
of the car. They were very close. Behind us on the
track twenty long trains, laden with shrilly screaming
women, were trying to back out of the yards all at
once, with a mighty hysterical tooting of whistles. Two
or three more shells followed, then we could hear "El
Niño" replying.

But the effect on the correspondents and newspaper
men was peculiar. No sooner had the first shell exploded than someone produced the whisky jug, entirely
of his own impulse, and we passed it around. No one
said a word, but everybody drank a stiff swig as it came
his way. Every time a shell would explode nearby we
would all wince and jump, but after a while we did not
mind it. Then we began to congratulate each other
and ourselves for being so brave as to stay by the car
under artillery fire. Our courage increased as the firing

grew far between and finally quit altogether, and as the whisky grew low. Everybody forgot dinner.

I remember that in the darkness two belligerent Anglo-Saxons stood at the door of the car, challenging the soldiers who passed and abusing them in the most discourteous language. We fell out among ourselves, too, and one man almost choked a driveling old fool who was with the moving-picture outfit. Late that night we were still trying earnestly to persuade two of the boys not to sally forth without the pass-word and reconnoiter the Federal lines at Torreon.

"Aw, what's there to be afraid of?" cried they. "A Mexican greaser hasn't any guts! One American can lick fifty Mexicans! Why, did you see how they ran this afternoon when the shells hit that grove? And how we—hic—we staid by the car?"

PART FIVE

CARRANZA—AN IMPRESSION

CARRANZA—AN IMPRESSION

WHEN the Treaty of Peace was signed in Juarez which ended the Revolution of 1910, Francisco Madero proceeded south toward Mexico City. Everywhere he spoke to enthusiastic and triumphant throngs of peons, who acclaimed him The Liberator.

In Chihuahua he addressed the people from the balcony of the Governor's palace. As he told of the hardships endured and the sacrifices made by the little band of men who had overthrown the dictatorship of Diaz forever, he was overcome with emotion. Reaching inside the room he pulled out a tall, bearded man of commanding presence, and, throwing his arm about his shoulder, he said, in a voice choked with tears:

"This is a good man! Love and honor him always."

It was Venustiano Carranza, a man of upright life and high ideals; an aristocrat, descended from the dominant Spanish race; a great land-owner, as his family had always been great land-owners; and one of those Mexican nobles who, like a few French nobles such as Lafayette in the French Revolution, threw themselves heart and soul into the struggle for liberty. When the Madero Revolution broke out Carranza took the

263

field in truly medieval fashion. He armed the peons who worked upon his great estates, and led them to war like any feudal overlord; and, when the Revolution was done, Madero made him Governor of Coahuila.

There he was when Madero was murdered at the Capital, and Huerta, seizing the Presidency, sent a circular letter to the Governors of the different States, ordering them to acknowledge the new dictatorship. Carranza refused even to answer the letter, declaring that he would have no dealings with a murderer and a usurper. He issued a proclamation calling the Mexican people to arms, proclaiming himself First Chief of the Revolution, and inviting the friends of liberty to rally around him. Then he marched out from his capital and took the field, where he assisted in the early fighting around Torreon.

After a short time Carranza marched his force from Coahuila, where things were happening, straight across the Republic into the State of Sonora, where nothing was happening. Villa had begun heavy fighting in Chihuahua State, Urbina and Herrera in Durango, Blanco and others in Coahuila, and Gonzales near Tampico. In times of upheaval like these it is inevitable that there shall be some preliminary squabbling over the ultimate spoils of war. Among the military leaders, however, there was no such dissension; Villa having just been unanimously elected General Chief of the Constitutionalist Army by a remarkable gathering of all the independent guerrilla leaders before Torreon, —an unheard-of event in Mexican history. But over in Sonora, Maytorena and Pesquiera were already

CARRANZA—AN IMPRESSION

squabbling over who should be Governor of the State, and threatening revolutions against each other. Carranza's reported purpose in crossing to the West with his army was to settle this dispute. But that doesn't seem possible.

Other explanations are that he desired to secure a seaport for the Constitutionalists on the West; that he wanted to settle the Yaqui land question; and that in the quiet of a comparatively peaceful State he could better organize the provisional government of the new Republic. He remained there six months, apparently doing nothing whatever, keeping a force of more than 6,000 good fighters practically inoperative, attending banquets and bull-fights, establishing and celebrating innumerable new national holidays, and issuing proclamations. His army, twice or three times as big as the disheartened garrisons of Guaymas and Mazatlan, kept up a lazy siege of those places. Mazatlan fell only a short time ago, I think; as did Guaymas. Only a few weeks ago Provisional-Governor Maytorena was threatening counter-revolutions against General Alvardo, Chief of Arms of Sonora, because he would not guarantee the Governor's safety, and evidently proposing to upset the Revolution because Maytorena was uncomfortable in the palace at Hermosillo. During all that time not a word was said about any aspect of the land question, as far as I could learn. The Yaqui Indians, the expropriation of whose lands is the blackest spot in the whole black history of the Diaz régime, got nothing but a vague promise. Upon that the whole tribe joined the Revolution. But a few

265

months later most of them went back to their homes
and began again their hopeless campaign against the
white man.

Carranza hibernated until early in the spring of
this year, when, the purpose of his Sonora sojourn
evidently having been accomplished, he turned his face
toward the territory where the real Revolution was
being fought.

Within that six months the aspect of things had
entirely changed. Except for the northern part of
Nueva Leon, and most of Coahuila, northern Mexico
was Constitutionalist territory almost from sea to
sea, and Villa, with a well-armed, well-disciplined force
of 10,000 men, was entering on the Torreon campaign.
All this was accomplished almost single-handed by
Villa; Carranza seems to have contributed nothing but
congratulations. He had, indeed, formed a provisional
government. An immense throng of opportunist politicians surrounded the First Chief, loud in their protestations of devotion to the Cause, liberal with proclamations, and extremely jealous of each other and of
Villa. Little by little Carranza's personality seemed
to be engulfed in the personality of his Cabinet, although his name remained as prominent as ever.

It was a curious situation. Correspondents who
were with him during these months have told me how
secluded the First Chief finally became. They almost
never saw him. Very rarely did they speak with him.
Various secretaries, officials, Cabinet members, stood
between them and him—polite, diplomatic, devious gen-

tlemen, who transmitted their questions to Carranza on paper and brought them back his answers written out; so that there would be no mistake.

But, whatever he did, Carranza left Villa strictly alone, to undergo defeats if he must, or make mistakes; so much so that Villa himself was forced to deal with foreign powers as if he were the head of the government.

There is no doubt that the politicians at Hermosillo sought in every way to make Carranza jealous of Villa's growing power in the north. In February the First Chief began a leisurely journey northward, accompanied by 3,000 troops, with the ostensible object of sending reinforcements to Villa and of making his provisional capital in Juarez when Villa left for Torreon. Two correspondents, however, who had been in Sonora, told me that the officers of this immense bodyguard believed that they were to be sent against Villa himself.

In Hermosillo Carranza had been remote from the world's new centers. No one knew but what he might be accomplishing great things. But when the First Chief of the Revolution began to move toward the American border, the attention of the world was concentrated upon him; and the attention of the world revealed so little to concentrate upon, that rumors rapidly spread of the non-existence of Carranza; for example, one paper said that he was insane, and another alleged that he had disappeared altogether.

I was in Chihuahua at the time. My paper wired me these rumors and ordered me to go and find Carranza. It was at the immensely exciting time of the Benton murder. All the protestations and half-veiled threats of the British and American governments converged upon Villa. But by the time I had received the message Carranza and his Cabinet had arrived at the Border and broken the six months' silence in a startling way. The First Chief's declaration to the State Department was practically this:

"You have made a mistake in addressing representations in the Benton case to General Villa. They should be addressed to me as First Chief of the Revolution and head of the Provisional Constitutionalist Government. Moreover, the United States has no business to address, even to me, any representations concerning Benton, who was a British subject. I have received no envoy from the government of Great Britain. Until I do I will make no answer to the representations of any other government. Meanwhile, a thorough investigation will be made of the circumstances of Benton's death, and those responsible for it will be judged strictly according to law."

At the same time Villa received a pretty plain intimation that he was to keep out of international affairs, and Villa gratefully shut up.

That was the situation when I went to Nogales. Nogales, Arizona, and Nogales, Sonora, Mexico, really form one big straggling town. The international boundary runs along the middle of the street, and at a small customs-house lounge a few ragged Mexican sentries, smoking interminable cigarettes, and evidently interfering with nobody, except to collect export taxes from everything that passes to the American side. The inhabitants of the American town go across the line to get good things to eat, to gamble, to dance, and to feel free; the Mexicans cross to the American side when somebody is after them.

I arrived at midnight and went at once to a hotel in the Mexican town where the Cabinet and most of the political hangers-on of Carranza were staying; sleeping four in a room, on cots in the corridors, on the floor, and even on the stairs. I was expected. A temperamental Constitutionalist consul up the line, to whom I had explained my errand, evidently considered it of great importance; for he had telegraphed to Nogales that the entire fate of the Mexican Revolution depended upon Mr. Reed's seeing the First Chief of the Revolution immediately upon his arrival. However, everybody had gone to sleep, and the proprietor, routed out of his back office, said that he hadn't the slightest idea what the names of any of the gentlemen were or where they slept. Yes, he said, he had heard that Carranza was in town. We went around kicking doors and Mexicans until we stumbled upon an unshaven but courteous gentleman who said that he was the Collector of Customs for the whole of Mexico under the new government. He waked up in turn the Secretary of the Navy, who routed out the Secretary of the Treasury; the Secretary of the Treasury finally flushed the Secretary of Hacienda, who finally brought us to the room of the Secretary of Foreign Relations, Señor Isidro Fabela. Señor Fabela said

269

that the First Chief had retired and couldn't see me; but that he himself would give me immediately a statement of just what Carranza thought about the Benton incident.

Now none of the newspapers had ever heard of Señor Fabela before. They were all clamoring to their correspondents, wanting to know who he was. He seemed to be such an important member of the provisional government, and yet his antecedents were not known at all. At different times he apparently filled most of the positions in the First Chief's Cabinet. Rather medium height and distinguished-looking, suave, courteous, and evidently very well educated, his face was decidedly Jewish. We talked for a long time, sitting on the edge of his bed. He told me what the First Chief's aims and ideals were; but in them I could discern nothing of the First Chief's personality whatever.

"Oh, yes," he said, "of course I could see the First Chief in the morning. Of course he would receive me."

But when we came right down to cases, Señor Fabela told me that the First Chief would answer no questions outright. They had all to be put in writing, he said, and submitted to Fabela first. He would then take them to Carranza and bring back his answer. Accordingly, the next morning I wrote out on paper about twenty-five questions and gave them to Fabela. He read them carefully.

"Ah!" he said; "there are many questions here that I know the First Chief will not answer. I advise you to strike them out."

CARRANZA—AN IMPRESSION

"Well, if he doesn't answer them," I said, "all right. But I would like to give him a chance to see them. He could only refuse to answer them."

"No," said Fabela, politely. "You had better strike them out now. I know exactly what he will answer and what he will not. You see, some of your questions might prejudice him against answering all the rest, and you would not want that to occur, would you?"

"Señor Fabela," I said, "are you sure that you know just what Don Venustiano won't answer?"

"I know that he won't answer these," he replied, indicating four or five which dealt rather specifically with the platform of the Constitutionalist government: such as land distribution, direct elections, and the right of suffrage among the peons.

"I will bring back your answers in twenty-four hours," he said. "Now I will take you to see the Chief; but you must promise me this: that you will not ask him any questions,—that you will simply go into the room, shake hands with him, and say 'How do you do,' and leave again immediately."

I promised, and, together with another reporter, followed him across the square to the beautiful little yellow municipal palace. We stood a while in the patio. The place was thronged with self-important Mexicans button-holing other self-important Mexicans who rushed from door to door with portfolios and bundles of papers. Occasionally, when the door of the Department of the Secretaryship opened, a roar of typewriters smote our ears. Officers in uniform stood about the portico waiting for orders. General Obregon,

Commander of the Army of Sonora, was outlining in a loud voice the plans for his march south upon Guadalajara. He started for Hermosillo three days afterward, and marched his army four hundred miles through a friendly country in three months. Although Obregon had shown no startling capacity for leadership, Carranza had made him General-in-Chief of the Army of the North-West, with a rank equal to Villa's. Talking to him was a stout, red-haired Mexican woman in a black satin princess dress embroidered with jet, with a sword at her side. She was Colonel Ramona Flores, Chief-of-Staff to the Constitutionalist General Carrasco, who operates in Tepic. Her husband had been killed while an officer in the first Revolution, leaving her a gold-mine, with the proceeds of which she had raised a regiment and taken the field. Against the wall lay two sacks of gold ingots which she had brought north to purchase arms and uniforms for her troops. Polite American concession-seekers shifted from one foot to the other, hat in hand. The ever-present arms and ammunition drummers poured into the ears of whoever would listen, praises of their guns and bullets.

Four armed sentries stood at the palace doors, and others lounged around the patio. There were no more in sight, except two who flanked a little door half-way down the corridor. These men seemed more intelligent than the others. Anybody who passed was scrutinized carefully, and those who paused at the door were questioned according to some thorough formula. Every two hours this guard was changed; the relief was in charge of a general, and a long colloquy took place before the change was effected.

"What room is that?" I asked Señor Fabela.

"That is the office of the First Chief of the Revolution," he answered.

I waited for perhaps an hour, and during that time I noticed that nobody entered the room except Señor Fabela and those he took with him. Finally he came over to me and said:

"All right. The First Chief will see you now."

We followed him. The soldiers on guard threw up their rifles.

"Who are these señores?" asked one.

"It's all right. They are friends," answered Fabela, and opened the door.

It was so dark within that at first we could see nothing. Over the two windows blinds were drawn. On one side was a bed, still unmade, and on the other a small table covered with papers, upon which stood a tray containing the remains of breakfast. A tin bucket full of ice with two or three bottles of wine stood in a corner. As our eyes became accustomed to the light, we saw the gigantic, khaki-clad figure of Don Venustiano Carranza sitting in a big chair. There was something strange in the way he sat there, with his hands on the arms of the chair, as if he had been placed in it and told not to move. He did not seem to be thinking, nor to have been working,—you couldn't imagine him at that table. You got the impression of a vast, inert body—a statue.

He rose to meet us, a towering figure, seven feet tall it seemed. I noticed with a kind of shock that in that dark room he wore smoked glasses; and, although ruddy and full-cheeked, I felt that he was not well,—the thing you feel about tuberculous patients. That tiny, dark room, where the First Chief of the Revolution slept and ate and worked, and from which he hardly ever emerged, seemed too small—like a cell.

Fabela had entered with us. He introduced us one by one to Carranza, who smiled a vacant, expressionless smile, bowed slightly, and shook our hands. We all sat down. Indicating the other reporter, who could not speak Spanish, Fabela said:

"These gentlemen have come to greet you on behalf of the great newspapers which they represent. This gentleman says that he desires to present his respectful wishes for your success."

Carranza bowed again slightly, and rose as Fabela stood up, as if to indicate that the interview was over.

"Allow me to assure the gentlemen," he said, "of my grateful acceptance of their good wishes."

Again we all shook hands; but as I took his hand I said in Spanish:

"Señor Don Venustiano, my paper is your friend and the friend of the Constitutionalists."

He stood there as before, a huge mask of a man. But as I spoke he stopped smiling. His expression remained as vacant as before, but suddenly he began to speak:

"To the United States I say the Benton case is none

of your business. Benton was a British subject. I will answer to the delegates of Great Britain when they come to me with representations of their government. Why should they not come to me? England now has an Ambassador in Mexico City, who accepts invitations to dinner from Huerta, takes off his hat to him, and shakes hands with him!

"When Madero was murdered the foreign powers flocked to the spot like vultures to the dead, and fawned upon the murderer because they had a few subjects in the Republic who were petty tradesmen doing a dirty little business."

The First Chief ended as abruptly as he had begun, with the same immobility of expression, but he clenched and unclenched his hands and gnawed his mustaches. Fabela hurriedly made a move toward the door.

"The gentlemen are very grateful to you for having received them," he said, nervously. But Don Venustiano paid no attention to him. Suddenly he began again, his voice pitched a little higher and louder:

"These cowardly nations thought they could secure advantages by standing in with the government of the usurper. But the rapid advancement of the Constitutionalists showed them their error, and now they find themselves in a predicament."

Fabela was plainly nervous.

"When does the Torreon campaign begin?" he asked, attempting to change the subject.

"The killing of Benton was due to a vicious attack on Villa by an enemy of the Revolutionists," roared the First Chief, speaking louder and louder and more rapidly; "and England, the bully of the world, finds herself unable to deal with us unless she humiliates herself by sending a representative to the Constitutionalists; so she tried to use the United States as a cat's paw. More shame to the United States," he cried, shaking his fists, "that she allowed herself to 'join with these infamous Powers!"

The unhappy Fabela made another attempt to dam the dangerous torrent. But Carranza took a step forward, and, raising his arm, shouted:

"I tell you that, if the United States intervenes in Mexico upon this petty excuse, intervention will not accomplish what it thinks, but will provoke a war which, besides its own consequences, will deepen a profound hatred between the United States and the whole of Latin America, a hatred which will endanger the entire political future of the United States!"

He ceased talking on a rising note, as if something inside had cut off his speech. I tried to think that here was the voice of aroused Mexico thundering at her enemies; but it seemed like nothing so much as a slightly senile old man, tired and irritated.

Then we were outside in the sunlight, with Señor Fabela agitatedly telling me not to publish what I had heard,—or, at least, to let him see the dispatch.

I stayed at Nogales a day or two longer. The next day after my interview, the typewritten paper upon which my questions had been printed was returned to me; the answers written in five different handwritings.

CARRANZA—AN IMPRESSION

Newspaper men were in high favor at Nogales; they were treated always with the utmost courtesy by the members of the Provisional Cabinet; but they never seemed to reach the First Chief. I tried often to get from these Cabinet members the least expression of what their plans were for the settlement of the troubles which caused the Revolution; but they seemed to have none, except a Constitutional Government. During all the times I talked with them I never detected one gleam of sympathy for, or understanding of, the peons. Now and again I surprised quarrels about who was going to fill the high posts of the new Mexican Government. Villa's name was hardly ever mentioned; when it was it was in this manner:

"We have every confidence in Villa's loyalty and obedience."

"As a fighting man Villa has done very well—very well, indeed. But he should not attempt to mingle in the affairs of Government; because, of course, you know, Villa is only an ignorant peon."

"He has said many foolish things and made many mistakes which we will have to remedy."

And scarcely a day passed but what Carranza would give out a statement from headquarters:

"There is no misunderstanding between General Villa and myself. He obeys my orders without question, as any common soldier. It is unthinkable that he would do anything else."

I spent a good deal of time loafing around the Municipal Palace; but I never saw Carranza again but once. It was toward sunset, and most of the Generals, drummers, and politicians had gone to dinner. I lounged on the edge of the fountain in the middle of the patio, talking with some soldiers. Suddenly the door of that little office opened, and Carranza himself stood framed in it, arms hanging loosely by his sides, his fine old head thrown back, as he stared blindly over our heads across the wall to the flaming clouds in the west. We stood up and bowed, but he didn't notice us. Walking with slow steps, he came out and went along the portico toward the door of the palace. The two guards presented arms. As he passed they shouldered their rifles and fell in behind him. At the doorway he stopped and stood there a long time, looking out on the street. The four sentries jumped to attention. The two men behind him grounded their arms and stopped. The First Chief of the Revolution clasped his hands behind his back, his fingers working violently. Then he turned, and pacing between the two guards, went back to the little dark room.

PART SIX

MEXICAN NIGHTS

CHAPTER I

EL COSMOPOLITA

EL COSMOPOLITA is Chihuahua's fashionable gambling hell. It used to be owned by Jacob La Touche—"The Turk"—a fat shambling man, who came to Chihuahua barefooted with a dancing bear twenty-five years ago, and became many times a millionaire. He owned an extravagant residence on the Paseo Bolivar, which was never called anything but "The Palace of Tears," because it was built with the proceeds of the Turk's gambling concessions, which ruined many families. But the wicked old man slunk away with Mercado's retreating Federal army; and when Villa came to Chihuahua he gave "The Palace of Tears" to General Ortega as a Christmas present, and confiscated El Cosmopolita.

Having a few idle pesos from my expense account, we used to frequent El Cosmopolita. Johnny Roberts and I stopped on our way from the hotel to take a few hot Tom-and-Jerries at a Chinese bar, run by a hoary Mongolian named Chee Lee. From there we proceeded to the gaming tables with the leisurely air of Russian Grand Dukes at Monte Carlo.

One entered first a long, low room, lighted with three smoky lanterns, where the roulette game was.

Above the table was a sign which read:

"Please do not get on the roulette table with your feet."

It was a vertical wheel, not a horizontal one, bristling with spikes which caught a flexible steel strip and finally stopped the wheel opposite a number. Each way the table extended twelve feet, always crowded with at least five rows of small boys, peons, and soldiers—excited and gesticulating, tossing a rain of small bills on the numbers and colors, and arguing violently over the winnings. Those who lost would set up terrible screams of rage as the croupier raked their money into the drawer, and often the wheel was quiet for three-quarters of an hour while some player, who had lost ten cents, exhausted his vocabulary upon the treasurer, the owner of the place and his ancestors and descendants ten generations each way, and upon God and his family, for allowing such injustice to go unpunished. Finally he would take himself off, muttering ominously: *"Á ver!* We shall see!" while the others would sympathetically make way for him, murmuring: *"Ah! Que mala suerte!"*

Near where the croupier sat was a worn place in the cloth with a small ivory button in the center. And when anyone was winning largely at the wheel the croupier would press this little button, which stopped the wheel where he wished, until the winner was discouraged from playing further. This was looked upon as perfectly legitimate by all present, since, *carramba!,* there is no sense in operating a gambling house at a loss!

EL COSMOPOLITA

The most amazing diversity of money was used.
Silver and copper had long since been forced out of
circulation in Chihuahua because of revolutionary
hard times. But there were still some Mexican bank-
bills; besides those there was *fiat* money, printed on
ordinary writing-paper by the Constitutionalist army,
and worth nothing; scrip issued by the mining companies; I. O. U.'s; notes of hand; mortgages; and a
hundred different *valés* of various railroads, planta-
tions, and public service corporations.

But the roulette table did not long interest us.
There was not enough action for your money. So
we shouldered our way into a small room, blue with
smoke, where a perpetual poker game was going at a
fan-shaped, baize-covered table. At a little recess at
the straight side of the table sat the dealer; chairs
were distributed around the circumference where the
players sat. One played against the bank, the dealer
scraping into the drawer a tenth of every pot—
the house's commission. Whenever anyone began to
plunge, and displayed a large wad, the dealer would
give a shrill, penetrating whistle and two suave gentlemen, who were employed by the house, would come
running and take a hand. There was no limit as long
as you had chips, or if your stack was underlaid with
bank-bills. The gentleman in possession of the "buck"
had the say whether it was to be draw poker (*cerrado*)
or stud (*abierto*). Stud was the most fun, because
a Mexican could never realize that the next card
would not give him a magnificent hand, and he bet

increasing amounts on every card with wildly growing excitement.

The strict rules of the American game, which so restrict freedom of action, were absent here. Johnny and I would lift a corner of our cards as soon as they were dealt, to show each other. And when I seemed to be drawing ahead Johnny would impulsively push his whole stack over to me; with the next card Johnny's hand would seem to have more promise than mine, and I would push both stacks back to him. By the time the last card was dealt all the chips would be laying neutrally between us, and whoever had the best hand bet our entire joint capital.

Of course nobody objected to this way of playing, but to offset it the dealer would whistle shrilly to the two house players and slyly deal them each a hand off the bottom of the pack.

Meanwhile a Chinaman would be dashing madly between the table and a lunch-counter across the street, bearing sandwiches, *chile con carne*, and cups of coffee to the players, who ate and drank loudly during the game, and spilled coffee and food into the jack-pot.

Occasionally some player who had traveled extensively in foreign lands got up and walked around his chair to dispel a run of bad luck; or asked for a new deck with an off-hand, expensive air. The dealer would bow politely, sweep the deck into his drawer and produce another one. He had only two decks of cards in the house. Both were about a year old, and largely decorated with the meals of former players.

Of course, the American game was played. But

there would sometimes enter a Mexican who was not intimately acquainted with the subtleties of the American deck. In the Mexican deck, for example, the seven, eight and nine spots are omitted. One such person, a pompous, pretentious Mexican, sat in one night just as I had called for a hand of stud. Before the dealer could whistle, the stranger had produced a great wad of money—all sorts, sizes and denominations, and bought one hundred pesos' worth of chips. The game was on. I drew three hearts in rapid succession, secured Roberts' pile, and began to play for a flush. The stranger gazed at his cards for a long time as if they were new to him. Then he flushed the deep red of intense excitement, and pushed in fifteen dollars. With the succeeding card he turned quite pale and pushed in twenty-five dollars, and when he looked at his last card he turned red again, and bet fifty dollars.

By some miracle I had filled a flush. But the man's wild betting scared me. I knew that a flush was good for almost anything in stud poker, but I couldn't keep up with that pace, so I passed the bet to him. He rose at that and protested violently.

"How do you mean 'Pass the bet?'" he cried, shaking both fists.

It was explained to him, and he subsided.

"Very well, then," he said. "Since this fifteen dollars is all I have, and you will not let me buy any more chips, I will bet everything," and he pushed it into the center.

I called him.

"What have you got?" he almost screamed, leaning

trembling over the table. I spread out my flush. With an excited laugh he banged the table a great blow.

"Straight!" he cried—and turned up four, five, six, ten, Jack.

He had already reached out an arm to gather in the money when the entire table burst into a clamor.

"It is wrong!"

"It is not a straight!"

"The money belongs to the Gringo!"

He lay sprawled out on the table with both arms round the pot.

"How?" he cried sharply, looking up. "It is not a straight? Look here—four, five, six, ten, knave!"

The dealer interposed:

"But it should have been four, five, six, seven, eight," he said. "In the American pack there are seven, eight and nine."

"How ridiculous!" sneered the man. "I have played cards all my life, and never, never have I seen a seven, eight or nine!"

By this time most of the roulette table throng had swarmed in at the door. They added their clamor to ours.

"Of course it is not a straight!"

"Of course it must be! Is there not four, five, six, ten, knave?"

"But the American pack is different!"

"But this is not the United States. This is Mexico!"

"Hey! Pancho!" shouted the dealer. "Go at once and notify the police!"

EL COSMOPOLITA

The situation remained the same. My opponent still lay upon the table with the jack-pot in his arms. A perfect pandemonium of argument filled the place; in some cases it had developed a personal note, and hands were stealing to hips. I unobtrusively pushed my chair against the wall. Presently the Chief of Police arrived with four or five gendarmes. He was a large, unshaven man whose mustaches twisted up to his eyes; dressed in a loose, dirty uniform with red plush epaulettes. As he came in everybody began explaining to him at once. The dealer made a megaphone out of his hands and shouted through the din; the man on the table turned up a livid face, insisting shrilly that it was an outrage for Gringo rules to spoil a perfectly good Mexican game like stud poker.

The chief listened, curling his mustaches, his chest swelling with the importance of being the deciding factor in an argument involving such large sums of money. He looked at me. I said nothing, but bowed politely. He returned the bow. Then, turning to his policeman he pointed a dramatic finger at the man at the table.

"Arrest this goat!" he said.

It was a fitting climax. Shrieking and protesting, the unfortunate Mexican was led into a corner, where he stood facing the table.

"The money belongs to this gentleman," continued the Chief of Police. "As for you, you evidently do not understand the rudiments of this game. I have a mind. . . ."

"Perhaps," said Roberts, politely, nudging me,

"the Señor Captain would like to show the gentle-man. . . . ?"

"I should be only too glad to loan him a few chips," I added, raking in the pile.

"*Oiga!*" said the Chief. "I will be glad to do so. Superlative thanks, sir!"

He drew up a chair, and, out of politeness, the buck was given to him.

"*Abierto!*" he said, with the air of an old hand.

We played. The Chief of Police won. He rattled his chips like a professional gambler, slapping the buck to his neighbor, and we played again.

"You see," said the Chief of Police, "it is easy if you observe the rules." He twisted his mustache, ruf-fled the cards, and pushed in twenty-five dollars. He won again.

After some time one of the policemen approached him respectfully and said:

"I beg you pardon, *mi capitan*, but what shall we do with the prisoner?"

"Oh!" said the Chief, staring. He waved his hand casually. "Just release him and return to your sta-tions."

Long after the last wheel had been spun on the roulette table, the lamps blown out, and the most feverish gambler ejected into the street, we sat play-ing in the poker room. Roberts and I were down to about three pesos apiece. We yawned and nodded with sleepiness. But the Chief of Police had his coat off and was crouched like a tiger over his cards. Now he was losing steadily. . . .

CHAPTER II

HAPPY VALLEY

IT happened to be the day of a fiesta, and, of course, nobody worked in Valle Allegre. The cock-fight was to take place at high noon in the open space back of Catarino Cabrera's drinking shop —almost directly in front of Dionysio Aguirre's, where the long burro pack-trains rest on their mountain journeys, and the muleteers swap tales over their *tequila*. At one, the sunny side of the dry arroyo that is called a street was lined with double rows of squatting peons—silent, dreamily sucking their corn-husk cigarettes as they waited. The bibulously inclined drifted in and out of Catarino's, whence came a cloud of tobacco smoke and a strong reek of *aguardiente*. Small boys played leap-frog with a large yellow sow, and on opposite sides of the arroyo the competing roosters, tethered by the leg, crew defiantly. One of the owners, an ingratiating, business-like professional, wearing sandals and one cerise sock, stalked around with a handful of dirty bank-bills, shouting:

"*Diez pesos*, señores! Only ten dollars!"

It was strange; nobody seemed too poor to bet ten dollars. It came on toward two o'clock, and still no one moved, except to follow the sun a few feet as it swung the black edge of the shadow eastward. The shadow was very cold, and the sun white hot.

On the edge of the shadow lay Ignacio, the violinist,

wrapped in a tattered serape, sleeping off a drunk. He can play one tune when intoxicated—Tosti's "Good-Bye." When very drunk he also remembers fragments of Mendelssohn's "Spring Song." In fact, he is the only high-brow musician in the whole State of Durango, and possesses a just celebrity. Ignacio used to be brilliant and industrious—his sons and daughters are innumerable—but the artistic temperament was too much for him.

The color of the street was red—deep, rich, red clay—and the open space where the burros stood, olive drab; there were brown crumbling adobe walls and squat houses, their roofs heaped high with yellow corn-stalks or hung with strings of red peppers. A gigantic green mesquite tree, with roots like a chicken's foot, thatched on every branch with dried hay and corn. Below, the town fell steeply down the arroyo, roofs tumbled together like blocks, with flowers and grass growing on them, blue feathers of smoke waving from the chimneys, and occasional palms sticking up between. They fell away to the yellow plain where the horse-races are run, and beyond that the barren mountains crouched, tawny as lions, then faintly blue, then purple and wrinkled, notched and jagged across the fierce, bright sky. Straight down and away through the arroyo one saw a great valley, like an elephant's hide, where the heat-waves buck-jumped.

A lazy smoke of human noises floated up: roosters crowing, pigs grunting, burros giving great racking sobs, the rustling crackle of dried corn-stalks being shaken out of the mesquite tree, a woman singing as she mashed her corn on the stones, the wailing of a myriad of babies.

The sun fairly blistered. My friend Atanacio sat upon the sidewalk thinking of nothing. His dirty feet were bare except for sandals, his mighty sombrero was of a faded dull brick color embroidered with tarnished gold braid, and his serape was of the pottery blue one sees in Chinese rugs, and decorated with yellow suns. He rose when he saw me. We removed our hats and embraced after the Mexican fashion, patting each other on the back with one hand while we shook the other.

"*Buenos tardes, amigo,*" he murmured. "How do you seat yourself?"

"Very well, much thanks. And you? How have they treated you?"

"Delicious. Superlative thanks. I have longed to see you again."

"And your family? How are they?" (It is considered more delicate in Mexico not to ask about one's wife, because so few people are married.)

"Their health is of the best. Great, great thanks. And your family?"

"*Bien, bien!* I saw your son with the army at Jimenez. He gave me many, many remembrances of you. Would you desire a cigarette?"

"Thanks. Permit me, a light. You are in Valle Allegre many days?"

"For the fiesta only, señor."

"I hope your visit is fortunate, señor. My house is at your orders."

"Thanks. How is it that I did not see you at the

baile last night, señor? You, who were always such a sympathetic dancer!"

"Unhappily Juanita is gone to visit her mother in El Oro, and now, therefore, I am a *platonico*. I grow too old for the señoritas."

"Ah, no, señor. A *caballero* of your age is in the prime of life. But tell me. Is it true what I hear, that the Maderistas are now at Mapimi?"

"*Si*, señor. Soon Villa will take Torreon, they say, and then it is only a matter of a few months before the Revolution is accomplished."

"I think that, yes. But tell me; I have great respect for your opinion. Which cock would you advise me to bet on?"

We approached the combatants and looked them over, while their owners clamored in our ears. They sat upon the curbing negligently herding their birds apart. It was getting toward three of the afternoon.

"But will there be a cock-fight?" I asked them.

"*Quien sabe?*" drawled one.

The other murmured that possibly it would be *mañana*. It developed that the steel spurs had been forgotten in El Oro, and that a small boy had gone after them on a burro. It was six miles over the mountains to El Oro.

However, no one was in any hurry, so we sat down also. Appeared then Catarino Cabrera, the saloon keeper, and also the Constitutionalist *jefe politico* of Valle Allegre, very drunk, walking arm in arm with Don Priciliano Saucedes, the former *jefe* under the Diaz government. Don Priciliano is a fine-looking, white-haired old Castilian who used to lend money to the peons at twenty per cent. Don Catarino is a former schoolmaster, an ardent Revolutionist—he lends money at a slightly less rate of usury to the same parties. Don Catarino wears no collar, but he sports a revolver and two cartridge-belts. Don Priciliano during the first Revolution was deprived of most of his property by the Maderistas of the town, and then strapped naked upon his horse and beaten upon his bare back with the flat of a sword.

"Aie!" he says to my question. "The Revolution! I have most of the Revolution upon my back!"

And the two pass on to Don Priciliano's house, where Catarino is courting a beautiful daughter.

Then, with the thunder of hoofs, dashes up the gay and gallant young Jesus Triano, who was a Captain under Orozco. But Valle Allegre is a three days' ride from the railroad, and politics are not a burning issue there; so Jesus rides his stolen horse with impunity around the streets. He is a large young man with shining teeth, a rifle and bandolier, and leather trousers fastened up the side with buttons as big as dollars—his spurs are twice as big. They say that his dashing ways and the fact that he shot Emetario Flores in the back have won him the hand of Dolores, youngest daughter of Manuel Paredes, the charcoal contractor. He plunges down the arroyo at a gallop, his horse tossing bloody froth from the cruel curb.

Captain Adolfo Melendez, of the Constitutionalist army, slouches around the corner in a new, bottle-green corduroy uniform. He wears a handsome gilded sword which once belonged to the Knights of Pythias. Adolfo came to Valle Allegre on a two weeks' leave, which he prolonged indefinitely in order to take to himself a wife—the fourteen-year-old daughter of a village aristocrat. They say that his wedding was magnificent beyond belief, two priests officiating and the service lasting an hour more than necessary. But this may have been good economy on Adolfo's part, since he already had one wife in Chihuahua, another in Parral, and a third in Monterey, and, of course, had to placate the parents of the bride. He had now been away from his regiment three months, and told me simply that he thought they had forgotten all about him by this time.

At half-past four a thunder of cheers announced the arrival of the small boy with the steel spurs. It seems that he had got into a card game at El Oro, and had temporarily forgotten his errand.

But, of course, nothing was said about it. He had arrived, which was the important thing. We formed a wide ring in the open space where the burros stood, and the two owners began to "throw" their birds. But at the first onslaught the fowl upon which we had all bet our money spread its wings, and, to the astonishment of the assembled company, soared screaming over the mesquite tree and disappeared toward the mountains. Ten minutes later the two owners unconcernedly divided the proceeds before our eyes, and we strolled home well content.

HAPPY VALLEY

Fidencio and I dined at Charlie Chee's hotel. Throughout Mexico, in every little town, you will find Chinamen monopolizing the hotel and restaurant business. Charlie, and his cousin Foo, were both married to the daughters of respectable Mexican villagers. No one seemed to think that strange. Mexicans appear to have no race prejudices whatever. Captain Adolfo, in a bright yellow khaki uniform and another sword, brought his bride, a faintly pretty brown girl with her hair in a bang, wearing chandelier lusters as earrings. Charlie banged down in front of each of us a quart bottle of *aguardiente*, and, sitting down at the table, flirted politely with Señora Melendez, while Foo served dinner, enlivened with gay social chatter in pidgin Mexican.

It seemed that there was to be a *baile* at Don Priciliano's that evening, and Charlie politely offered to teach Adolfo's wife a new step which he had learned in El Paso, called the Turkey Trot. This he did until Adolfo began to look sullen and announced that he didn't think he would go to Don Priciliano's, since he considered it a bad thing for young wives to be seen much in public. Charlie and Foo also tendered their regrets, because several of their countrymen were due in the village that evening from Parral, and said that they would, of course, want to raise a little Chinese hell together.

So Fidencio and I finally departed, after solemnly promising that we would return in time for the Chinese festivities after the dance.

Outside, strong moonlight flooded all the village.

The jumbled roofs were so many tipped-up silvery planes, and the tree-tops glistened. Like a frozen cataract the arroyo fell away, and the great valley beyond lay drowned in rich, soft mist. The life-sounds quickened in the dark—excited laughter of young girls, a woman catching her breath at a window to the swift, hot torrent of a man's speech as he leaned against the bars, a dozen guitars syncopating each other, a young buck hurrying to meet his *novia*, spurs ringing clear. It was cold. As we passed Cabrera's door a hot, smoky, alcoholic breath smote us. Beyond that you crossed on stepping-stones the stream where the women wash their clothes. Climbing the other bank we saw the brilliant windows of Don Priciliano's house, and heard the far strains of Valle Allegre's orchestra.

Open doors and windows were choked with men—tall, dark, silent peons, wrapped to the eyes in their blankets, staring at the dance with eager and solemn eyes, a forest of sombreros.

Now Fidencio had just returned to Valle Allegre after a long absence, and as we stood on the outside of the group a tall young fellow caught sight of him, and, whirling his serape like a wing, he embraced my friend, crying:

"Happy return, Fidencio! We looked for you many months!"

The crowd swayed and rocked like a windy wheat field, blankets flapped dark against the night. They took up the cry:

"Fidencio! Fidencio is here! Your Carmencita is inside, Fidencio. You had better look out for your sweetheart! You can't stay away as long as that and expect her to remain faithful to you!"

Those inside caught the cry and echoed it, and the dance, which had just begun, stopped suddenly. The peons formed a lane through which we passed, patting us on the back with little words of welcome and affection; and at the door a dozen friends crowded forward to hug us, faces alight with pleasure.

Carmencita, a dumpy, small Indian girl, dressed in a screaming blue ready-made dress that didn't fit, stood over near the corner by the side of a certain Pablito, her partner, a half-breed youth about sixteen years old with a bad complexion. She affected to pay no attention to Fidencio's arrival, but stood dumbly, with her eyes on the ground, as is proper for unmarried Mexican women.

Fidencio swaggered among his *compadres* in true manly fashion for a few minutes, interspersing his conversation with loud virile oaths. Then, in a lordly manner, he went straight across the room to Carmencita, placed her left hand within the hollow of his right arm, and cried: "Well, now; let's dance!" and the grinning, perspiring musicians nodded and fell to.

There were five of them—two violins, a cornet, a flute and a harp. They swung into "Tres Piedras," and the couples fell in line, marching solemnly round the room. After parading round twice they fell to dancing, hopping awkwardly over the rough, hard, packed-dirt floor with jingling spurs; when they had danced around the room two or three times they walked again, then danced, then walked, then danced, so that each number took about an hour.

It was a long, low room, with whitewashed walls and a beamed ceiling wattled with mud above, and at one end was the inevitable sewing-machine, closed now, and converted into a sort of an altar by a tiny embroidered cloth upon which burned a perpetual rush flame before a tawdry color print of the Virgin which hung on the wall. Don Priciliano and his wife, who was nursing a baby at her breast, beamed from chairs at the other end. Innumerable candles had been heated on one side and stuck against the wall all around, whence they trailed sooty snakes above them on the white. The men made a prodigious stamping and clinking as they danced, shouting boisterously to one another. The women kept their eyes on the floor and did not speak.

I caught sight of the pimply youth glowering with folded arms upon Fidencio from his corner; and as I stood by the door, fragments of the peons' conversation floated in to me:

"Fidencio should not have stayed away so long."

"*Carramba!* See the way Pablito scowls there. He thought surely Fidencio was dead and that Carmencita was his own!"

And then a hopeful voice:

"Perhaps there will be trouble!"

The dance finally ended and Fidencio led his betrothed correctly back to her seat against the wall. The music stopped. The men poured out into the night where, in the flare of a torch, the owner of the losing rooster sold bottles of strong drink. We toasted each other boisterously in the sharp dark. The mountains around stood dazzling in the moon. And then, for the intervals between dances were very short, we heard the music erupt again, volcanically and exuberantly, into a waltz. The center of twenty curious and enthusiastic youths—for he had traveled—Fidencio strutted back into the room. He went straight to Carmencita, but as he led her out upon the floor Pablito glided up behind, pulling out a large obsolete revolver. A dozen shouts rang:

"*Cuidado*, Fidencio! Look out!"

He whirled, to see the revolver pointed at his stomach. For a moment no one moved. Fidencio and his rival looked at each other with wrathful eyes. There was a subdued clicking of automatics everywhere as the gentlemen drew and cocked their weapons, for some of them were friends of Pablito's. I heard low voices muttering:

"Porfirio! Go home and get my shotgun!"

"Victoriano! My new rifle! It lies on the bureau in mother's room."

A shoal of small boys like flying-fish scattered through the moonlight to get firearms. Meanwhile, the *status quo* was preserved. The peons had squatted out of the range of fire, so that just their eyes showed above the window-sills, where they watched proceedings with joyous interest. Most of the musicians were edging toward the nearest window; the harpist, however, had dropped down behind his instrument. Don Priciliano and his wife, still nursing the infant, rose and majestically made their way to some interior part of the house. It was none of their business; besides, they did not wish to interfere with the young folks' pleasure.

With one arm Fidencio carefully pushed Carmencita away, holding his other hand poised like a claw. In the dead silence he said:

"You little goat! Don't stand there pointing that thing at me if you're afraid to shoot it! Pull the trigger while I am unarmed! I am not afraid to die, even at the hand of a weak little fool who doesn't know when to use a gun!"

The boy's face twisted hatefully, and I thought he was going to shoot.

"Ah!" murmured the peons. "Now! Now is the time!"

But he didn't. After a few minutes his hand wavered, and with a curse he jammed the pistol back into his pocket. The peons straightened up again and crowded disappointedly around the doors and windows. The harpist got up and began to tune his harp. There was much thrusting back of revolvers into holsters, and the sprightly social conversation grew up again. By the time the small boys arrived with a perfect arsenal of rifles and shotguns, the dance had been resumed. So the guns were stacked in a corner.

As long as Carmencita claimed his amorous attention and there was a prospect of friction, Fidencio stayed. He swaggered among the men and basked in the admiration of the ladies, outdancing them all in speed, abandon and noise.

But he soon tired of that, and the excitement of meeting Carmencita palled upon him. So he went out into the moonlight again and up the arroyo, to take part in Charlie Chee's celebration.

As we approached the hotel we were conscious of a curious low moaning sound which seemed akin to music. The dinner-table had been removed from the dining-room into the street, and around the room turkey-trotted Foo and another Celestial. A barrel of *aguardiente* had been set up on a trestle in one corner, and beneath it sprawled Charlie himself, in his mouth a glass tube which syphoned up into the barrel. A tremendous wooden box of Mexican cigarettes had been smashed open on one side, the packages tumbling out upon the floor. In other parts of the room two more Chinamen slept the profound sleep of the very drunk, wrapped in blankets. The two who danced sang meanwhile their own version of a once popular ragtime song called "Dreamy Eyes." Against this marched magnificently "The Pilgrim's Chorus" from Tann-häuser, rendered by a phonograph set up in the kitchen. Charlie removed the glass tube from his mouth, put a thumb over it, and welcomed us with a hymn which he sang as follows:

> *"Pooll for the shore, sailor,*
> *Pooll for the shore!*
> *Heed not the lowling lave*
> *But pooll for the shore!"*

He surveyed us with a bleary eye, and remarked: "Bledlau! Je' Calist is wid us here toni'?"

After which he returned the syphon to his mouth.

We blended into these festivities. Fidencio offered to exhibit the steps of a new Spanish *fandango*, the way it was danced by the damned "grasshoppers" (as Mexicans call the Spaniards). He stamped bellowing around the room, colliding with the Chinamen, and roaring "La Paloma." Finally, out of breath, he collapsed upon a nearby chair, and began to descant upon the many charms of Adolfo's bride, whom he had seen for the first time that day. He declared that it was a shame for so young and blithe a spirit to be tied to a middle-aged man; he said that he himself represented youth, strength and gallantry, and was a much more fitting mate for her. He added that as the evening advanced he found that he desired her more and more. Charlie Chee, with the glass tube in his mouth, nodded intelligently at each of these statements. I had a happy thought. Why not send for Adolfo and his wife and invite them to join our festivities? The Chinamen asleep on the floor were kicked awake and their opinion asked. Since they could understand neither Spanish nor English, they answered fluently in Chinese. Fidencio translated.

"They say," he said, "that Charlie ought to be sent with the invitation."

We agreed to that. Charlie rose, while Foo took his place at the glass tube. He declared that he would invite them in the most irresistible terms, and, strapping on his revolver, disappeared.

Ten minutes later we heard five shots. We discussed the matter at length, not understanding why there should be any artillery at that time of night, except that probably two guests returning from the *baile* were murdering each other before going to bed. Charlie took a long time, in the meanwhile, and we were just considering the advisability of sending out an expedition to find him when he returned.

"Well, how about it, Charlie?" I asked. "Will they come?"

"I don't think so," he replied doubtfully, swaying in the doorway.

"Did you hear the shooting?" asked Fidencio.

"Yes, very close," said Charlie. "Foo, if you will kindly get out from under that tube. . . ."

"What was it?" we asked.

"Well," said Charlie, "I knocked at Adolfo's door and said we were having a party down here and wanted him to come. He shot at me three times and I shot at him twice."

So saying, Charlie seized Foo by the leg and composedly lay down under the glass tube again.

We must have stayed there some hours after that. I remember that toward morning Ignacio came in and played us Tosti's "Good-bye," to which all the Chinamen danced solemnly around.

At about four o'clock Atanacio appeared. He burst open the door and stood there very white, with a gun in one hand.

"Friends," he said, "a most disagreeable thing has

happened. My wife, Juanita, returned from her mother's about midnight on an ass. She was stopped on the road by a man muffled up in a *poncho*, who gave her an anonymous letter in which were detailed all my little amusements when I last went for recreation to Juarez. I have seen the letter. It is astonishingly accurate! It tells how I went to supper with Maria and then home with her. It tells how I took Ana to the bull-fight. It describes the hair, complexion and disposition of all those other ladies and how much money I spent upon them. *Carramba!* It is exact to a cent!

"When she got home I happened to be down at Catarino's taking a cup with an old friend. This mysterious stranger appeared at the kitchen door with another letter in which he said I had three more wives in Chihuahua, which, God knows, is not true, since I only have one!

"It is not that I care, *amigos*, but these things have upset Juanita horribly. Of course, I denied these charges, but, *valgame Dios!* women are so unreasonable!

"I hired Dionysio to watch my house, but he has gone to the *baile*, and so, arousing and dressing my small son, that he may carry me word of any further outrages, I have come down to seek your help in preserving my home from this disgrace."

We declared ourselves willing to do anything for Atanacio—anything, that is, that promised excitement. We said that it was horrible, that the evil stranger ought to be exterminated.

HAPPY VALLEY

"Who could it be?"

Atanacio replied that it was probably Flores, who had had a baby by his wife before he married her, but who had never succeeded in quite capturing her affections. We forced *aguardiente* upon him and he drank moodily. Charlie Chee was pried loose from the glass tube, where Foo took his place, and sent for weapons. And in ten minutes he returned with seven loaded revolvers of different makes.

Almost immediately came a furious pounding on the door, and Atanacio's young son flung himself in.

"Papa!" he cried, holding out a paper. "Here is another one! The man knocked at the back door, and when Mamma went to find out who it was she could only see a big red blanket covering him entirely up to the hair. He gave her a note and ran away, taking a loaf of bread off the window."

With trembling hands Atanacio unfolded the paper and read aloud:

Your husband is the father of forty-five small children in the State of Coahuila.

   (Signed) Some One Who Knows Him.

"Mother of God!" cried Atanacio, springing to his feet, in a transport of grief and rage. "It is a lie! I have always discriminated! Forward, my friends! Let us protect our homes!"

Seizing our revolvers we rushed out into the night. We staggered panting up the steep hill to Atanacio's house—sticking close together so no one would be mistaken by the others for the Mysterious Stranger. Ata-

nacio's wife was lying on the bed weeping hysterically. We scattered into the brush and poked into the alleys around the house, but nothing stirred. In a corner of the corral lay Dionysio, the watchman, fast asleep, his rifle by his side. We passed on up the hill until we came to the edge of the town. Already dawn was coming. A never-ending chorus of roosters made the only sound, except the incredibly soft music from the *baile* at Don Priciliano's, which would probably last all that day and the next night. Afar, the big valley was like a great map, quiet, distinct, immense. Every wall corner, tree branch and grass-blade on the roofs of the houses were pricked out in the wonderful clear light of before-dawn.

In the distance, over the shoulder of the red mountain, went a man covered up in a red serape.

"Aha!" cried Atanacio. "There he goes!"

And with one accord we opened up on the red blanket. There were five of us, and we had six shots apiece. They echoed fearfully among the houses and clapped from mountain to mountain, reproduced each one a hundred times. Of a sudden the village belched half-dressed men and women and children. They evidently thought that a new revolution was beginning. A very ancient crone came out of a small brown house on the edge of the village rubbing her eyes.

"*Oiga!*" she shouted. "What are you shooting at?"

"We are trying to kill that accursed man in the red blanket, who is poisoning our homes and making Valle Allegre a place unfit for a decent woman to live in!" shouted Atanacio, taking another shot.

LOS PASTORES

The old woman bent her bleary eyes upon our target. "But," she said gently, "that is not a bad man. That's only my son going after the goats."

Meanwhile, the red-blanketed figure, never even looking back, continued his placid way over the top of the mountain and disappeared.

CHAPTER III

LOS PASTORES

THE romance of gold hangs over the mountains of Northern Durango like an old perfume. There, it is rumored, was that mythical Ophir whence the Aztecs and their mysterious predecessors drew the red gold that Cortez found in the treasury of Moctezuma. Before the dawn of Mexican history the Indians scratched these barren hillsides with dull copper knives. You can still see the traces of their workings. And after them the Spaniards, with flashing, bright helmets and steel breast-plates, filled from these mountains the lofty treasure-ships of the Indies. Almost a thousand miles from the Capital, over trackless deserts and fierce stony mountains, a tiny colorful fringe of the most brilliant civilization in Europe flung itself among the canyons and high peaks of this desolate land; and so far was it from the seat of change that long after Spanish rule had disappeared from Mexico forever, it persisted here. The Spaniards enslaved the Indians of the region, of course, and the

torrent-worn, narrow valleys are still sinister with
legend. Almost anybody around Santa Maria del Oro
can tell you stories of the old days when men were
flogged to death in the mines, and the Spanish over-
seers lived like princes.

But they were a hardy race, these mountaineers.
They were always rebelling. There is a legend of how
the Spaniards, finally discovering themselves alone, two
hundred leagues from the seacoast, in the midst of an
overwhelmingly hostile native race, attempted one night
to leave the mountains. Fires sprang up on the high
peaks, and the mountain villages throbbed to the sound
of drums. Somewhere in the narrow defiles the Spaniards disappeared forever. And from that time, until
certain foreigners secured mining concessions there,
the place had an evil name. The authority of the
Mexican government barely reached it.

There are two villages which were the capitals of
the gold-seeking Spaniards in this region, and where
the Spanish tradition is still strong: Inde, and Santa
Maria del Oro,—usually called El Oro. Inde, the
Spaniards romantically named from their persistent
dream that this new world was India; Santa Maria del
Oro was called so on the same principle that one sung
a *Te Deum* in honor of bloody victory—a grateful-
ness to heaven for the finding of red gold, Our Lady of
the Gold.

In El Oro one can still see the ruins of a monastery
—they call it now, vaguely, the Collegio—the pathetic little arched roofs of a row of monkish cells built
of adobe, and now fast crumbling under hot suns and

LOS PASTORES

torrential rains. It partly surrounds what was once the patio of the cloister, and a great mesquite tree towers there over the forgotten headstone of an ancient grave, inscribed with the lordly name of Doña Isabella Guzman. Of course, everybody has entirely forgotten who Doña Isabella was, or when she died. There still stands in the public square a fine old Spanish church with a beamed ceiling. And over the door of the tiny Palacio Municipal is the almost erased carving of the arms of some ancient Spanish house.

Here is romance for you. But the inhabitants have no respect for tradition, and hardly any memory of the ancients who left these monuments. The exuberant Indian civilization has entirely obliterated all traces of the *conquistadores*.

El Oro is noted as the gayest town of all the mountain region. There are *bailes* almost every night, and far and near it is a matter of common knowledge that El Oro is the home of the prettiest girls in Durango. In El Oro, too, they celebrate feast days with more ebullience than in other localities. All the charcoal-burners and goat-herds and pack-train drivers and ranchers for miles around come there on holidays,—so that one feast-day generally means two or three without work, since there must be one day for celebrating, and at least another for coming and returning home.

And what *Pastorellas* they have in El Oro! Once a year, on the Feast of the Santos Reyes, they perform Los Pastores all over this part of the country. It is an ancient miracle play of the kind that used to take place all over Europe in the Renaissance,—the

309

kind that gave birth to Elizabethan drama, and is now extinct everywhere in the world. It is handed down by word of mouth from mother to daughter, from the remotest antiquity. It is called "Luzbel," the Spanish for Lucifer, and depicts Perverse Man in the Midst of His Deadly Sin, Lucifer, the Great Antagonist of Souls, and the Everlasting Mercy of God Made Flesh in the Child Jesus.

In most places there is only one performance of Los Pastores. But in El Oro there are three or four on the night of the Santos Reyes, and others at different times of the year, as the spirit moves. The *cura*, or village priest, still trains the actors. The play takes place no longer in the church, however. It is added to from generation to generation, sometimes being twisted to satirize persons in the village. It has become too profane, too realistic, for the Church; but still it points the great moral of medieval religion.

Fidencio and I dined early on the night of the San tos Reyes. Afterward, he took me along the street to a narrow alley-way between adobe walls, which led through a broken place into a tiny corral behind a house hung with red peppers. Under the legs of two meditative burros scurried dogs and chickens, a pig or so, and a swarm of little naked brown children. A wrinkled old Indian hag, smoking a cigarette made of an entire corn-husk, squatted upon a wooden box. Upon our appearance she arose, muttering toothless words of greeting, lifted the lid of the box, and produced an *olla* full of new-made *aguardiente*. The dis-

310

tillery was in the kitchen. We paid her a silver peso, and circulated the jug among the three of us, with many polite wishes for health and prosperity. Over our heads the sunset sky yellowed and turned green, and a few large mountain stars blazed out. We heard laughter and guitars from the lower end of the town, and the uproarious shouts of the charcoal-burners finishing their holiday strong. The old lady consumed much more than her share. . . .

"Oh, mother!" said Fidencio. "Where are they going to give the Pastores to-night?"

"There are many Pastores," she answered with a leer. "*Carramba!* what a year it is for Pastores! There is one in the schoolhouse, and another back of Don Pedro's, and another in the *casa* of Don Mario, and still another in the house of Perdita, who was married to Thomas Redondo, who was killed last year in the mines; may God have mercy on his soul!"

"Which will be the best?" demanded Fidencio, kicking a goat which was trying to enter the kitchen.

"*Quien sabe!*" she shrugged vaguely. "Were my old bones not so twisted I would go to Don Pedro's. But I would be disappointed. There are no Pastores nowadays such as the ones we used to give when I was a girl."

We went, then, to Don Pedro's, down a steep, uneven street, stopped every few feet by boisterous bankrupts who wanted to know where a man could establish credit for liquor. Don Pedro's was a considerable house, for he was the village rich man. The open square which his buildings enclosed would have been a corral ordinarily; but Don Pedro could afford a patio, and it was full of fragrant shrubs and barrel cacti,— a rude fountain pouring from an old iron pipe in the center. The entrance to this was a narrow, black archway, in which sat the town orchestra playing. A pine torch was stuck by its pitch against the outside wall, and under this a man took up fifty-cent pieces for the entrance fee. We watched for some time, but nobody seemed to be paying anything. A clamorous mob stood around him, pleading special privilege—that *they* ought to get in free. One was Don Pedro's cousin; another his gardener; a third had married the daughter of his mother-in-law by his first marriage; one woman insisted that she was the mother of a performer. There were other entrances at which no guardian stood; and through these, when they found themselves unable to cajole the gentleman at the main door, the crowd placidly sifted. We paid our money amid an awed silence and entered.

White, burning moonlight flooded the place. The patio sloped upward along the side of the mountain, where there was no wall to stop the view of great planes of shining upland, tilted to meet the shallow jade sky. To the low roof of the house a canopy of canvas drooped out over a flat place, supported by slanting poles, like the pavilion of a Bedouin king. Its shadow cut the moonlight blacker than night. Six torches stuck in the ground around the outside of the place sent up thin lines of pitchy smoke. There was no other light under the canopy, except the restless gleams of innumerable cigarettes. Along the wall of

the house stood black-robed women with black man-
tillas over their heads, the men-folks squatting at their
feet. Wherever there was space between their knees
were children. Men and women alike smoked their
cigarros, handing them placidly down so that the little
ones might take a puff. It was a quiet audience, speaking little and softly, perfectly content to wait, watching the moonlight in the patio, and listening to the
music, which sounded far away in the arch. A night-
ingale burst into song somewhere among the shrubs,
and all of us fell ecstatically silent, listening to it.
Small boys were dispatched to tell the band to stop
while the song went on. That was very exciting.

During all this time there was no sign whatever of
the performers. I don't know how long we sat there,
but nobody made any comment on the fact. The audience was not there primarily to see the Pastores; it
was there to see and hear whatever took place, and
everything interested it. But being a restless, practical Westerner, alas! I broke the charmed silence to
ask a woman next to me when the play would begin.

"Who knows?" she answered tranquilly.

A newcomer, after turning my question and the answer over in his mind, leaned across.

"Perhaps to-morrow," he said. I noticed that the
band was playing no longer. "It appears," he continued, "that there are other Pastores at Doña Perdita's
house. They tell me that those who were to have per-
formed here have gone up there to see them. And the
musicians have also gone up there. For the past half-

hour I have been considering seriously going up there myself."

We left him, still considering seriously; the rest of the audience had settled down for an evening of pleasant gossip, having apparently forgotten the Pastores altogether. Outside, the ticket-taker with our peso had long since gathered his companions to him and sought the pleasing hilarity of a cantina.

And so we strolled slowly up the street toward the edge of town where the whitewashed plaster walls of rich men's houses give way to the undecorated adobes of the poor. There all pretense of streets ended, and we went along burro paths between huts scattered according to their owners' whims, through dilapidated corrals to the house of the widow of Don Tomas. It was built of sun-dried mud bricks, jutting part way into the mountain itself, and looked as the stable of Bethlehem must have looked. As if to carry out the analogy, a great cow lay in the moonlight just beneath the window, breathing and chewing her cud. Through the window and the door, over a throng of heads, we could see candle light playing on the ceiling and hear a whining chant sung by girlish voices, and the beat of crooks keeping time on the floor with jingling bells.

It was a low, dirt-floored, whitewashed room, raftered and wattled with mud above, like any peasant dwelling in Italy or Palestine. At the end farthest from the door was a little table heaped with paper flowers where two tall church candles burned. Above it, on the wall, hung a chromo of the Virgin and Child. And in the middle of the flowers was set a tiny wooden

314

model of a cradle in which lay a leaden doll to represent the Infant Jesus. All the rest of the room, except for a small space in the middle of the floor, was packed with humanity: a fringe of children sitting cross-legged around the stage, half-grown-ups and girls kneeling, and behind them, until they choked the doorway, blanketed peons with their hats off, eager and curious. By some exquisite chance, a woman sat next to the altar, her breast exposed as she nursed her baby. Other women with their babies stood along the wall on both sides of her, except for a narrow, curtained entrance into another room where we could hear the giggling of the performers.

"Has it begun?" I asked a boy next to me.

"No," he answered; "they just came out to sing a song to see if the stage was big enough."

It was a merry, noisy crowd, bandying jokes and gossip across each others' heads. Many of the men were exhilarated with *aguardiente*, singing snatches of ribald songs with their arms around each other's shoulders, and breaking out every now and then into fierce little quarrels that might have led to anything—for they were all armed. And right in the middle of everything a voice said:

"S-s-sh! They are going to begin now!"

The curtain was lifted, and *Lucifer*, hurled from Heaven because of his invincible pride, stood before us. It was a young girl—all the performers are girls, in distinction to the pre-Elizabethan miracle plays, where the actors were boys. She wore a costume whose every part had been handed down from immeas-

urable antiquity. It was red, of course—red leather—
the conventional medieval color for devils. But the
exciting thing about it was that it was evidently the
traditional rendering of the uniform of a Roman
legionary ('and the Roman soldiers who crucified
Christ were considered a little less than devils in the
Middle Ages). She wore a wide, skirted doublet of
red leather, under which were scalloped trousers, falling almost to the shoe tops. There doesn't seem to be
much connection here until you remember that the
Roman legionaries in Britain and in Spain wore leather
trousers. Her helmet was greatly distorted, because
feathers and flowers had been fastened to it; but underneath you could trace the resemblance to the Roman
helmet. A cuirass covered her breast and back; instead of steel it was made of small mirrors. And a
sword hung at her side. Drawing the sword, she strutted about, pitching her voice to imitate a man's:

> "*Yo soy luz; ay en mi nombre se ve!*
> *Pues con la luz*
> *Que baje*
> *Todo el abismo encendi——*"

A splendid soliloquy of Lucifer hurled from heaven:

"Light am I, as my name proclaims—and the light
of my fall kindled all the great abyss. Because I
would not humble myself, I, who was the Captain General, be it known to all men, am to-day the accursed
of God. . . . To thee, O mountains, and to thee, O
sea, I will make my complaint, and thus—alas!—re-

lieve my overburdened breast. . . . Cruel fortune, why art thou so inflexibly severe? . . . I who yesterday dwelt serene in yonder starry vault am to-day disinherited, abandoned. Because of my mad envy and ambition, because of my rash presumption, gone is my palace of yesterday, and to-day finds me sad among these mountains, mute witnesses of my grievous and pitiful state. . . . O mountains! happy art thou!—happy art thou in all, whether bleak and bare, or gay with leafy verdure! O ye swift brooks flowing free, behold me! . . ."

"Good! good!" said the audience.

"That's the way Huerta is going to feel when the Maderistas enter Mexico City!" shouted one irrepressible revolutionist, amid laughter.

"Behold me in my affliction and guilt——" continued Luzbel.

Just then a large dog came through the curtain, cheerfully wagging his tail. Immensely pleased with himself, he nosed among the children, licking a face here and there. One baby slapped him violently, and the dog, hurt and astonished, made a rush between *Lucifer's* legs in the midst of that sublime peroration. A second time *Lucifer* fell, and, rising amid the wild hilarity of the house, laid about her with her sword. At least fifty of the audience descended upon the dog and ejected him howling, and the play went on.

Laura, married to *Arcadio*, a shepherd, appeared singing at the door of her cottage—that is to say, through the curtain. . . .

317

"How peacefully falls the light of the moon and the stars this supremely beautiful night! Nature appears to be on the point of revealing some wonderful secret. The whole world is at peace, and all hearts, methinks, are overflowing with joy and contentment. . . . But —who is this—of such pleasing presence and fascinating figure?"

Lucifer prinked and strutted, avowing with Latin boldness his love for her. She replied that her heart was *Arcadio's;* but the Arch-devil dwelt upon her husband's poverty, and himself promised her riches, towering palaces, jewels and slaves.

"I feel that I am beginning to love thee," said *Laura.* "Against my will—I cannot deceive myself ____"

At this point there was smothered laughter in the audience: "Antonia! Antonia!" said everybody, grinning and nudging. "That's just the way Antonia left Enrique! I always thought the Devil was in it!" remarked one of the women.

But *Laura* had pangs of conscience about poor *Arcadio.* Lucifer insinuated that *Arcadio* was secretly in love with another, and that settled it.

"So that thou mayst not be troubled," *Laura* said calmly, "and, so that I may be free from him, I shall even watch for an opportunity to kill him."

This was a shock, even to *Lucifer.* He suggested that it would be better to make *Arcadio* feel the pangs of jealousy, and in an exultant aside remarked with satisfaction that "her feet are already in the direct pathway to Hell."

The women, apparently, felt a good deal of satisfaction at this. They nodded virtuously to one another. But one young girl leaned over to another, and, sighing, said:

"Ah! But it must be wonderful to love like that!"

Arcadio returned, to be reproached by *Laura* with his poverty. He was accompanied by *Bato*, a combination of *Iago* and *Autolycus*, who attended the dialogue between the shepherd and his wife with ironical asides. By means of the jeweled ring that *Lucifer* had given *Laura*, *Arcadio's* suspicions were aroused, and, when *Laura* had left him in haughty insolence, he gave vent to his feelings:

"Just when I was happy in her fidelity, she with cruel reproaches embitters my heart! What shall I do with myself?"

"Look for a new mate," said *Bato*.

That being rejected, *Bato* gave the following modest prescription for settling the difficulty:

"Kill her without delay. This done, take her skin and carefully fold it away. Shouldst thou marry again, let the bride's sheet be that skin, and thus prevent another jilting. To still further strengthen her virtue, tell her gently but firmly: 'Sweetheart, this thy sheet was once my wife; see that thou dost carry thyself circumspectly lest thou, too, come to the same end. Remember that I am a hard and peevish man who does not stick at trifles.'"

At the beginning of this speech the men began to

snicker, and when it ended they were guffawing loudly. An old peon, however, turned furiously on them:

"There is a proper prescription!" he said. "If that were done more often there would not be so many domestic troubles."

But *Arcadio* didn't seem to see it, and *Bato* recommended the philosophic attitude.

"Stop thy complaining and leave Laura to her lover. Free thus from obligations, thou wilt become rich, and be able to eat well, dress well, and truly enjoy life. The rest matters but little. . . . Seize, therefore, this opportunity toward thine own good fortune. And do not forget, I beg thee, once thy fortune is made, to regale this meager paunch of mine with good cheer."

"Shame!" cried the women, clucking. "How false!" "The *desgraciado!*" A man's voice piped up: "There is some truth in that, señoras! If it weren't for the women and children we all might be able to dress in fine clothes and ride upon a horse."

A fierce argument grew up around this point.

Arcadio lost patience with *Bato,* and the latter plaintively said:

"If thou hast any regard for poor *Bato,* let us go to supper."

Arcadio answered firmly, not until he had unburdened his heart.

"Unburden and welcome," said *Bato,* "until thou art tired. As for me, I shall put such a knot in my tongue that even shouldst thou chatter like a parrot I shall be mute." He seated himself on a large rock and pretended to sleep; and then for fifteen minutes Arcadio unburdened himself to the mountains and the stars.

"Oh, Laura, inconstant, ungrateful and inhuman, why hast thou caused me such woe? Thou hast wounded my faith and my honor and hast put my soul in torment. Why dost thou mock my ardent love? Oh, thou steep stills and towering mountains, help me to express my woe! And thou, stern, immovable cliffs, and thou, silent woods, help me to ease my heart of its pain. . . ."

Amid heartfelt and sympathetic silence the audience mourned with *Arcadio*. A few women sobbed openly.

Finally *Bato* could stand it no longer.

"Let us go to supper," he said. "Better it is to suffer a little at a time!"

A perfect gale of laughter cut off the end of the sentence.

Arcadio: "To thee only, Bato, have I confided my secret."

Bato (aside): "I do not believe I can keep it! Already my mouth itches to tell it. This fool will learn that 'a secret and a pledge to none should be entrusted.' "

Enter a group of shepherds with their shepherdesses, singing. They were dressed in their feminine Sunday best with flowery summer hats, and carried enormous wooden apostolic crooks, hung with paper flowers and strings of bells.

"Beautiful is this night beyond compare,—
Beautiful and peaceful as never before,
And happy the mortal who beholds it.
Everything proclaims that the Son of God,
The Word Divine made human flesh,
Will soon be born in Bethlehem
And mankind's ransom be complete."

Then followed a dialogue between ninety-year-old, miserly *Fabio* and his sprightly young wife, to which all present contributed, upon the subject of the great virtues of women and the great failings of men.

The audience joined violently in the discussion, hurling the words of the play back and forward—men and women drawing together in two solid hostile bodies. The women were supported by the words of the play, but the men had the conspicuous example of *Laura* to draw from. It passed soon into an argument about the virtues and failings of certain married couples in El Oro. The play suspended for some time.

—— *Bras*, one of the shepherds, stole *Fabio's* wallet from between his knees as he slept. Then came gossip and backbiting. *Bato* forced *Bras* to share with him the contents of the stolen wallet, which they opened, to find none of the food they expected. In their disappointment, both declared their willingness to sell their souls to the Devil for a good meal. *Lucifer* overheard the declaration and attempted to bind them to it. But after a battle of wits between the rustics and the Devil—the audience solid to a man against the underhanded tactics of *Lucifer*—it was decided by a

322

throw of the dice, at which the Devil lost. But he had told them where food could be obtained, and they went for it. *Lucifer* cursed God for interfering in behalf of two worthless shepherds. He marveled that "a hand mightier than *Lucifer's* has been stretched out to save." He wondered at the Everlasting Mercy toward worthless Man, who has been a persistent sinner down the ages, while he, *Lucifer*, had felt God's wrath so heavily. Sweet music was suddenly heard—the shepherds singing behind the curtain—and *Lucifer* mused upon Daniel's prophecy that "the Divine Word shall be made Flesh." The music continued, announcing the birth of Christ among the shepherds. *Lucifer*, enraged, swore that he would use all his power to the end that all mortals shall at some time "taste Hell," and commanded Hell to open and receive him "in its center."

At the birth of Christ the spectators crossed themselves, the women muttering prayers. *Lucifer's* impotent raging against God was greeted with shouts of "Blasphemy! Sacrilege! Death to the Devil for insulting God!"

Bras and *Bato* returned, ill from overeating, and, believing they were about to die, called wildly for help. Then the shepherds and shepherdesses came in, singing and pounding the floor with their crooks, as they promised they would cure them.

At the beginning of Act II, *Bato* and *Bras*, fully restored to health, were discovered again plotting to steal and eat the provisions laid by for a village festival, and as they went out to do so *Laura* appeared, singing of her love for *Lucifer*. Heavenly music was heard, rebuking her for her "adulterous thoughts," whereupon she renounced all desire for guilty love and declared that she would be content with *Arcadio*.

The women of the audience rustled and nodded and smiled at these exemplary sentiments. Sighs of relief were heard all over the house that the play was coming out right.

But just afterward the sound of a falling roof was heard, and Comic Relief, in the persons of *Bras* and *Bato*, entered, carrying a basket of food and a bottle of wine. Everybody brightened up at the appearance of these beloved crooks; anticipatory mirth went around the room. *Bato* suggested that he eat his half while *Bras* stood guard, whereupon *Bato* ate *Bras's* share, too. In the midst of the quarrel that followed, before they could hide the traces of their guilt, the shepherds and shepherdesses came back in search of the thief. Many and absurd were the reasons invented by *Bato* and *Bras* to explain the presence of the food and drink, which they finally managed to convince the company was of diabolical origin. In order to further cover their traces they invited the others to eat what is left.

This scene, the most comic of the whole play, could hardly be heard for the roars of laughter that interrupted every speech. A young fellow reached over and punched a *compadre*.

"Do you remember how we got out of it when they caught us milking Don Pedro's cows?"

LOS PASTORES

Lucifer returned, and was invited to join the feast. He incited them maliciously to continue discussion of the robbery, and little by little to place the blame upon a stranger whom they all agreed having seen. Of course they meant *Lucifer*, but, upon being invited to describe him, they depicted a monster a thousand times more repulsive than the reality. None suspected that the apparently amiable stranger seated in their midst was *Lucifer*.

How *Bato* and *Bras* were at last discovered and punished, how *Laura* and *Arcadio* were reconciled, how *Fabio* was rebuked for his avariciousness and saw the error of his ways, how the Infant Jesus was shown lying in his manger, with the three strongly individualized Kings out of the East, how *Lucifer* was finally discovered and cast back into hell—I have not space here to describe.

The play lasted for three hours, absorbing all the attention of the audience. *Bato* and *Bras*—especially *Bato*—received their enthusiastic approbation. They sympathized with *Laura*, suffered with *Arcadio*, and hated *Lucifer* with the hatred of gallery gods for the villain in the melodrama. Only once was the play interrupted, when a hatless youth rushed in and shouted:

"A man has come from the army, who says that Urbina has taken Mapimi!"

Even the performers stopped singing—they were pounding the floor with jingling crooks at the time—and a whirlwind of questions beat upon the newcomer.

INSURGENT MEXICO

But in a minute the interest passed, and the shepherds took up their song where they had dropped it.

When we left Doña Perdita's house, about midnight, the moon had already gone behind the western mountains, and a barking dog was all the noise in the dark sharp night. It flashed upon me, as Fidencio and I went home with our arms about each others' shoulders, that this was the kind of thing which had preceded the Golden Age of the Theater in Europe—the flowering of the Renaissance. It was amusing to speculate what the Mexican Renaissance would have been if it had not come so late.

But already around the narrow shores of the Mexican Middle Ages beat the great seas of modern life— machinery, scientific thought, and political theory. Mexico will have to skip for a time her Golden Age of Drama.

(1)

RY

d on

_____

Lightning Source UK Ltd.
Milton Keynes UK
UKHW022037230421
382536UK00003B/179

9 781296 499594